Installing and Configuring Windows 10: 70-698 Exam Guide

Learn to deploy, configure, and monitor Windows 10
effectively to prepare for the 70-698 exam

Bekim Dauti

BIRMINGHAM - MUMBAI

Installing and Configuring Windows 10: 70-698 Exam Guide

Commissioning Editor: Vijin Boricha
Acquisition Editor: Rahul Nair
Content Development Editor: Abhishek Jadhav
Technical Editor: Mohd Riyan Khan
Copy Editor: Safis Editing
Project Coordinator: Jagdish Prabhu
Proofreader: Safis Editing
Indexer: Pratik Shirodkar
Graphics: Tom Scaria
Production Coordinator: Nilesh Mohite

First published: January 2019

Production reference: 1310119

Published by Packt Publishing Ltd.
Livery Place
35 Livery Street
Birmingham
B3 2PB, UK.

ISBN 978-1-78899-086-8

www.packtpub.com

Like the big ship that sails the ocean, the planet Earth sails the universe. So, as the ship's crew cares for the ship to not sink into the ocean, people also have to take care for the planet to not sink into the universe. Then, save the planet to save yourself.

– Bekim Dauti

`mapt.io`

Mapt is an online digital library that gives you full access to over 5,000 books and videos, as well as industry leading tools to help you plan your personal development and advance your career. For more information, please visit our website.

Why subscribe?

- Spend less time learning and more time coding with practical eBooks and Videos from over 4,000 industry professionals

- Improve your learning with Skill Plans built especially for you

- Get a free eBook or video every month

- Mapt is fully searchable

- Copy and paste, print, and bookmark content

Packt.com

Did you know that Packt offers eBook versions of every book published, with PDF and ePub files available? You can upgrade to the eBook version at `www.packt.com` and as a print book customer, you are entitled to a discount on the eBook copy. Get in touch with us at `customercare@packtpub.com` for more details.

At `www.packt.com`, you can also read a collection of free technical articles, sign up for a range of free newsletters, and receive exclusive discounts and offers on Packt books and eBooks.

Contributors

About the author

Bekim Dauti works mainly with the administration of computer systems and networks, as well as vocational training in Cisco and Microsoft technologies. He holds a bachelor's degree from the University of Tirana and a master's from UMUC Europe, both in information technology. He also holds numerous IT certifications from vendors including ECDL, MOS, CompTIA, Cisco, Microsoft, and Sun Microsystems. Bekim has contributed to over 10 computer books and dozens of articles for PCWorld Albanian and CIO Albania. He is the founder of Dautti Sh.p.k. Currently, he works as a system administrator at Kosovo Telecom JSC.

I thank God for giving me life, health, and the opportunity to contribute through knowledge sharing. May God Almighty reward my family, friends, the folks at Packt Publishing, my teammates at Kosovo Telecom's JSC Sys Admin team, my colleagues both at Dautti Sh.p.k. and InfoTech and everyone who supported me in writing this book. Last, but not least, peace and blessings to every reader.

About the reviewer

Rishalin Pillay, with in excess of 11 years of cybersecurity experience, has acquired a vast number of skills while consulting for Fortune 500 companies and participating in projects related to network security design, implementation, and vulnerability analysis.
He holds many certifications that demonstrate his knowledge and expertise in the cybersecurity field, such as CISSP, CCNP Security, CCSPA, MCSE, MCT, A+, and Network+.

Rishalin currently works at a large-scale software company as a senior cybersecurity engineer.

Packt is searching for authors like you

If you're interested in becoming an author for Packt, please visit `authors.packtpub.com` and apply today. We have worked with thousands of developers and tech professionals, just like you, to help them share their insight with the global tech community. You can make a general application, apply for a specific hot topic that we are recruiting an author for, or submit your own idea.

Table of Contents

Preface

The *Installing and Configuring Windows 10: 70-698 Exam Guide* is designed to consolidate what you already know, while also updating your knowledge of Windows 10. With its easy-to-follow guidance, you will quickly learn the user interface and discover steps to work efficiently in Windows 10 to rule out delays and obstacles.

This book begins by covering various ways of installing Windows 10, followed by instructions on post-installation tasks. You will learn about the deployment of Windows 10 in Enterprise and also see how to configure networking in Windows 10. You'll understand how to leverage Disk Management and Windows PowerShell to configure disks, volumes, and file system options. As you progress through the chapters, you will be able to set up remote management in Windows 10 and learn more about Windows update usage, behavior, and settings. You will also gain insights that will help you monitor and manage data recovery and explore how to configure authentication, authorization, and advanced management tools in Windows 10.

By the end of this book, you will be equipped with sufficient knowledge to take the 70-698 exam and explore different study methods to improve your chances of passing the exam with ease.

Who this book is for

This book is for IT professionals who perform installation, configuration, general local management, and maintenance of Windows 10 core services, and are preparing to undertake the Windows 10: 70-698 exam.

What this book covers

Chapter 1, *Preparing for Installation*, explains pre-installation preparation and requirements.

Chapter 2, *Installing Windows 10*, covers the installation of Windows 10.

Chapter 3, *Configuring Devices and Device Drivers*, covers devices and device drivers.

Chapter 4, *Performing Post-Installation Configuration*, explains Windows 10 post-installation tasks.

Chapter 5, *Implementing Windows in an Enterprise Environment*, explains the Windows 10 deployment in Enterprise.

Chapter 6, *Configuring Networking*, covers Windows 10 networking.

Chapter 7, *Configuring Storage*, explains storage in Windows 10.

Chapter 8, *Configuring Data Access and Usage*, covers data access and usage in Windows 10.

Chapter 9, *Implementing Apps*, explains app installation and configuration in Windows 10.

Chapter 10, *Configuring Remote Management*, explains remote management in Windows 10.

Chapter 11, *Configuring Updates*, explains Windows 10 updates, as well as Windows Update usage, behavior, and settings.

Chapter 12, *Monitoring Windows 10*, explains Windows 10 monitoring.

Chapter 13, *Configuring System and Data Recovery*, explains system and data recovery in Windows 10.

Chapter 14, *Configuring Authorization and Authentication*, explains authorization and authentication in Windows 10.

Chapter 15, *Configuring Advanced Management Tools*, explains those advanced management tools that are available in Windows 10.

Chapter 16, *Studying and Passing Exam 70-698*, helps you become familiar with the 70-698 exam and learn about study methods to improve your odds of passing the exam.

To get the most out of this book

For few chapter labs you need Windows 10 Enterprise or Windows Education with 8 GB of RAM. Whereas for most of the chapter labs Windows 10 Pro with 4 GB of RAM will do the work.

Conventions used

There are a number of text conventions used throughout this book.

`CodeInText`: Indicates code words in text, database table names, folder names, filenames, file extensions, pathnames, dummy URLs, user input, and Twitter handles. Here is an example: "Click the search box in the taskbar and enter `cmd`."

Any command-line input or output is written as follows:

```
Get-SmbShareAccess
Grant-SmbShareAccess
```

Bold: Indicates a new term, an important word, or words that you see on screen. For example, words in menus or dialog boxes appear in the text like this. Here is an example: "Click **Done** to close the **File Sharing Wizard**."

Warnings or important notes appear like this.

Tips and tricks appear like this.

Get in touch

Feedback from our readers is always welcome.

General feedback: If you have questions about any aspect of this book, mention the book title in the subject of your message and email us at `customercare@packtpub.com`.

Errata: Although we have taken every care to ensure the accuracy of our content, mistakes do happen. If you have found a mistake in this book, we would be grateful if you would report this to us. Please visit `www.packt.com/submit-errata`, selecting your book, clicking on the Errata Submission Form link, and entering the details.

Piracy: If you come across any illegal copies of our works in any form on the internet, we would be grateful if you would provide us with the location address or website name. Please contact us at `copyright@packt.com` with a link to the material.

If you are interested in becoming an author: If there is a topic that you have expertise in, and you are interested in either writing or contributing to a book, please visit `authors.packtpub.com`.

Reviews

Please leave a review. Once you have read and used this book, why not leave a review on the site that you purchased it from? Potential readers can then see and use your unbiased opinion to make purchase decisions, we at Packt can understand what you think about our products, and our authors can see your feedback on their book. Thank you!

For more information about Packt, please visit `packt.com`.

Preparing for Installation

Welcome to Windows 10! This chapter is designed to provide you with an introduction to Windows 10. As you might know, Windows 10 is the newest operating system for PCs developed by Microsoft as part of the Windows NT family. As such, it is necessary for your computer to meet the minimum system requirements to install Windows 10. Therefore, this chapter will explain the system's minimum requirements as well as the recommended ones. Also, you will get familiar with installation options, such as upgrade and clean install. Then, you will be able to get to know the Windows 10 editions and their unique features. Definitions such as clients, servers, hosts, and nodes are also covered in this chapter. Last but not least, after getting acquainted with the installation media concept, you will have the option to download Windows 10 and create installation media, depending on the format your computer supports.

In this chapter, we will cover the following topics:

- Understanding hardware requirements
- Understanding clean install
- Understanding upgrade
- Understanding Windows 10 editions
- Understanding Windows 10 features
- Understanding installation media
- Understanding client, server, host, and node
- Chapter lab—downloading Windows 10

Technical requirements

In order to complete the labs for this chapter, you will need one of the following pieces of equipment:

- PC with Windows 10 Pro, at least 4 GB of RAM, 500 GB of HDD, and access to the internet

Determining hardware requirements

Windows 10 (codenamed Threshold) was released on July 29, 2015. Windows 10 represents another of Microsoft's Windows NT family **operating system** (**OS**) that merges Windows 7 and Windows 8/8.1 into a single OS. Windows 10 provides support for two physical processors, 32-bit and 64-bit, and ARM architecture. According to Microsoft, Windows 10 is the last OS released for **personal computers** (**PCs**). That said, Windows 10 new releases are offered through the **Windows as a Service** format. For the first anniversary in July 2016, Microsoft released Windows 10 Anniversary Update (codenamed Redstone 1), introducing a number of new features and enhancements. And so the practice of releasing new Windows 10 versions continues to be present even today. Recently, Microsoft has released the Windows 10 October 2018 Update (version 1809), which is included in this book.

As far as the **minimum system requirements** are concerned, Windows 10 can be installed on a PC with the following technical specifications:

- **Processor**: 1 GHz or faster processor
- **RAM**: 1 GB for 32-bit or 2 GB for 64-bit
- **HDD**: 16 GB for 32-bit OS 20 GB for 64-bit OS
- **Graphics card**: DirectX 9 or later with WDDM 1.0 driver
- **Monitor**: SVGA (800x600)

However, be aware that those are just bare minimum specifications, meaning that your computer will only be able to run the most basic tasks. Hence, if you want to avoid slow performance on your computer, then you'd better stick to the following **recommended system requirements**:

- **Processor**: 2 GHz or faster processor
- **RAM**: 4 GB for 32-bit or 8 GB for 64-bit
- **HDD**: 1 TB
- **Graphics card**: Microsoft DirectX 9 with WDDM driver
- **Monitor**: XGA (1024x768) and above

- **Other hardware**: Has support for optical disk drives such as DVDs and support for SSDs with USB, keyboard, and mouse
- **Internet connection**: Cable or DSL connection

Choosing between an upgrade and a clean install

As the name indicates, whether you are installing Windows 10 on a new hard disk or on an existing disk, the **clean install** (see *Figure 1.1*) formats the new disk so it can install the new OS, or reformats the existing disk by erasing the existing OS, users' data, and apps to install the new OS. To summarize, a clean install (re)builds the OS and its utilities entirely from scratch, thus overwriting all the previous content on a disk:

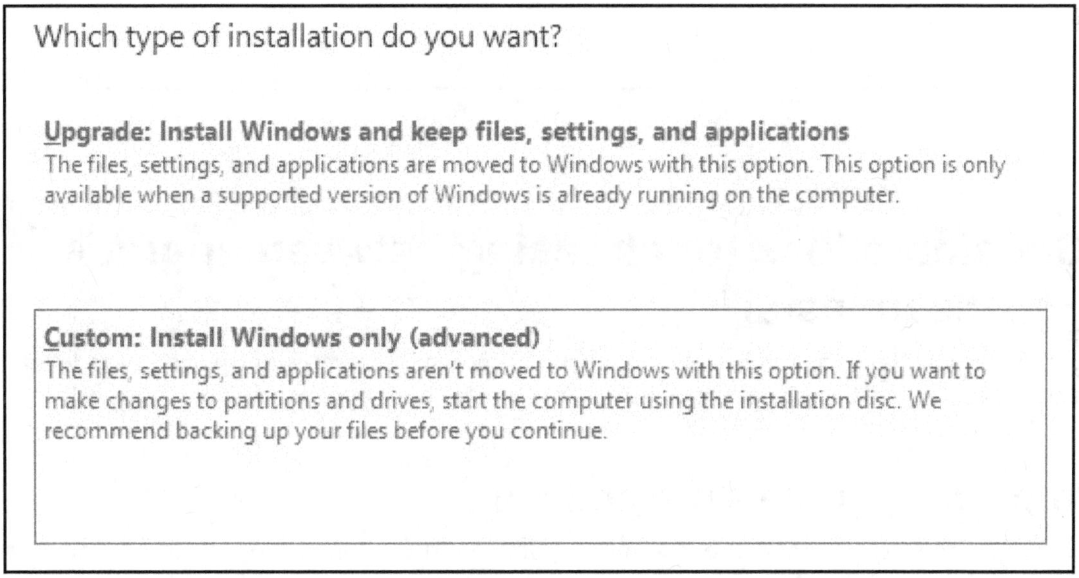

Which type of installation do you want?

Upgrade: Install Windows and keep files, settings, and applications
The files, settings, and applications are moved to Windows with this option. This option is only available when a supported version of Windows is already running on the computer.

Custom: Install Windows only (advanced)
The files, settings, and applications aren't moved to Windows with this option. If you want to make changes to partitions and drives, start the computer using the installation disc. We recommend backing up your files before you continue.

Figure 1.1 Clean install option from Windows 10 setup

Unlike clean install, upgrade (as in *Figure 1.2*) replaces your existing OS with a new one. That means that you retain your files and settings. It is often called an **in-place upgrade** because it takes place on a machine with an already installed OS. Prior to running an upgrade, it is recommended that you make a backup of Windows system states, files, and folders:

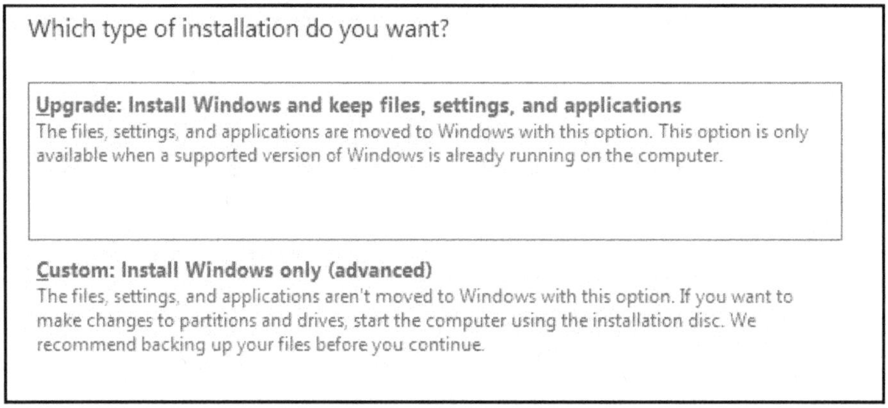

Which type of installation do you want?

Upgrade: Install Windows and keep files, settings, and applications
The files, settings, and applications are moved to Windows with this option. This option is only available when a supported version of Windows is already running on the computer.

Custom: Install Windows only (advanced)
The files, settings, and applications aren't moved to Windows with this option. If you want to make changes to partitions and drives, start the computer using the installation disc. We recommend backing up your files before you continue.

Figure 1.2 Upgrade option from Windows 10 setup

Considerations for choosing between upgrade and clean install

In the previous section, you learned about the difference between an in-place upgrade and a clean install. The following lists the pros and cons of both upgrade and clean install.

In-place upgrade – pro and cons

One of the most common methods to move from an old version of Windows to the newest version of Windows and be able to keep all of your files and apps is by doing an **in-place upgrade**. In addition, an in-place upgrade is suitable for less-experienced users. Here are the pros and cons of an upgrade:

- **Pros**:
  - No bootable media is required
  - Keep all of your files, settings, and apps
  - Roll back to previous versions of Windows

- **Cons**:
  - Apps and drivers may not work correctly
  - May not perform as expected
  - May contain bloatware from a previous Windows version

Clean install – pro and cons

If you have purchased a new computer with no preloaded OS on it, or a new computer with an old OS on it, then definitely you can opt for **clean install** if you do not want an in-place upgrade. In addition, a clean install is suitable for experienced users. Here are the pros and cons of a clean install:

- **Pros**:
  - It is a fresh Windows 10 installation
  - Enables you to configure disk partitioning
  - Enables you to change editions by providing a product key
- **Cons**:
  - Requires bootable media
  - Requires formatting the partition of a disk or the entire disk
  - May take time to install apps and migrate files

Determining appropriate editions according to device type

Never in the history of Windows OS has a single version had more editions than Windows 10. There are altogether **12 editions** of Windows 10, each with unique features:

- **Windows 10 Home**: Designed to be used by home users.
- **Windows 10 Pro**: Designed to be used by business users.
- **Windows 10 Enterprise**: A full-featured edition designed to be used by business users in an enterprise environment. It is distributed through Volume Licensing.
- **Windows 10 Education**: Another full-featured edition designed to be used in education. It is distributed through Academic Volume Licensing.
- **Windows 10 Pro Education**: A special edition designed to be used by schools. It is distributed through a discounted K-12 Academic License.

- **Windows 10 Enterprise LTSB**: Stands for Windows 10 Enterprise **Long Term Servicing Branch** and receives standard monthly security and reliability updates for an extended 10-year support period.
- **Windows 10 Mobile Enterprise**: A full-featured edition that is optimized for mobile devices in an enterprise environment.
- **Windows 10 Mobile**: Designed for smartphones and tablets. This edition has replaced Windows Phone 8.1.
- **Windows 10 IoT**: Stands for Windows 10 **Internet of Things** and is primarily designed to replace Windows Embedded.
- **Windows 10 in S mode**: Designed to only run apps from the Microsoft Store.
- **Windows 10 Team**: Designed as a device-specific version. It is loaded onto the Surface Hub (an interactive whiteboard designed by Microsoft).
- **Windows 10 Pro for Workstations**: Designed for high-end hardware for intensive computing tasks.

 Since the release of the Windows 10 April 2018 Update, Microsoft is working on the Windows 10 Lean edition for end devices with limited storage.

How to determine which Windows 10 version your PC is running?

To find out which version of Windows 10 is running on your PC, do the following:

1. Click the search icon in the taskbar.
2. Enter about as a keyword, and select **About your PC** from the search results, as shown in *Figure 1.3*:

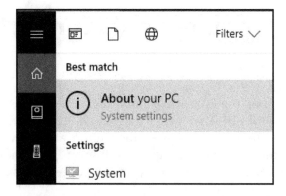

Figure 1.3 Finding out information about Windows 10 using the About your PC option

3. Under **Windows specifications** on the **About** page of **Windows Settings**, you will find information about the Windows 10 edition, version, when it was installed, and the OS build.

Another way to find out which version of Windows 10 your PC is running, is as follows:

1. Press the Windows logo key + R.
2. Enter `winver` and then select **OK**, as shown in *Figure 1.4*:

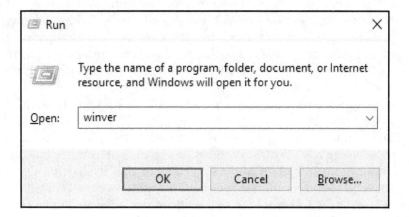

Figure 1.4 Finding out information about of Windows 10 using the winver command

3. From the **About** Windows dialog box, you will find information about the Windows 10 version, the OS build, edition, and to whom the product is licensed.

Determining requirements for particular features

As you may have noticed in the *Determining appropriate editions according to device type* section earlier in this chapter, the **Enterprise** and **Education** editions are the only full-featured editions of Windows 10. That means that not all features work or are available in each edition of Windows 10. So, depending on the edition, at your disposal are some of the unique Windows 10 features, such as Cortana, Windows Hello, Continuum, Secure Boot, BitLocker/BitLocker To Go, Client Hyper-V, Skype, and other features.

You can learn more about Windows 10 specifications and systems requirements at `https://www.microsoft.com/en-us/windows/windows-10-specifications#additional-requirements`.

Determining and creating appropriate installation media

An **installation media** is a medium that contains the operating system files. Whether you are making a clean install or an upgrade to Windows 10, you will definitely need an installation media. You can have a fabricated installation media that you have probably purchased from Microsoft or its channel partners, or you can create one. Before you go on and purchase a fabricated installation media or create one on your own, it is recommended to assess what format of an installation media your device supports. Nowadays, while most end devices are equipped with USB ports (including micro USB ports), not all devices have a DVD drive. Therefore, it is your device that determines the format of an installation media. With that in mind, when opting for a fabricated installation media, in most cases you will end up receiving a DVD disk. Whereas, if you decide to create one on your own then you need a Windows 10 ISO file and a DVD disk or USB flash drive. Due to the size of the Windows 10 ISO file, it is recommended that the capacity of the DVD disk and USB flash drive be at least 8 GB. To learn how to download the Windows 10 ISO file and how to burn an ISO file to a DVD disk or create a bootable USB flash drive on your own, see the *Chapter lab – downloading Windows 10* section later in this chapter.

To create a bootable USB flash drive on your own, download the **Windows USB/DVD Download Tool** from `https://www.microsoft.com/en-us/download/details.aspx?id=56485`.

What are clients, servers, hosts, and nodes?

When talking about clients, servers, hosts, and nodes, we are actually talking about computer network components. At first glance, it may seem like, more or less, we are talking about the same component, but in fact each component is unique in itself. Hence, to understand these components correctly, the following sections will explain clients, servers, hosts, and nodes.

Understanding clients and servers

As you may know, the network world recognizes two architectures: **peer-to-peer** (**P2P**) and **client/server** architecture. While a P2P network architecture consists of hosts that, depending on network activity, switch roles from client to server and vice versa, in a client/server architecture, hosts have predefined roles where some are clients and some are servers. **Clients** are the hosts who make requests for network services, whereas the **servers** are hosts that provide network services. Both clients and servers play an active role in computer networks. In *Figure 1.5*, the server with a shared printer acts as a print server, and as such it provides print services to the clients in a network. Whereas, the PC, laptop, and smartphone represent the clients that request services:

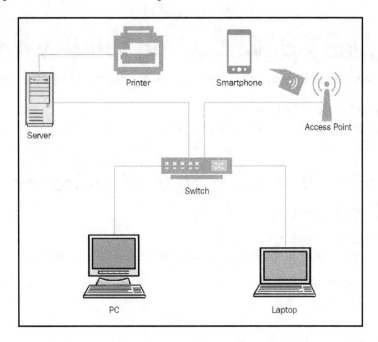

Figure 1.5 Client/server network architecture

The origin of the word **server** originates from the word **serve**. If you search for the word **serve** in the *Merriam-Webster* dictionary, among the results you will find is the one that says: *to provide services that benefit or help*. Thus, a server in a computer network means a computer that provides services to the clients. From that, the server serves the clients.

Understanding hosts and nodes

When talking about hosts and nodes, although their first impression might drive us towards thinking that they are the same thing, in fact, they are not! The difference between hosts and nodes is that while all hosts can be nodes, not every node can act as a host. That way, to every host an IP address is assigned. So, a **host** is any device with an IP address that requests or provides networking resources to any other host or node on the network. However, there are devices such as hubs, bridges, switches, modems, and access points that have no IP address assigned, but are still used for communication. That said, a **node** is any device that can generate, receive, and transmit the networking resources on a computer network, and as such it has no communication interface with an IP address. Based on that, in *Figure 1.5*, the server, smartphone, PC, and laptop are acting as hosts in a network, while the switch and **access point** (**AP**) act as nodes.

Chapter lab – downloading Windows 10

In this chapter lab, you will learn how to download Windows 10 from the following:

- Microsoft Evaluation Center
- Through the Windows 10 media creation tool

Downloading Windows 10 from Microsoft Evaluation Center

The steps to download Windows 10 Enterprise (90-day free evaluation) and burn the ISO file to a DVD are fairly simple. To do so, perform the following steps:

1. Open your browser and enter `https://www.microsoft.com/en-us/evalcenter/` in the address bar.
2. In the upper-right corner, locate the search icon and enter `Windows 10 Enterprise`, and then press *Enter*.

3. From the list of results, select **Windows 10 Enterprise**.
4. After selecting the evaluation file type, click the **Continue** button.
5. After you have completed the form, click the **Continue** button.
6. Select the platform and language, and then click the **Download** button.
7. Specify the location on you computer or on a network share when prompted to save the Windows 10 Enterprise file (see *Figure 1.6*):

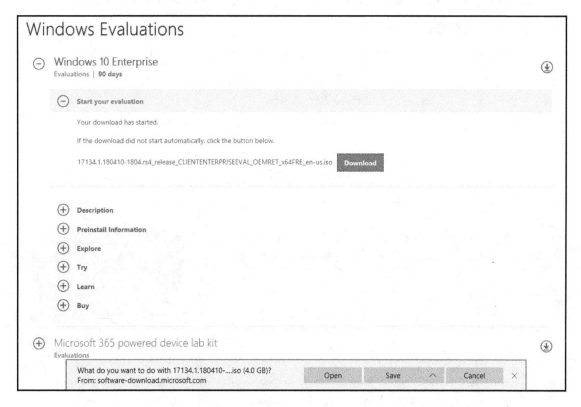

Figure 1.6 Downloading Windows 10 Enterprise from Microsoft Evaluation Center

Once your Windows 10 Enterprise download completes, you can then burn the ISO file to a DVD or create a bootable USB flash drive. Remember, Windows 10 Enterprise is valid only for 90 days from the day that you install it. Afterward, if you want to continue to use it then you should purchase a license.

To find out how to mount and burn ISO files in Windows 10 and previous versions of Windows, navigate to `https://www.laptopmag.com/articles/mount-burn-iso-files-windows`.

Downloading Windows 10 through the media creation tool

To download Windows 10 and make a bootable USB flash drive, do the following:

1. Open your browser and enter `https://www.microsoft.com/en-us/software-download/windows10` in the address bar.

2. In the **Create Windows 10 installation media** section, click on **Download tool now**.

3. Specify the location on you computer or on a network share when prompted to save the media creation tool (see *Figure 1.7*):

Figure 1.7 Downloading the media creation tool for Windows 10

4. Once the download completes, click on **Run**.
5. Shortly, the **Windows 10 Setup** window will display the **Applicable notices and license terms** view. Click on **Accept**.
6. In the **What do you want to do?** view, select **Create Installation media (USB flash drive, DVD, or ISO file) for another PC** and click on **Next**.
7. The next view enables you to **Select language, architecture, and edition**, and then click on **Next**.
8. In the **Choose which media to use** view, select **USB flash drive** and click **Next**.
9. **Select a USB flash drive** and click **Next**.
10. The next view shows that **Downloading Windows 10** has started.
11. Once Windows 10 is downloaded, the next view indicates that the Windows 10 setup is **Creating Windows 10 media**.
12. Finally, click **Finish** when you notice the **Your USB flash drive is ready** view (see *Figure 1.8*):

Figure 1.8 Windows 10 setup indicating that a bootable USB flash drive is ready

Summary

We can summarize the chapter with the following points:

- Windows 10 represents another Microsoft's Windows NT family operating system (OS) that merges Windows 7 and Windows 8/8.1 into a single OS
- Windows 10 new releases are offered through Windows as a service format

- Clean install (re)builds the OS and its utilities entirely from scratch, thus overwriting all the previous content on a disk
- An upgrade replaces your existing OS with a new one
- There are altogether 12 editions of Windows 10, each with unique features
- The Enterprise and Education editions are the only full-featured editions of Windows 10
- An installation media is a medium that contains the operating system files
- Clients are computers that request the resources in a computer network
- Servers are a network component that provides resources to clients
- A host is any device with an IP address that requests or provides networking resources to any other host or node on the network
- A node is any device that can generate, receive, and transmit the networking resources on the computer network and as such it has no communication interface with an IP address

Questions

1. Windows 10 new releases are offered through Windows as a Service format.
    1. True
    2. False

2. There are altogether _____ of Windows 10, each with unique features.

3. Which of the following are full-featured editions of Windows 10? (Choose two):
    1. Windows 10 Home
    2. Windows 10 Pro
    3. Windows 10 Enterprise
    4. Windows 10 Education

4. An installation media is a medium that contains the MS Office files.
    1. True
    2. False

5. _____ replaces your existing OS with a new one.

6. Which of the following are pros and cons of a clean install?
    1. Enables you to configure disk partitioning
    2. Enables you to change editions by providing product key
    3. May take time to install apps and migrate files
    4. All of the above

7. Clients are computers that request the resources in a computer network.
    1. True
    2. False

8. _____ is any device that can generate, receive, and transmit the networking resources on the computer network, and as such it has no communication interface with an IP address.

9. Which of the following are pros and cons of an upgrade?
    1. Rolling back to the previous version of Windows
    2. Apps and drivers may not work correctly
    3. May contain bloatware from a previous Windows version
    4. All of the above

10. Discuss the minimum system requirements versus the recommended system requirements.

Further reading

- **Windows 10 upgrade paths**: https://docs.microsoft.com/en-us/windows/deployment/upgrade/windows-10-upgrade-paths
- **Windows 10 edition upgrade:** https://docs.microsoft.com/en-us/windows/deployment/upgrade/windows-10-edition-upgrades
- **What's new for IT pros in Windows 10, version 1803**: https://techcommunity.microsoft.com/t5/Windows-IT-Pro-Blog/What-s-new-for-IT-pros-in-Windows-10-version-1803/ba-p/188568

Installing Windows 10 2

This chapter is designed to provide you with detailed instructions regarding Windows 10 installation. The step-by-step instructions, driven by easy-to-understand graphics, show you how to master the installation of Windows 10. With that in mind, this chapter covers the following installation types: upgrade using installation media, clean installation using a bootable USB flash drive, and configuring a native boot. With the guidance provided by this easy-to-follow chapter, you will quickly learn the installation process without obstacles. In addition, you will learn about Windows 10 valid upgrade paths, as well as getting to know the tools required to migrate from Windows 2000, XP, or Vista to Windows 10. Other than that, you will get to know how to turn Windows features on or off, and configure regional and language settings in Windows 10. With all that, this chapter proves to be an excellent collection of how-to tips to get the job done in Windows 10.

In this chapter, we will cover the following topics:

- Configuring native boot
- Identifying upgrade paths
- Migrating from previous versions of Windows
- Installing additional Windows 10 features
- Configuring Windows 10 for additional regional and language support
- Chapter labs—performing upgrade and clean installation

Technical requirements

In order to complete the labs for this chapter, you will need the following equipments:

- PC with at least Windows 7, 2 GB of RAM, 30 GB of HDD, and access to the internet
- PC with Windows 10 Enterprise, 8 GB of RAM, Hyper-V feature turned on, 500 GB of HDD, and access to the internet

Upgrade using installation media

So, if you have already assessed the minimum system requirements for installing Windows 10 and backed up your data in your Windows 7 computer, then it looks like you are ready to rock and roll the upgrade process. As explained in Chapter 1, *Preparing for Installation*, in the *Determining and creating appropriate installation media* section, usually a DVD disc or a USB flash drive act as the installation media. With that in mind, the upgrade from an existing Windows version to Windows 10 requires an installation media to be inserted/plugged into the computer prior to running the upgrade process. To insert a DVD disc into a DVD drive or plug a USB flash drive into a USB port, complete the following steps:

1. Open the *DVD drive tray*, insert the **DVD disc**, and close the *DVD drive tray*. Wait until the **DVD disc** has been read.

Or:

1. Locate a free *USB port* on your PC and plug in the **USB flash drive**.
2. Wait until your PC recognizes the **USB flash drive** and click **setup**, as shown in *Figure 2.1*:

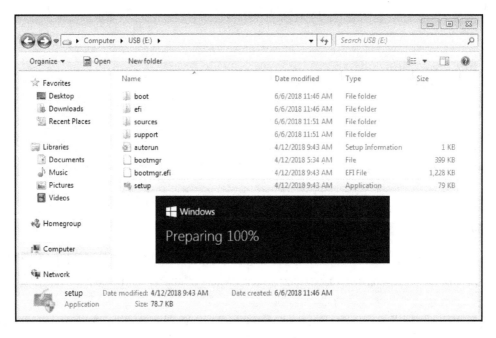

Figure 2.1 Upgrading Windows 7 to Windows 10

Check out the *Chapter lab – performing upgrade, and clean installation* section later on this chapter to continue with the steps of the upgrade process from a previous version of Windows to Windows 10 using an installation media.

 If you want to know how to upgrade to Windows 10, and what you need to know before upgrading to Windows 10, check out the following URL: https://www.pcworld.com/article/2928286/windows/how-to-upgrade-to-windows-10-what-you-need-to-know.html.

Configuring native boot scenarios

Native boot is a method that enables the computer to boot from the **virtual hard disk (VHD)** without the need for virtualization. It works in a way that adds VHD to a boot loader and boots from it. On the VHD disk, the Windows 10 deployment image is applied. Then, you have to configure your computer to boot from the VHD disk. Once you restart your computer, you will be prompted to boot from the VHD disk instead.

 You can learn about deploying Windows with a VHDX (native boot) at https://docs.microsoft.com/en-us/windows-hardware/manufacture/desktop/deploy-windows-on-a-vhd--native-boot.

Installing to VHD

To deploy the Windows 10 image to the VHD disk, complete the following steps:

1. Press Windows key + X to display the administrator's menu (known also as the secret Start menu), as shown in *Figure 2.2*:

Figure 2.2 Administrator's menu (a secret Start menu)

2. Select **Disk Management**.

3. Right-click on the volume that has the most free space, and select **Shrink Volume**.

4. In the **Enter the amount of space to shrink in MB** textbox, enter the value `30000`, and click **Shrink**.

5. Right-click on the unallocated volume and select **New Simple Volume**.

6. Complete the **New Simple Volume Wizard** by clicking a few times on **Next**, and finally **Finish**.

7. Your newly created volume (named **BootFromVHD**) is shown in *Figure 2.3*:

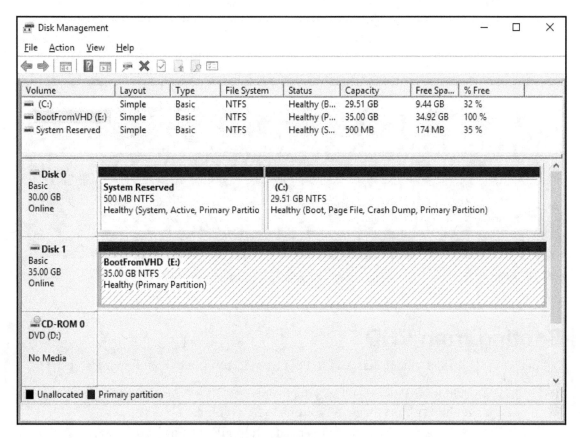

Figure 2.3 New volume created using Disk Management

8. Make sure to extract the Windows 10 ISO file to an accessible folder anywhere in your computer.
9. Press Windows key + X to display the administrator's menu, and select **Windows PowerShell (Admin)**.

10. Enter `DISM /Apply-Image`
    `/ImageFile:C:\Windows10\sources\install.wim /Index:1`
    `/ApplyDir:E:\` to apply the Windows 10 image to the VHD disk (define the
    path according to your scenario; mine
    is `C:\Windows10\sources\install.wim`), as shown in *Figure 2.4*:

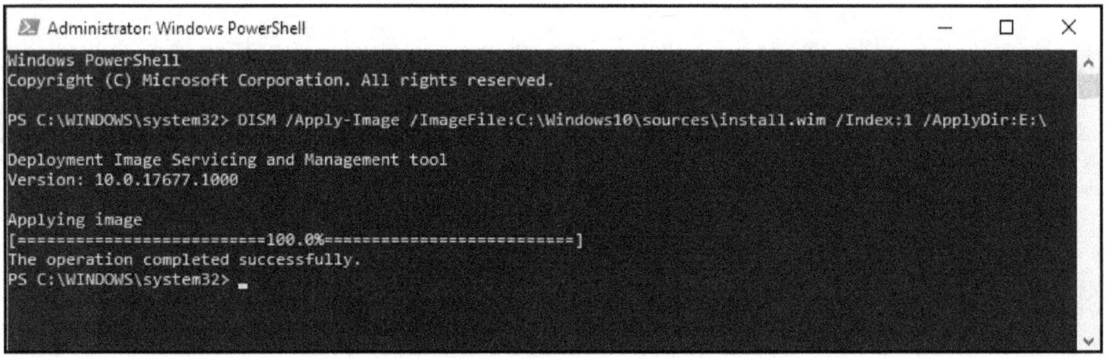

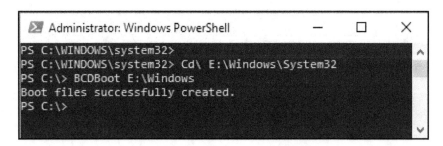

Figure 2.4 Applying the Windows 10 image to the VHD disk

Booting from VHD

To specify VHD disk as a boot disk and to boot from it, complete the following steps:

1. With Windows PowerShell still open, enter `Cd\ E:\Windows\System32` to
   change the directory from `C:` volume to `E:` volume.
2. Enter `BCDBoot E:\Windows` to specify the VHD disk as a boot disk, as shown in
   Figure 2.5:

Figure 2.5 Changing directory from C: volume to E: volume, and specifying the VHD disk as a boot disk

3. Close Windows PowerShell and **restart** your computer.
4. You will be prompted to **start up from the VHD disk**, as shown in *Figure 2.6* (in my scenario, volume 3 is the VHD disk):

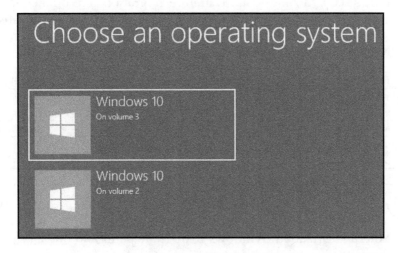

Figure 2.6 Starting up from the VHD disk

5. As it is a new installation of Windows 10, you will be **prompted to set up** the region and keyboard, accept the Windows 10 License Agreement and set up an account (offline or online), Cortana, and privacy settings.
6. After you have completed all the preconfigurations, then *voila*, you have logged in to Windows 10 running out of the VHD disk (see *Figure 2.7*):

Figure 2.7 Running Windows 10 from the VHD disk

Identifying valid upgrade paths

While you can upgrade from Windows 7 and 8/8.1 to Windows 10, you will not be able to do it from Windows 2000, XP, and Vista. Therefore, migration is recommended for the latter. It is interesting to note that in the first year of the release of Windows 10, the upgrade from Windows 7 and 8/8.1 to Windows 10 was available for free through Windows Update. *Table 2.1* lists the Windows versions that can be upgraded or migrated to Windows 10:

Previous Windows version	Upgrade to Windows 10	Migration to Windows 10
Windows 2000	No	Yes
Windows XP	No	Yes
Windows Vista	No	Yes
Windows 7	Yes	No
Windows 8	Yes	No
Windows 8.1	Yes	No

Table 2.1 Windows 10 upgrade paths

 You can learn about Windows 10 upgrade paths and find a list of deprecated features with alternatives at `https://www.askvg.com/ windows-10-upgrade-paths-and-things-to-know-before-upgrading/`.

Migrating from previous versions of Windows

Usually, there are two reasons why you cannot upgrade an old version of Windows to Windows 10. First, the old version of Windows (such as Windows 2000, XP, or Vista) is not supported by Microsoft as an in-place upgrade to Windows 10, and second, the computer hardware might not meet the minimum system requirements. So, you have no choice but to migrate your old version of Windows to Windows 10. A migration requires bringing in a new computer where you would install Windows 10. Once the installation of Windows 10 is completed on a new computer, you would want to run **Windows Easy Transfer** (**WET**) or **User State Migration Tool** (**USMT**) to move stuff from your old computer to a new computer. However, while WET is not available in Windows 10 (it was removed in Windows 8.1), USMT is intended for large-scale automated deployments.

Thus, Microsoft recommends the PCmover Express application developed by Laplink. But, like the Zinstall and EaseUS Todo PCTrans (the EaseUS Todo PCTrans free version can be downloaded for free but with limited features) applications, PCmover Express is not available free of charge. So, the choice is yours depending on the version of Windows you are migrating from and what type of data you want to migrate to Windows 10.

 You can learn how to migrate users and user data step-by-step from Windows XP, Vista, 7, and 8/8.1 to Windows 10 using the USMT at `http:/ /itproguru.com/expert/2016/01/step-by-step-how-to-migrate-users- and-user-data-from-xp-vista-windows-7-or-8-to-windows-10-using- microsoft-tool-usmt-user-state-migration-toolkit/`.

Installing from a bootable USB

Installing from bootable USB associates with clean install. That is because the computer needs to be booted from a bootable installation media and not from the **hard disk drive** (**HDD**). As explained in `Chapter 1`, *Preparing for Installation*, in the *Determining and creating appropriate installation media* section, usually a DVD disc and USB flash drive act as an installation media. With that in mind, the clean install requires setting up the boot order in **basic input/output system** (**BIOS**) or **Unified Extensible Firmware Interface** (**UEFI**), depending on which program your computer uses. To access BIOS or UEFI, different keys on a keyboard can be used, however, that very much depends on the manufacturer of your computer's BIOS or UEFI. The most frequently used keys are *Del* and *F2*, although it does not mean that you should not try keys like *F9*, *F10*, and *F11*. Once you access the BIOS or UEFI, you will be presented with the following boot options:

- **Boot from DVD**: Prior to accessing the BIOS or UEFI, insert the bootable DVD disc into the DVD drive. Access the BIOS or UEFI, set the DVD as the first boot option, and then save the changes and exit the BIOS or UEFI.
- **Boot from generic USB**: Similar to the bootable DVD disc, plug in your bootable USB flash drive prior to accessing BIOS or UEFI. Access the BIOS or UEFI, set the USB flash drive as the first boot option, and then save the changes and exit the BIOS or UEFI.
- **Boot over network**: This does not require bootable installation media. Instead, it requires the **Windows Deployment Services** (**WDS**), which has bootable and installation images. Access the BIOS or UEFI, and set boot over the network as the first boot option. Save the changes and exit the BIOS or UEFI.

Since, in our case, we are using a bootable USB flash drive as an installation media, then once the computer restarts, it will attempt to boot from the bootable USB. Once it boots, Windows 10 installation files are loaded into the RAM memory from a bootable USB flash drive.

Check out the *Chapter lab – performing upgrade and clean installation* section later in this chapter to continue with the steps of the clean install using a bootable USB flash drive.

 Learn the easy way to clean install Windows 10 on your computer at `https://www.howtogeek.com/224342/how-to-clean-install-windows-10/`.

Installing additional Windows 10 features

Let's say that you have just completed the installation of Windows 10 Enterprise and that you want to access client Hyper-V. Scrolling through the Start menu, you will notice that client Hyper-V is not there. A further search in **Administrative Tools** does not match the requested result as well. However, knowing that client Hyper-V is part of the Enterprise edition, then the question is how do you add this feature to your Windows 10? The answer to that question can be found in **Turn Windows Features On or Off**. To do this, perform the following steps:

1. Click the search icon on a taskbar and enter `Turn Windows features on or off`.
2. Click the best match, which is **Turn Windows features on or off**.
3. On a **Windows Features** window, locate and check **Hyper-V** (as shown in *Figure 2.8*):

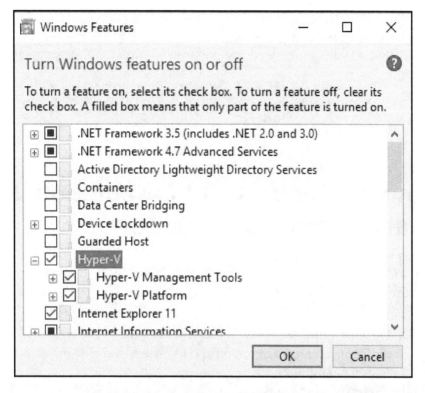

Figure 2.8. Turning Windows Features on or off

4. Make sure that both **Hyper-V Management Tools** and **Hyper-V Platform** are checked too, and then click **OK**.

5. **Windows Features** will start to **Apply Changes**.

6. Once completed, **Windows Features** displays the message **Windows completed the requested changes**.

7. Click **Close** to close the **Windows Features** window.

Whatever feature you need that is not preloaded by default in Windows 10 can be added through the **Turn Windows features On or Off** option. And, as the name indicates, any added feature that you do not need anymore can be turned off with the same option.

 Learn about all the available Windows features in Windows 10 and how you can turn them on or off at `https://windowsinstructed.com/turn-windows-features-windows/`.

Configuring Windows 10 for additional regional and language support

It has never been easier and more convenient to add a second preferred language to your PC in addition to the default language, or to make Windows localization in the second preferred language by adding the language pack. With that in mind, to add the second preferred language and the language pack, complete the following steps:

1. Click the Start button and click Settings in the Start menu.
2. Click the **Time & Language** option and in the left and side navigation menu, click **Region & language**.
3. In the **Preferred languages** section, click **Add a language**.
4. In the **Choose a language to install screen**, either select **Type a language name** or scroll down to choose a preferred language.
5. Once you choose the preferred language, click **Next** and on the **Install language features** screen, click **Install**.

6. Once the installation completes, the added second preferred language is shown, as can be seen in *Figure 2.9*:

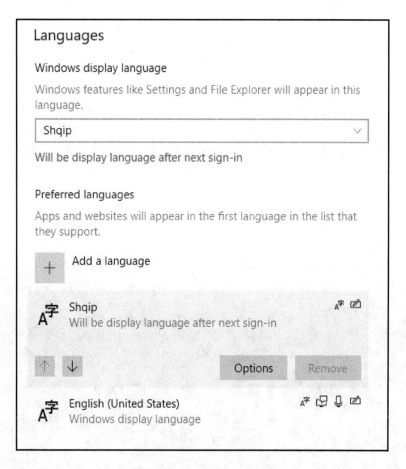

Figure 2.9 Configuring an additional language in Windows 10

 Learn how to configure Windows regional and language settings in Windows 10 in two ways at `https://www.iris.co.uk/support/windows-regional-and-language-settings/`.

Chapter labs – performing upgrade and clean installation

In these chapter labs, you will learn how to do the following:

- Perform an upgrade using installation media
- Perform clean installation

Performing an upgrade using installation media

To continue with the upgrade, following the steps explained in the *Upgrading using installation media* section, perform the following steps:

1. Select **Download and install updates (recommended)** and click **Next**, as shown in *Figure 2.10*:

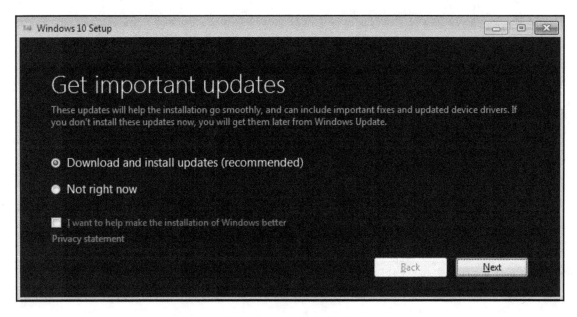

Figure 2.10. Windows 10 upgrade updates help the upgrade go smoothly

2. Enter **Product key** if your copy of Windows 7 is not activated and click **Next**.

3. Take your time to read the **Applicable notices and license terms** and click **Accept**.

4. When **Windows 10 Setup** determines that you are ready to install Windows 10, click the **Install** button (see *Figure 2.11*):

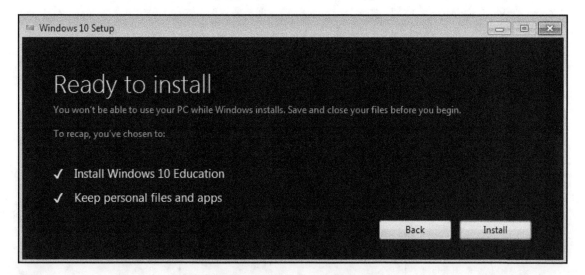

Figure 2.11 Keeping personal files is very important when running an upgrade

5. Installing Windows 10 installation has started and your PC will reboot several times to complete the upgrade process.

6. After the first restart, the upgrade process is working on updates.

7. After several restarts, the famous Windows 10 welcome screen indicates that the upgrade is complete.

8. Click *Ctrl + Alt + Del* to display the login screen, type your password, and press *Enter*.

9. After preparing the desktop for the first-time login, Windows 10 asks you to set up services.

10. *Voila*, you have reached the **Windows 10 desktop**.

Performing a clean installation

To continue with the clean install after you have booted your computer from a bootable USB, as explained in the *Installing on a bootable USB* section, do the following:

1. In the **Windows Setup** window, enter your language and other preferences and click **Next**.
2. Click the **Install now** button to install your copy of Windows 10.
3. Enter the **Product key** and click **Next**.
4. Select the **operating system** you want to install and click **Next**.
5. Take your time to read the **Microsoft Software License Terms**, then check **I accept the license terms** and click **Next**.
6. Select the **Custom** type of installation and select the **drive** where you want to install Windows 10. Click **Next**.
7. Installing Windows 10 has **started up** (see *Figure 2.12*), so sit back and relax:

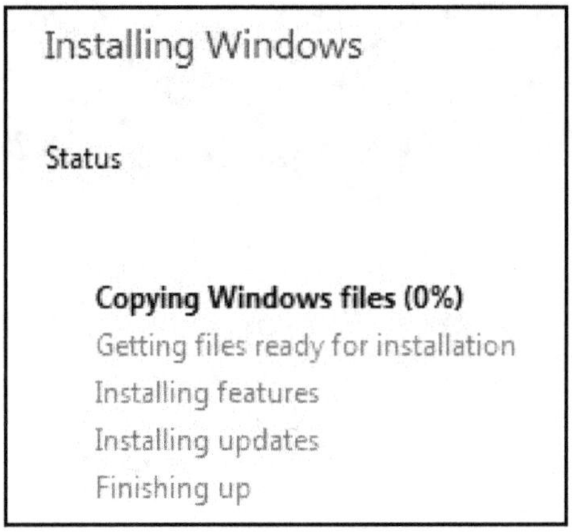

Figure 2.12 Installing Windows 10 files on your computer's hard drive

8. Windows needs to **restart** to continue installing Windows 10 files on your computer.
9. After the restart, Windows will try to **get ready** and it will automatically restart again.
10. After the restart, Windows will ask you to **set up** basic settings, networks, accounts, and services.
11. Once the **required pre-configurations** are completed, the Windows 10 desktop will appear.

Summary

We can summarize the chapter with the following points:

- Prior to running an in-place upgrade, make sure to back up your data.
- An installation media is a bootable DVD disc or bootable USB flash drive.
- Native boot is a method that enables the computer to boot from the VHD without the need for virtualization.
- A combination of Windows key + X displays the administrator's menu, also known as the secret Start menu.
- While Windows 7 and 8/8.1 can be upgraded to Windows 10, Windows 2000, XP, and Vista need to be migrated to Windows 10.
- A migration requires getting a new computer and installing Windows 10.
- Zinstall, EaseUS Todo PCTrans, and PCmover Express are some of the paid apps that help migrate user settings and data from an older versions of Windows to Windows 10.
- Clean install requires setting up the boot order in BIOS or UEFI.
- Any features you need that aren't preloaded by default in Windows 10, you can add through the **Turn Windows features on or off** option.
- **Region & language** helps you configure additional languages in Windows 10.

Questions

1. It is recommended to back up user data before running an in-place upgrade from Windows 7 and 8/8.1 to Windows 10.
    1. True
    2. False
2. A _____ requires getting a new computer and installing Windows 10.
3. Which of the following versions of Windows can be upgraded to Windows 10?
    1. Windows 7
    2. Windows 8
    3. Windows 8.1
    4. All of the above

4. **Region & language** helps you configure **Network & Internet** in Windows 10.
    1. True
    2. False

5. _____ requires setting up the boot order in BIOS or UEFI.

6. Which of the following versions of Windows can be migrated to Windows 10?
    1. Windows 2000
    2. Windows XP
    3. Windows Vista
    4. All of the above

7. A combination of Windows key + X displays the administrator's menu.
    1. True
    2. False

8. _____ is a method that enables the computer to boot from the **virtual hard disk (VHD)** without the need for virtualization.

9. Which of the following is required to run a clean installation of Windows 10?
    1. Facebook account
    2. Laser printer
    3. Bootable USB flash drive
    4. Movie DVD disc

10. Zinstall, EaseUS Todo PCTrans, and PCmover Express are some of the free apps that help migrate user settings and data from an older versions of Windows to Windows 10.
    1. True
    2. False

11. Any features that you need and that are not preloaded by default in Windows 10, then you can add them through the _____ option.

12. Which of the following helps in adding or removing features to/from Windows 10?
    1. Turn system icons on or off
    2. Turn wireless devices on or off
    3. Turn Windows features on or off
    4. Turn app notifications on or off

Further reading

- **Preparing a PC**: https://docs.microsoft.com/en-us/windows-hardware/manufacture/desktop/prepare-a-pc
- **Installing Windows from a USB flash drive**: https://docs.microsoft.com/en-us/windows-hardware/manufacture/desktop/install-windows-from-a-usb-flash-drive
- **Booting to a virtual hard disk**: https://docs.microsoft.com/en-us/windows-hardware/manufacture/desktop/boot-to-vhd--native-boot--add-a-virtual-hard-disk-to-the-boot-menu

3
Configuring Devices and Device Drivers

This chapter is designed to provide you with detailed instructions regarding Windows 10 post-installation tasks, particularly managing devices and device drivers. With that in mind, this chapter explains the importance of device drivers after every installation of an operating system. Tasks such as installation, removal, disabling, updating/upgrading, rollback, and other related things concerning device drivers are part of an IT help desk member's day-to-day job. This requires good knowledge of the triangle composed of the operating system, hardware, and device driver. This chapter also addresses signed and unsigned device drivers by featuring the File Signature Verification tool. The chapter covers the DISM tool too by listing the steps required to add driver packages to the Windows image. Each topic is accompanied with step-by-step instructions driven by targeted, easy-to-understand graphics. The chapter concludes with a chapter labs on operating with device drivers.

In this chapter, we will cover the following topics:

- Understanding devices and drivers
- Resolving device driver issues
- Configuring device driver settings
- Managing driver packages
- Downloading and importing driver packages
- Using the DISM tool to add driver packages
- Chapter labs–operating with device drivers

Technical requirements

In order to complete the labs for this chapter, you will need the following equipment:

- PC with Windows 10 Pro, at least 4 GB of RAM, 500 GB of HDD, and access to the internet

Understanding devices and drivers

As you know, the hardware and software are the two main components that constitute the **personal computer** (**PC**). The **hardware** represents the physical component of the PC, whereas the **software** constitutes the logical component of the PC. The hardware is a collection of physical devices, and the software is a collection of programmed instructions. Since the hardware and software are two components of a completely different nature, there is the need for an intermediate component to help establish communication between these components. That need encouraged **device driver** development. A **device driver** is a program that acts as a bridge between computer hardware and an operating system. It helps the operating system to recognize and control a certain device (that is, hardware) on the computer. Generally, device drivers are distributed through CD or DVD discs that accompany the devices, or through the manufacturer's website. However, the Windows 10 **driver store** as a file is rich with device drivers, thus minimizing the need for device drivers. Simply, you insert, attach, or plugin the device to your computer and, through the **Plug and Play** (**PnP**) feature, your device will get recognized by Windows 10.

Computer devices

Today, apparently, the PC consists mostly of a computer case, monitor, keyboard, and mouse, as shown in *Figure 3.1*. However, as simple as it may seem, computer devices are categorized depending on their function and where they are located in the so-called computer system. So, depending on their function, computer devices are categorized as follows:

- **Input devices**: These devices create input for computer processing architecture
- **Output devices**: These devices create output from what has been processed by computer processing architecture
- **Input/output devices**: These devices are touch-enabled devices that act as an input and output device at the same time

The other categorization, based on the location of the devices, is as follows:

- **Internal devices**: These devices are located exclusively inside the computer's case. Power supply, motherboard, and accompanying components, hard drives, extension cards, and other internal hardware components are examples of internal devices.

- **External devices**: These devices are connected to the computer's case, and are essential devices of a computer system as a whole. A keyboard, monitor, mouse, speakers, earphones, webcam, microphone, and other external hardware components are examples of external devices.

- **Peripheral devices**: These devices are located near to the computer, and as such are not an essential part of the computer system as a whole. Printers, scanners, projectors, plotters, and other such devices are examples of peripheral devices.

- **Network devices**: These devices are connected to a computer over a network cable. Network printers, network scanners, network backup libraries, **Network Attached Storage (NAS)**, **Storage Area Network (SAN)**, and other network devices are examples of network devices:

Figure 3.1 The computer system

In today's literature, authors often refer to any device outside of the computer case as a peripheral device. That perspective includes the keyboard and mouse too.

Device drivers

In Windows 10, you have the ability to manage devices through **Devices** in **Windows Settings**, and manage devices and their drivers by using **Device Manager** from **Computer Management**. Unlike **Devices**, **Device Manager** uses a slightly different representational approach for device drivers. Other than the proper representation of device drivers, there are also the following representations (as shown in *Figure 3.2*):

- The **generic** status indicates that a generic device driver is installed. A generic driver is an alternative driver applied by an operating system from its driver store in a situation when the original driver from the manufacturer is missing.
- The **black exclamation mark on a yellow triangle** status indicates that either the device driver is missing, or an installed device driver is not installed properly.
- The **downward black arrow** status indicates a disabled driver. To enable it, you simply right-click on the device driver and select **Enable**:

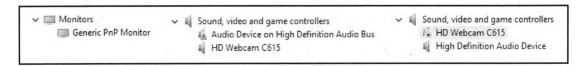

Figure 3.2 Three famous statuses of device drivers in Device Manager

Resolving driver issues

Generally, as you may know, **Device Manager** enables you to manage both the internal and external devices of your computer. Whenever there are problems associated with device drivers, there are several options available in **Device Manager** to resolve those issues. So, if you right-click any of the device drivers of the listed devices and select **Properties** (see *Figure 3.3*) from the context menu, from within **Driver** tab, you will have access to the following options:

- **Update Driver**: It enables you to update the driver by searching automatically for updated driver software or browsing your computer for driver software.

- **Roll Back Driver**: It enables you to roll back to the previously installed driver if the updated driver is not performing properly.
- **Disable Device**: It enables you to disable the device driver by putting the device into a lower-power state if the current driver is causing major issues.
- **Uninstall Device**: It enables you to uninstall the current driver if is not performing properly:

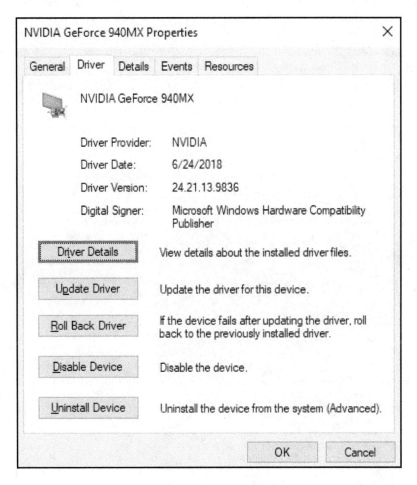

Figure 3.3. Options for resolving driver issues

Configuring driver settings including signed and unsigned drivers

From **Device Manager**, right-click any of the device drivers of the listed devices and select **Properties**. Notice that the device driver's **Properties** dialog box for the majority of devices mostly contain the **General**, **Driver**, **Details**, **Events**, and **Power Management** tabs. However, if you do the same for the device driver of your network adapter, you will see that the network adapter's **Properties** dialog box contains two lines of tabs, as shown in *Figure 3.4*. It is obvious the availability of the Advanced tab as opposed to the device driver for your keyboard. Thus, the **Advanced** tab enables you to configure driver settings by selecting the **Property** you want to change on the left of the **Properties** dialog box, and then selecting its **Value** on the right of the **Properties** dialog box:

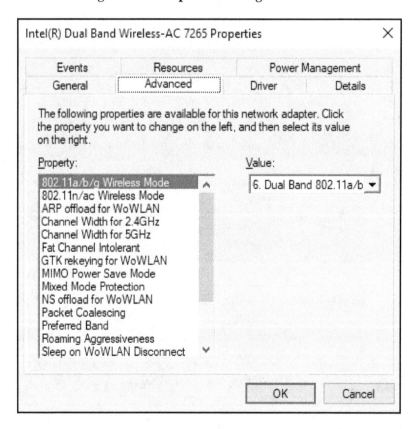

Figure 3.4. The Advanced tab in the network adapter's Properties dialog box

A **signed driver** represents a driver's **digital signature** (see *Figure 3.5*) which identifies the publisher of the driver package. Technically speaking, a signed driver proves that the manufacturer has tested the driver package at **Windows Hardware Quality Labs (WHQL)** and that Microsoft has certified it, ensuring that its installation will not cause any reliability or security issues. That way, the signed driver provides authenticity by guaranteeing the identity of the device driver, and integrity by ensuring that the device driver is intact and has not been altered. To view a driver's digital signing information in Windows 10, complete the following steps:

1. Press Windows key + *X* and select **Device Manager**.
2. Expand **network adapters**.
3. Right-click the **Realtek PCIe FE Family Controller** network adapter and select **Properties**.
4. Select the **Driver** tab and then click **Driver Details** to view the **Digital Signer** information, as shown in *Figure 3.5*:

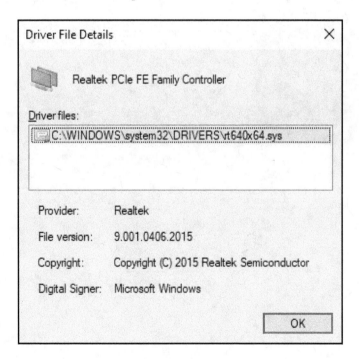

Figure 3.5. A signed driver

Microsoft has developed a tool called **File Signature Verification** (`sigverif.exe`), which will help you identify both signed and unsigned drivers on your Windows 10 computer. `sigverif.exe`, as shown in *Figure 3.6*, works in a way that it scans all device drivers installed on your Windows 10 computer and then generates a log file called `SIGVERIF.TXT`, which contains information about both unsigned drivers and signed drivers. **Unsigned drivers** are device drivers that have not been tested in WHQL and as such have not been certified by Microsoft. In Windows 10, `SIGVERIF.TXT` is located in the `C:\Users\Public\Documents\SIGVERIF.TXT` path. It is good to keep in mind that the installation of unsigned drivers on Windows 10 64-bit is not supported:

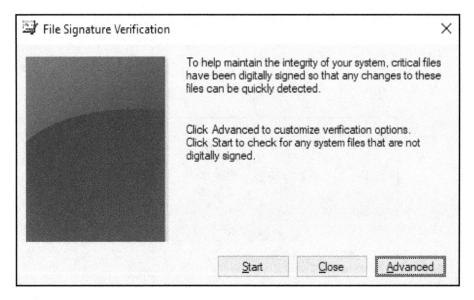

Figure 3.6. File Signature Verification tool

To run the File Signature Verification tool in Windows 10, complete the following steps:

1. Press Windows key + *R* to open the **Run** dialog box.
2. Enter `sigverif.exe` and press *Enter*.
3. Click **Start** and wait until the drivers scan completes.
4. Once the driver scan completes, the **Signature Verification Results** dialog box pops ups automatically (see *Figure 3.7*):

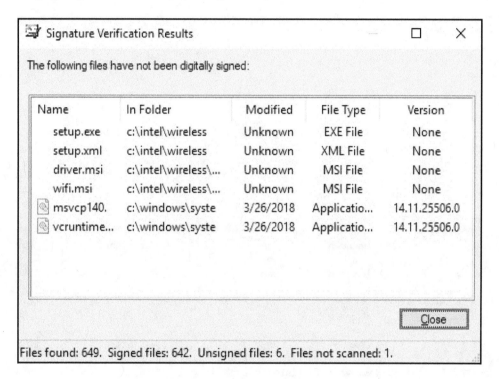

Figure 3.7. Signature Verification Results

To access the **log file** (SIGVERIF.TXT) after the driver scan completes, complete the following steps:

1. With the File Signature Verification tool open, click the **Advanced** button.
2. In the **Advanced File Signature...** dialog box, click the **View Log** button.
3. Shortly, the Microsoft Signature Verification log file SIGVERIF.TXT opens, as shown in *Figure 3.8*:

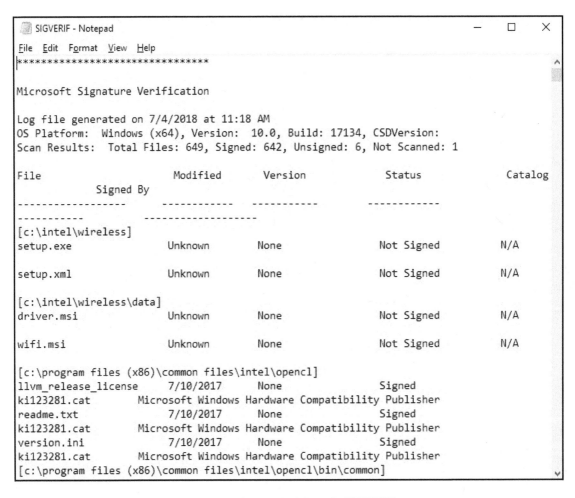

Figure 3.8. Microsoft Signature Verification log file, SIGVERIF.TXT

Managing driver packages

When a device is manufactured, the manufacturer is obliged to adhere to **industry hardware standards**. That implies that the manufacturer is obliged to provide the device driver along with the device. A device driver is a set of files that represent the so-called **driver package**. It is **device-specific** and enables Windows 10 to communicate with the device:

- **Driver files** are **dynamic-link library** (DLL) files with the `.sys` filename extension. The `.sys` file is a system file that provides the I/O interface for a device. Every time a device driver is installed, Windows 10 copies the `.sys` file to `C:\Windows\System32\drivers`.

- **Installation files** supply a *device setup information* (`.inf`) file and a *driver catalog* (`.cat`) file. The `.inf` file is a plain-text file that contains the information that Windows 10 uses to install a device driver. Every time a device driver is installed, Windows 10 copies the `.inf` file to `C:\Windows\INF`. By contrast, the `.cat` file is a catalog file that contains a cryptographic hash that is used by Windows 10 to verify that the package was not altered once it was published.

- **Other related files**, such as a device installation application, a device icon, device property pages, and other files, can also be part of a driver package.

So, whenever a device is plugged into a computer and its device driver is installed, the device's driver package ends up in the Windows 10 driver store. If a user plugs a device into a computer and its driver happens to be in the driver store, the device is immediately recognized by Windows 10. The driver store is a secure and trusted repository that stores all Windows and third-party device drivers. In Windows 10, the driver store is located at `C:\Windows\System32\DriverStore`. In a business environment, system administrators can pre-load driver packages for the most commonly used devices in the driver store so that when users plugin their devices, they are automatically recognized by Windows 10. In Microsoft's Windows world, the concept of recognizing a device without the need to install device drivers is known as **Plug and Play** (**PnP**). PnP has tremendously simplified the work with devices and device drivers in such a way that as soon as the device is connected to the computer, the operating system automatically recognizes the device by using the device driver from the driver store.

Downloading and importing driver packages

In Windows 10, downloading device drivers can be done in several ways. **Windows Update**, a service in Windows 10, enables you to automatically download device drivers once you have plugged the device into the computer. However, if you are provisioning systems, then you can opt for a method of **downloading and importing** driver packages into the driver store prior to deploying the PC. PnPUtil.exe is a command-line tool that enables system administrators to managed driver packages in the driver store. Thus, a system administrator can add, delete, and enumerate a driver package in the driver store, and it can install a driver package on the computer.

To add a driver package into the driver store using the PnPUtil.exe command-line tool, complete the following steps:

1. Access the manufacturer's website.
2. Download the right driver package.
3. Extract the downloaded file to your computer.
4. Identify the path to the .inf file.
5. Open Command Prompt with elevated privileges.
6. Enter the PnPUtil.exe /add-driver <path-to-.inf-file> command (see *Figure 3.9*):

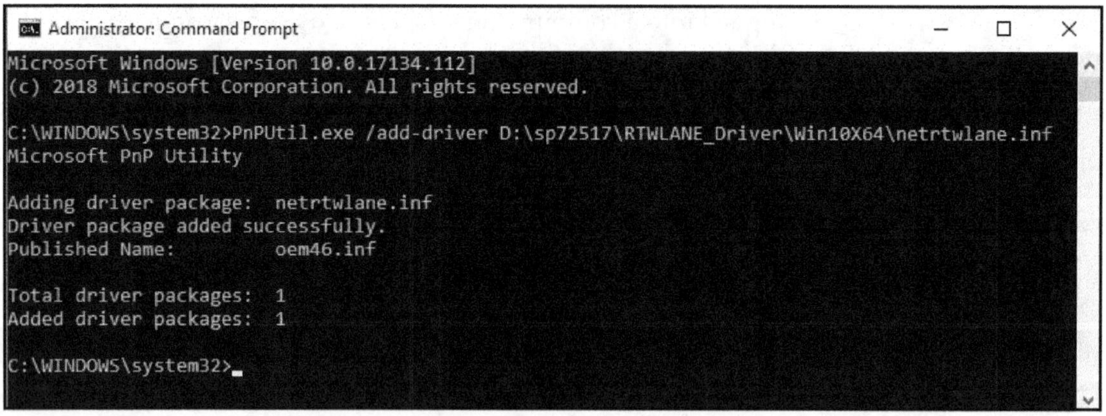

```
Administrator: Command Prompt                                          —    □    ✕
Microsoft Windows [Version 10.0.17134.112]
(c) 2018 Microsoft Corporation. All rights reserved.

C:\WINDOWS\system32>PnPUtil.exe /add-driver D:\sp72517\RTWLANE_Driver\Win10X64\netrtwlane.inf
Microsoft PnP Utility

Adding driver package:  netrtwlane.inf
Driver package added successfully.
Published Name:         oem46.inf

Total driver packages:  1
Added driver packages:  1

C:\WINDOWS\system32>
```

Figure 3.9. Importing the driver package into the driver store using PnPUtil.exe

To verify that the recently added driver package is in the driver store, complete the following steps:

1. Press Windows key + *E* to open **File Explorer**.
2. Navigate to the `C:\Windows\System32\DriverStore\FileRepository` path.
3. Find your recently added driver package, as shown in *Figure 3.10*:

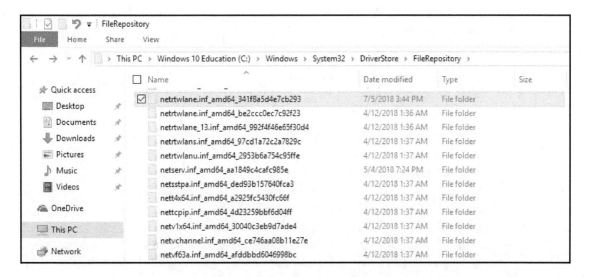

Figure 3.10. Verifying that the driver package has been added successfully to the driver store

Using the DISM tool to add packages

Deployment Image Servicing and Management (**DISM**) is a command-line tool that enables system administrators to prepare and service Windows images. DISM can be accessed either through Command Prompt or from Windows PowerShell. It can capture, deploy, service, and manage Windows images used for **Windows Preinstallation Environment** (**WinPE**), **Windows Recovery Environment** (**WinRE**), and Windows Setup. Most commonly, DISM is used to apply updates, drivers, and language packs to a Windows image both offline and online. In Windows 10, DISM is located at `C:\Windows\System32\DISM`. Unlike DISM, **Windows System Image Manager** (**Windows SIM**) is a graphical tool that system administrators can use to create unattended installation answer files. An answer file has an `.xml` extension and can be used for Windows installation without the presence of help desk technician.

In addition, an answer file enables you to automate the **Out-of-Box Experience (OOBE)**, which represents the first experience that a user has when using the Windows OS for the first time. It consists of initial configurations steps, such as picking a region, selecting a keyboard and adding a second keyboard, accepting the Windows license agreement, getting connected to wired or wireless networks, setting up a Microsoft account, setting up privacy, and setting up Cortana.

To add a driver package to the Windows image using the DISM command-line tool, complete the following steps:

1. Press Windows key + *X* to open the administrator's menu.
2. Select **Windows PowerShell (Admin)**.
3. Locate the folder where your Windows 10 image is located (`install.wim`) and write down the path.
4. Create a folder in any of your disk partitions and name it accordingly (mine is `DISM_Test`).
5. In Windows PowerShell, enter the `DISM /Get-Imageinfo /ImageFile:D:\Windows10\sources\install.wim` command to gather information about all of the images in a WIM file.
6. Then, enter the `DISM /Mount-Image /ImageFile:D:\Windows10\sources\install.wim /Name:"Windows 10 Pro" /MountDir:D:\DISM_Test` command to mount a Windows image.
7. And to add the driver package to the Windows image, enter the `DISM /Image:D:\DISM_Test /Add-Driver /Driver:D:\sp72517\RTWLANE_Driver\Win10X64\netrtwlane.inf` command, as shown in *Figure 3.11*:

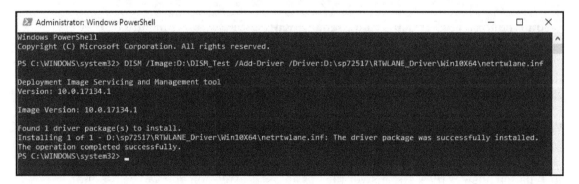

Figure 3.11. Adding a driver package to the Windows image using DISM

Chapter labs – Operating with device drivers

In these chapter labs, you will learn how to do the following:

- Access **Devices** and **Device Manager**
- Add devices and install device drivers
- Update device drivers
- Remove devices and uninstall device drivers
- Manage devices and disable device drivers
- Roll back device drivers

Accessing Devices and Device Manager

To access **Devices**, complete the following steps:

1. Press Windows key + *X*.
2. Select **Settings** from the administrator's menu.
3. In **Windows Settings**, select **Devices**.

To access **Device Manager**, complete the following steps:

1. Press Windows key + *R*.
2. Enter `devmgmt.msc` and press *Enter*.
3. Shortly, the **Device Manager** will open.

Adding devices and installing device drivers

To add a device using **Devices** from **Windows Settings**, complete the following steps:

1. In the **Devices** navigation menu, click **Printers & scanners**.
2. To add a printer or a scanner, click **Add a printer or scanner**.
3. If Windows 10 cannot identify the added device, then click **The printer that I want isn't listed**.

4. The **Add Printer** wizard (see *Figure 3.12*) opens to walk you through the process of adding the printer and installing the appropriate driver:

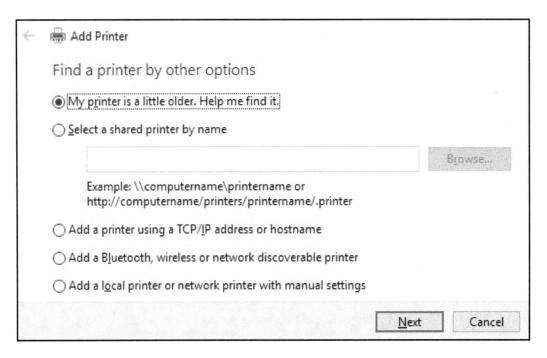

Figure 3.12. Add Printer wizard enables you to add printers and install its driver

5. Follow the onscreen instructions of the **Add Printer** wizard and click **Next** after each step.
6. Finally, you will reach the **Finish** button, which completes the installation of the device.

To install a device driver using either the installation media or a file downloaded from the internet, complete the following steps:

1. Insert the DVD disk into the DVD drive or locate the downloaded **device driver file** on your computer.
2. Using **File Explorer**, run the setup or install file.
3. Follow the onscreen instructions and click **Next** after each step.
4. Finally, click the **Finish** button, which completes the installation of the device driver.

Updating device drivers

To update a device driver using **Device Manager**, complete the following steps:

1. Expand the device's category.
2. Right-click on the device and select **Update driver** (see *Figure 3.13*):

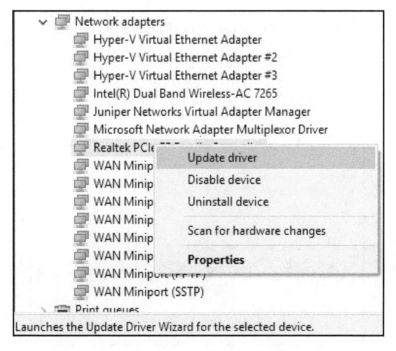

Figure 3.13. Updating the device driver using Device Manager

3. Either search automatically for a device driver from the internet or browse your computer for a device driver.
4. Follow the onscreen instructions and click **Next** after each step.
5. Finally, you will reach the **Finish** button, which completes the installation of the device driver.

Removing devices and uninstalling device drivers

To remove a device using **Devices** from **Windows Settings**, complete the following steps:

1. In the **Devices** navigation menu, click **Printers & scanners** and select the device that you want to remove.

2. Click the **Remove device** button, as shown in *Figure 3.14*:

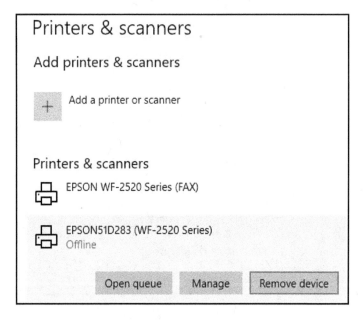

Figure 3.14. Removing a device using Devices

To uninstall a device driver using **Device Manager**, complete the following steps:

1. Expand the device's category.
2. Right-click the device and select **Uninstall device** (see *Figure 3.15*):

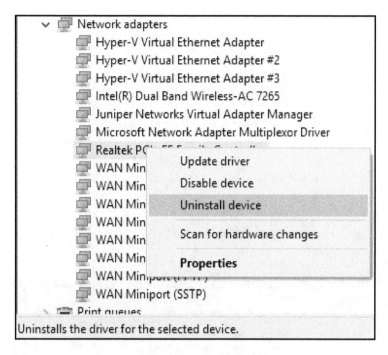

Figure 3.15. Uninstalling a device driver using Device Manager

Managing devices and disabling device drivers

To manage a device using **Devices** from **Windows Settings**, complete the following steps:

1. In the **Devices** navigation menu, click **Printers & scanners** and select the device that you want to manage.

2. Click the **Manage** button, as shown in *Figure 3.16*:

Figure 3.16. Managing a device using Devices

To disable a device driver using **Device Manager**, complete the following steps:

1. Expand the device's category.
2. Right-click on the device and select **Disable device** (see *Figure 3.17*):

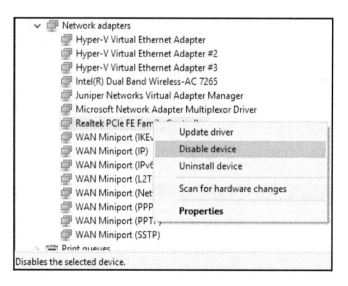

Figure 3.17. Disabling a device driver using Device Manager

Rolling back device drivers

To roll back a device driver using **Device Manager**, complete the following steps:

1. Expand the device's category.
2. Right-click on the device and select **Properties**.
3. Select the **Driver** tab and then click the **Roll Back Driver** button, as shown in *Figure 3.18*:

Figure 3.18. Rolling back a device driver using Device Manager

Summary

We can summarize the chapter with the following points:

- In Windows 10, you have the ability to manage devices through **Devices** in **Windows Settings**, and manage devices and their drivers by using **Device Manager** from **Computer Management**.
- A signed driver represents a driver's digital signature, which identifies the publisher of the driver package.
- File Signature Verification (`sigverif.exe`) will help you identify both signed and unsigned drivers on your Windows 10 computer.
- Unsigned drivers are device drivers that have not been tested in WHQL and as such have not been certified by Microsoft.
- Driver files are **dynamic-link library** (**DLL**) files with the `.sys` filename extension.
- Installation files supply device setup information (`.inf`) file and a driver catalog (`.cat`) file.
- Other related files, such as a device installation application, a device icon, device property pages, and other files, can also be part of a driver package.
- A driver package is a set of files that make up a device driver and enables Windows 10 to communicate with the device.
- `PnPUtil.exe` is a command-line tool that enables system administrators to manage driver packages in the driver store.
- **Deployment Image Servicing and Management** (**DISM**) is a command-line tool that enables system administrators to prepare and service Windows images.
- **Windows System Image Manager** (**Windows SIM**) is a graphical tool that system administrators can use to create unattended installation answer files.
- An answer file has an `.xml` extension and can be used for Windows installation without the presence of the help desk technician.
- **Out-Of-Box Experience** (**OOBE**) represents the first experience that a user has when using Windows OS for the first time.

Questions

1. A driver package is a set of files that make up a device driver and enables Windows 10 to communicate with the device.
    1. True
    2. False

2. An _____ has an .xml extension and can be used for Windows installation without the presence of the help desk technician.

3. Which of the following files contains the driver package?
    1. Driver files
    2. Installation files
    3. Other files
    4. All of the above

4. **Deployment Image Servicing and Management (DISM)** is a command-line tool that enables system administrators to prepare and service Windows images.
    1. True
    2. False

5. _____ is a command-line tool that enables system administrators to manage driver packages in the driver store.

6. Which of the following tools enables system administrators to create unattended installation answer files?
    1. PnPUtil
    2. DISM
    3. WSIM
    4. OOBE

7. Unsigned drivers are device drivers that have not been tested in WHQL and as such have not been certified by Microsoft.
    1. True
    2. False

8. In Windows 10, you have the ability to manage devices through _____ in **Windows Settings**, and manage devices and their drivers by using _____ from **Computer Management**.

9. Which of the following statuses are valid for device drivers in **Device Manager**?
    1. Generic
    2. Black exclamation mark on a yellow triangle
    3. Downward black arrow
    4. All of the above

10. A signed driver represents a driver's digital signature, which identifies the publisher of the driver package.
    1. True
    2. False

11. _____ represents the first experience that a user has when using Windows OS for the first time.

12. Which of the following options are available in the **Drivers** tab of the device driver's **Properties** dialog box? (Choose three).
    1. Install driver
    2. Update driver
    3. Disable device
    4. Uninstall device

Further reading

- **Driver installation**: https://docs.microsoft.com/en-us/windows-hardware/drivers/3dprint/driver-installation
- **Tools for testing drivers**: https://docs.microsoft.com/en-us/windows-hardware/drivers/devtest/tools-for-testing-drivers
- **Test signing**: https://docs.microsoft.com/en-us/windows-hardware/drivers/install/test-signing
- **Components of a driver package**: https://docs.microsoft.com/en-us/windows-hardware/drivers/install/components-of-a-driver-package
- **DISM overview**: https://docs.microsoft.com/en-us/windows-hardware/manufacture/desktop/what-is-dism

4
Performing Post-Installation Configuration

In contrast to Chapter 3, *Configuring Devices and Device Drivers*, this chapter is designed to provide you with detailed instructions regarding Windows 10 post-installation tasks, particularly those pertaining to common configurations and customization. That being said, this chapter provides the step-by-step explanations of configuring accessibility options, Cortana, Microsoft Edge, Internet Explorer, and **Power & sleep** settings. These and many others present a way of configuring and customizing many aspects of your Windows 10 computer for the sake of stimulating work with the computer, performance, and productivity. As such, it requires a sound knowledge of all OS features, options, and components. Among the accessibility options covered in this chapter are **Magnifier**, **Narrator**, **Audio**, **Speech**, and **On-Screen Keyboard**. These options enable Windows to see, hear, use, and focus on tasks to make it easier to type. Likewise, this chapter is accompanied with step-by-step instructions driven by targeted, easy-to-understand diagrams. This chapter concludes with disabling Internet Explorer as a chapter lab.

In this chapter, we will cover the following topics:

- Common configurations and customizations
- Configuring accessibility options
- Configuring Cortana
- Configuring Microsoft Edge
- Configuring Internet Explorer
- Configuring **Power & sleep** settings
- Chapter lab - Turning off Internet Explorer

Technical requirements

In order to complete the labs for this chapter, you'll need the following equipment:

- PC with Windows 10 Pro, at least 4 GB of RAM, 500 GB of HDD, and access to the internet.

Common configurations and customizations

The most enjoyable thing in Windows 10 is undoubtedly the return of the Start menu. But not just that because, this time, Microsoft with Windows 10 brings you a Start menu that can fit your personal style. In addition, Windows 10 comes with handy tools to personalize the Windows desktop, Windows **Taskbar**, and the **Notification Area**. These and many others present the true potential of Windows 10 in providing plenty of tools, settings, and ways to configure and customize the working area on your Windows 10 computer.

Configuring and customizing the Start menu

Ever since the introduction of the Start menu in Windows 95 (with the exception of Windows 8/8.1) until now in Windows 10, there have only been minor changes here and there. The Start menu remains the unique element that embodies the Windows operating system. Having said that, the Start menu in Windows 10 represents a combination of the Windows Start menu (Windows 95 to Windows 7) and the Windows Start screen (Windows 8/8.1). As a result, on touch-enabled devices, Windows 10 automatically enables the **Tablet mode,** displaying the Windows 10 Start menu in a format of a Windows Start screen. Otherwise, on non-touch-enabled devices, Windows 10 automatically enables the **Desktop mode**, hence displaying the redesigned Windows Start menu.

To turn on and off the **Tablet mode** in Windows 10 using Windows **Settings**, complete the following steps:

1. Click the Start button.
2. Select **Settings** on the Start menu.
3. Select **Personalization** on the Windows **Settings** dialog box.
4. Select **Start** on the **Personalization** setting's navigation menu.

5. And then turn on **Use Start full screen,** as shown in the following screenshot, to enable the **Tablet mode**:

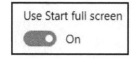

Figure 4.1. Enabling the Use Start full screen from Windows Settings

6. Turn off **Use Start full screen** in order to enable the redesigned Windows 10 Start menu (that is, the **Desktop mode**).

 Continuum is the feature that enables Windows to automatically switch between the **Desktop mode** and **Tablet mode**. It does so based on what OS you use. You can also use the **Tablet mode** tile in the **Action Center** to toggle between the **Desktop** and **Tablet** modes.

To resize the Start menu by making it taller or wider, complete the following steps:

1. Select the top border of the Start menu and drag it up to make it taller or drag it down to make it smaller.
2. Select the side border of the Start menu and drag it on the right to make it wider or drag it on the left to make it narrower.

To list **All apps** on the Start screen, complete the following steps:

1. On the far right of the Windows **Taskbar**, right behind the system clock, click the **Action Center** icon.
2. With the **Action Center** open, click on the **Tablet mode** tile.
3. Click on the Start button to open the Start screen, and then click **All Apps** almost on top of the of Windows 10 Start screen, shown in the following screenshot:

Figure 4.2. Listing all apps on the Windows 10 Start screen

To access your apps in a faster way from within the Start menu using letters, complete the following steps:

1. Click the Start button.
2. With the Start menu open, click on any of the letters.
3. The alphabet will appear, as shown in the following screenshot:

Figure 4.3. Using the alphabet to access your apps faster

4. Select the letter that the app begins with.

To pin your favorite app on the right panel of the Start menu, complete the following steps:

1. Click the Start button.
2. With the Start menu open, right-click the app that you want to pin.
3. Select **Pin to Start** from the context menu, as shown in the following screenshot:

Figure 4.4. Pinning the favorite app on the right panel of the Start menu

To resize the **Apps** tiles on the right panel of the Start menu, complete the following steps:

1. Click the Start button.
2. With the Start menu open, right-click the favorite app tile on the right panel of the Start menu.
3. Select **Resize** from the **Context** menu, as shown in the following screenshot, and then choose the size that you want:

Figure 4.5. Resizing the app tiles on the right panel of the Start menu

To group your favorite apps on the right panel of the Start menu, complete the following steps:

1. Click the Start button to open the Start menu.
2. On the right panel of the Start menu, select your favorite app tile.
3. Drag the tile up or down until a group divider appears.
4. Release the tile.
5. Repeat steps 1 to 3 to add more tiles in the group.
6. Select the top of the group to label it, as shown in the following screenshot:

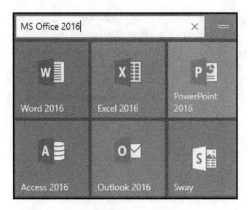

Figure 4.6. Grouping apps on the right panel of the Start menu

The **Action Center** is a new tool introduced with Windows 10. It's a slide-out pane that appears when you click the **Action Center** icon on the **Taskbar**. As such, the **Action Center** enables you to view all system notifications and have quick access to various settings. It is customizable, hence enabling you to determine how your computer will report problems.

Configuring and customizing the Windows desktop

There may be many reasons why you would like to customize the Windows Desktop on your computer. However, a common reason for, I guess, every user could be the fact that the working area of a computer screen is the desktop that stimulates everyone's work. The Windows Desktop was first introduced in Windows 95 and since then it has been an integral component of Windows OSes. It consists of the work area and the taskbar. As we organize things on a physical desktop, almost in a similar format, we also organize icons in the Windows Desktop. So, in Windows 10, the most common icon that you can find on the Windows desktop is the **Recycle Bin**. However, you can also add many favorite icons and hence create shortcuts to your favorite apps.

To configure and customize the background for your Windows Desktop, complete the following steps:

1. Click the Start button.
2. With the Start menu open, select **Settings**.
3. Select **Personalization** from the Windows **Settings** dialog box.
4. You'll notice that **Background** is opened by default, as it's the first item listed in the **Personalization** setting's navigation menu.
5. From the **Background** drop-down list, you can select such options as **Picture**, **Solid Color**, and **Slideshow,** as shown in the following screenshot:

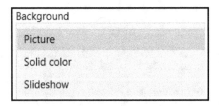

Figure 4.7. Customizing the Windows desktop background

Since it is analogous to a physical desktop, perhaps that's the reason why Microsoft engineers named it the Windows Desktop!

To configure and customize the colors for your Windows Desktop, complete the following steps:

1. Click the Start button.
2. With the Start menu open, select **Settings**.
3. Select **Personalization** from the Windows **Settings** dialog box.
4. Select **Colors** on the **Personalization** setting's navigation menu.
5. Select your favorite **Windows colors** from the color palette, as shown in the following screenshot:

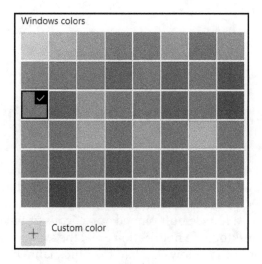

Figure 4.8. Configuring Windows colors in Windows 10

To configure and customize the theme for your Windows Desktop, complete the following steps:

1. Click the Start button.
2. With the Start menu open, select **Settings**.
3. Select **Personalization** from the Windows **Settings** dialog box.
4. Select **Themes** on the **Personalization** navigation menu.

5. Either select any of the available themes or select **Get more themes in Microsoft Store,** as shown in the following screenshot:

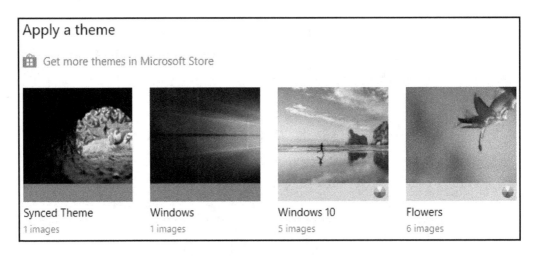

Figure 4.9. Configuring themes in Windows 10

Configuring and customizing the Windows Taskbar

The Windows **Taskbar** is a ribbon that, by default, is located at the bottom of the screen. It was introduced in Windows 95 and since then has been included in each new version of Windows OS that followed. As such, the Windows **Taskbar** contains the Start button, the Cortana icon or search box, a few default pinned apps, icons of the programs currently opened in the Windows desktop, the notification area, the system clock, and the action center icon. Earlier versions of Windows OS had the quick launch on the Windows **Taskbar**.

To configure and customize the Windows **Taskbar**, complete the following steps:

1. Click the Start button.
2. With the Start menu open, select **Settings**.
3. Select **Personalization** from the Windows **Settings** dialog box.
4. Select **Taskbar** on the **Personalization** setting's navigation.
5. You'll have plenty of controls to configure and customize so you can make the Windows **Taskbar** look how you want.

To pin your favorite app on the Windows **Taskbar**, complete the following steps:

1. Click the Start button.
2. With the Start menu open, right-click the favorite app tile on the right panel of the Start menu.
3. Select **More** from the context menu, as shown in the following screenshot, and then select the **Pin to taskbar** option:

Figure 4.10. Pinning a favorite app on the Windows Taskbar

Configuring and customizing the notification area

As mentioned earlier, the **Notification area** (see *Figure 4.11*) is part of the Windows **Taskbar** and is located on the far right side, to the **Action Center**. It mainly contains items running in the background. That way, it provides information to users about the network, battery level, volume level, and system clock status. All of these icons are also referred to as system icons. Depending on the applications installed on your computer, the **Notification area** can contain other background items too:

Figure 4.11. Windows 10 **Notification area**

To configure and customize the **Notification area**, complete the following steps:

1. Click the Start button.
2. With the Start menu open, select **Settings**.
3. Select **Personalization** from the Windows **Settings** dialog box.

4. Select **Taskbar** on the **Personalization** setting's navigation menu.

5. From the **Notification area** section (see *Figure 4.12*), you can opt for **Select which icons appear on the taskbar** and **Turn system icons on or off**:

Notification area

Select which icons appear on the taskbar

Turn system icons on or off

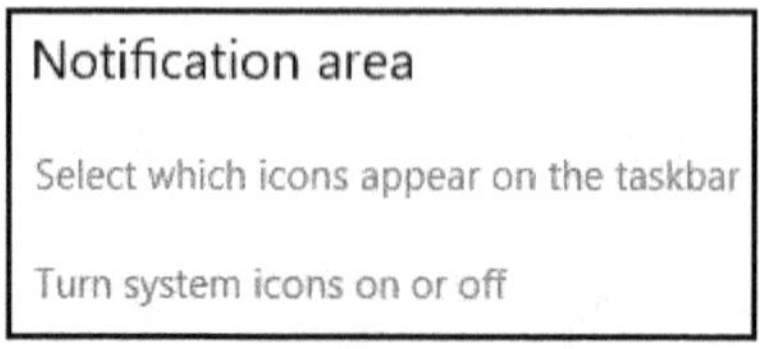

Figure 4.12. Notification area options in Windows 10

Configuring accessibility options

Windows 10, through **Ease of Access** in Windows **Settings,** enables your computer to see, hear, use, and focus on tasks. With that being said, you can use **Magnifier** to zoom in on parts of your display, **Narrator** to control your device, **Audio** to allow your device to hear, **Speech** to make you device easier to use, and **On-screen Keyboard** to make it easier to type. In addition to these accessibility features, **Ease of Access** enables you to access and configure a dozen other accessibility features.

Configuring Narrator

Narrator enables you to control your device. Hence, **Narrator** reads the elements displayed on the screen, including text and buttons, and can be controlled by the keyboard, touch, and mouse. In addition, **Narrator** enables you to customize it so that you can select your favorite voice, change how much content you want to hear, use the **Narrator** cursor, and use Braille.

To hear text and controls on the screen, complete the following steps:

1. Press the Windows key + *I* to open Windows **Settings**.
2. With the Windows **Settings** open, select **Ease of Access**.
3. Select **Narrator** on the **Ease of Access** navigation menu.
4. From the **Use Narrator** section (as shown in the following screenshot), you can turn on **Narrator**:

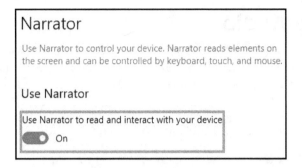

Figure 4.13. Turning on Narrator in Windows 10

Configuring Magnifier

If you're interested in zooming in certain parts of your screen, then **Magnifier** enables you to do that. **Magnifier** can run in full screen, in a separate window, or even as a lens that follows your mouse cursor around the screen. Hence, **Magnifier** enables you to customize it so that you can change the zoom level; change the **Magnifier** view between full screen, docked, and lens; and specify what you want **Magnifier** to follow.

To magnify things on the screen, complete the following steps:

1. Press the Windows key + *I* to open Windows **Settings**.
2. With Windows **Settings** open, select **Ease of Access**.
3. Select **Magnifier** on the **Ease of Access** navigation menu.
4. From the **Use Magnifier** section (as in the following screenshot), you can turn on **Magnifier**:

Figure 4.14. Turning on Magnifier in Windows 10

Configuring Audio

The **Audio** feature is a very useful accessibility feature that makes your device easier to hear or use without sound. As such, the **Audio** accessibility feature enables you to personalize it by changing the device **volume**, turning on **mono** audio, and displaying audio **alerts visually**.

To combine left and right audio channels into one channel, complete the following steps:

1. Press the Windows key + *I* to open Windows **Settings**.
2. With the Windows **Settings** open, select **Ease of Access**.
3. Select **Audio** on the **Ease of Access** navigation menu.
4. From the **Turn on mono audio** section (as shown in the following screenshot), you can turn on mono audio:

Figure 4.15. Turning on mono audio in Windows 10

Configuring the On-Screen Keyboard

The **On-Screen keyboard** is very useful for any device in general, particularly touch-based devices, because it enables you to use your device without a physical keyboard. The **On-Screen Keyboard** provides considerable options to personalize it so that you can use **sticky**, **toggle** and **filter** keys; change how keyboard **shortcuts** work; and make it easier to type. To access it quickly and easily, the small icon of a keyboard is available in the system tray too.

To enable the **On-Screen Keyboard**, complete the following steps:

1. Press the Windows key + *I* to open Windows **Settings**.
2. With Windows **Settings** open, select **Ease of Access**.

3. Select **Keyboard** on the **Ease of Access** navigation menu.

4. From the **Use your device without a physical keyboard** section (as shown in the following screenshot), you can turn on the keyboard:

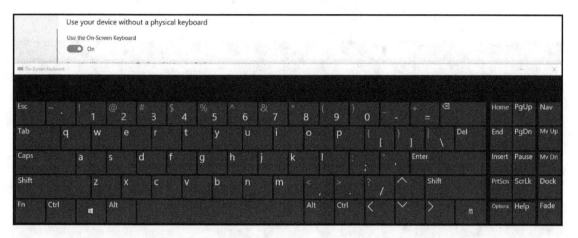

Figure 4.16. Turning on the On-Screen Keyboard in Windows 10

You can use the `osk` keyword to launch the **On-Screen Keyboard** from the **Run** window, Command Prompt, and Windows PowerShell.

Configuring Cortana

We live in the age that pioneers **artificial intelligence** (**AI**). As such, applications such as Siri, Alexa, and Assistant represent the IT industry's efforts to bring AI to the level of applications. Just like these apps, **Cortana** is a Microsoft effort to apply AI at a general-purpose level. Introduced in Windows 8.1, Cortana is a virtual personal assistant that comes with Windows 10, enabling you to find help, apps, files, settings, and other stuff on your computer and from the internet.

Setting up Cortana

Initially, you can set up Cortana while you're installing Windows 10. At this stage, you are asked to make Cortana your personal assistant. You can do that by clicking on the **Yes** button, as shown in the following screenshot:

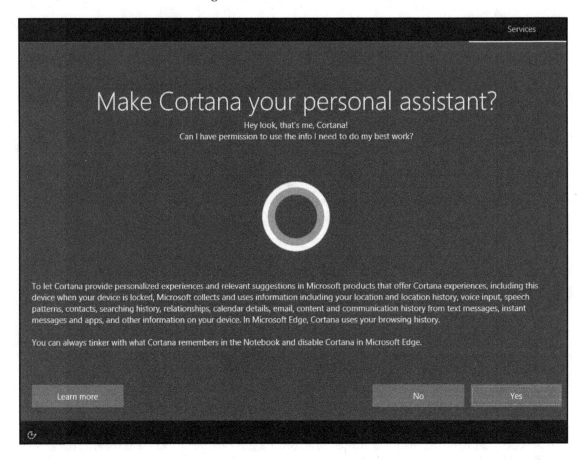

Figure 4.17. Making Cortana your personal assistant

But, if you clicked the **No** button in the previous step, then no worries, as after completing the Windows 10 installation, you can enable Cortana by completing the following steps:

1. Press the Windows key + *S* to open Cortana.
2. With Cortana open, select **Cortana can do much more...**.
3. Cick the **Personalize** button to enable Cortana, as shown in the following screenshot:

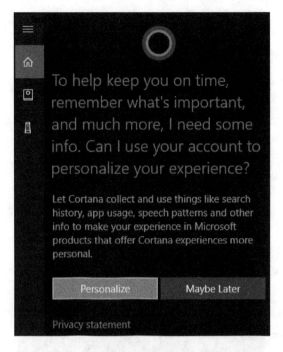

Figure 4.18. Enabling Cortana as your personal assistant

As you may know, Cortana requires the appropriate equipment to communicate with you and to be able to accept your commands. With that being said, your PC needs to be equipped with a microphone and speakers. As soon as you make sure that you have these devices on your PC, then you can continue setting up Cortana. So, after enabling Cortana, the first thing to do is to make sure that Cortana can hear you. To check the microphone, complete the following steps:

1. Click the search box on the taskbar.
2. With Cortana open, select **Settings,** as shown in the following screenshot:

Figure 4.19. Opening Windows **Settings** from Cortana's menu

3. From the **Microphone** section, you can select **Check the microphone**.

To enable the **Hey Cortana** option, complete the following steps:

1. Click the search box on the taskbar.
2. With Cortana open, select **Settings**.
3. From the **Hey Cortana** section, you can turn on **Hey Cortana**.
4. Select **Learn how I say "Hey Cortana"**.
5. Click the Start button so that Cortana can get familiar with your voice (see the following screenshot):

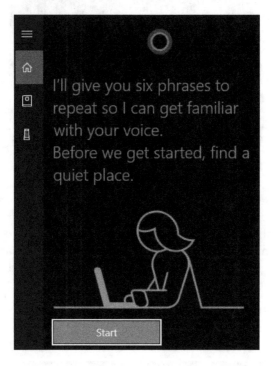

Figure 4.20. Learning how to say "Hey Cortana"

Running Cortana

Before starting to issue commands to Cortana, you must first set it up to listen to your commands.

To let Cortana listen for your commands, complete the following steps:

1. Press the Windows key + *S* to open Cortana.
2. With Cortana open, select **Settings**.
3. From the **Keyboard shortcut** section, you can turn on **Let Cortana listen for my commands** (see the following screenshot):

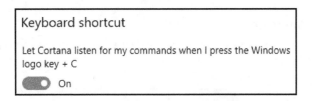

Figure 4.21. Configuring Cortana to listen your commands

To issue commands to Cortana, complete the following steps:

1. Press the Windows key + *C* to make Cortana listen to your commands.
2. With Cortana in listening mode (see the following screenshot), begin saying your commands:

Figure 4.22. Issuing commands to Cortana

Because, at this stage, Cortana is already enabled, then you may just want to say *Hey Cortana* without pressing the Windows key + C in order to begin issuing commands to Cortana.

Searching for help

Cortana's search box offers you a quick and easy way to search for help whenever you need to.

To search for help, complete the following steps:

1. Click the search box on the taskbar.
2. With Cortana open, enter the keyword of what you're looking for (see the following screenshot):

Figure 4.23. Searching for help with Cortana

Getting help about computer problems

In addition to the search box, Windows 10, through the **Get Help** application, offers you the option to get help about computer problems from Microsoft's Virtual Agent.

To get help about computer problems, complete the following steps:

1. Click the search box on the taskbar.
2. With Cortana open, enter **Get Help**.
3. With Microsoft's Virtual Agent open, type the keyword of what you're looking for (see the following screenshot):

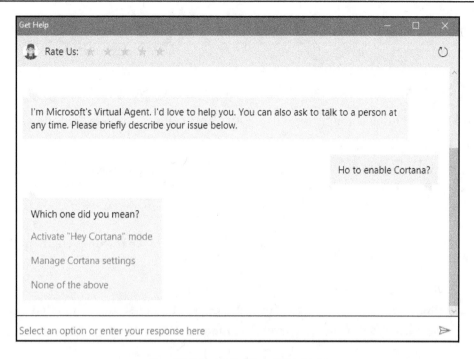

Figure 4.24. Getting help from Microsoft's Virtual Agent

Configuring Microsoft Edge

In Windows 10, Microsoft has introduced a brand new browser to surf the web. In contrast to Internet Explorer, **Microsoft Edge** provides a completely new approach in finding stuff, reading, and writing on the web, and getting help from Cortana from within the browser. The fact that Microsoft Edge is the default browser in Windows 10, indicates that Microsoft intends to replace Internet Explorer with it. Even so, Internet Explorer in its 11th version continues to be part of Windows 10 as well.

Running Microsoft Edge

As you know, in Windows 10 there are many ways to run applications. This also applies to Microsoft Edge. Therefore, in the following sections, you will be familiar with several ways to run this app.

To open the Microsoft Edge using a pinned tile on the Start menu, complete the following steps:

1. Click the Start button
2. Select Microsoft Edge from the pinned tile on the Start menu

To open Microsoft Edge using the app list on the Start menu, complete the following steps:

1. Click the Start button
2. Scroll down the app list until you reach the section that begins with the letter **M**
3. Select **Microsoft Edge**

To open Microsoft Edge using Cortana's search box on the taskbar, complete the following steps:

1. Click the search box on the taskbar
2. Enter `Microsoft Edge` and instantly Cortana will list the **Best match**
3. Select **Microsoft Edge** from the **Best match** list and press *Enter*

Searching from within the address bar

As you know, the search engine **Bing** is also Microsoft's product. So, don't be surprised that once you start Microsoft Edge and you start entering keywords into the address bar that immediately Bing is listing your search results.

To search from the Microsoft Edge address bar, complete the following steps:

1. Once Microsoft Edge is open, begin entering your keywords on the address bar.
2. Bing automatically lists the search results, as shown in the following screenshot:

Figure 4.28. Automatic listing of search results from the Microsoft Edge address bar

All your stuff is in the Hub

In Microsoft Edge, the Hub is the place where all of your stuff collected on the web is kept. That being said, the Hub holds your favorites, reading lists, books, history, and downloads.

To access the Hub in Microsoft Edge, complete the following steps:

1. With Microsoft Edge opened, select the **Hub** on the menu bar located at the top-right corner of the Microsoft Edge window (see the following screenshot):

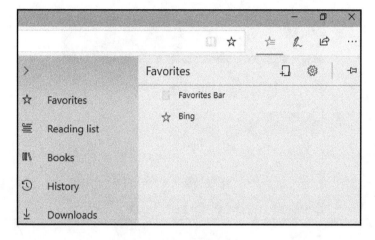

Figure 4.29. Microsoft Edge Hub

2. Navigate to any of the options (from **Favorites** to **Downloads**) available on the Hub.

Reading without distraction

If you have missed **Reading View** in Internet Explorer (except Internet Explorer 10 for Windows 8/8.1), then you have it available in Microsoft Edge. Such a view enables you to enjoy the reading of your favorite sites. It is pretty simple and straightforward and a very valuable feature.

To read without distractions in Microsoft Edge, complete the following steps:

1. Once Microsoft Edge is open, navigate to a favorite site on the web.
2. Select **Reading View** on the address bar located at the top-right corner of the Microsoft Edge window, as shown in the following screenshot:

Figure 4.30. Microsoft Edge Reading View enables you to enjoy reading

Adding items on the Reading list

In addition to adding your favorite sites, a feature that has also been available in Internet Explorer, Microsoft Edge enables you to add items in the **Reading list**. That way, whenever you want to read them it is enough to just open the **Reading list**.

To save articles on Microsoft Edge Reading list, complete the following steps:

1. From Microsoft Edge window, select the star icon next to **Reading view** icon on the address bar located at the top-right corner of Microsoft Edge window.
2. Select the **Reading list** tab.
3. Click the **Add** button (see the following screenshot):

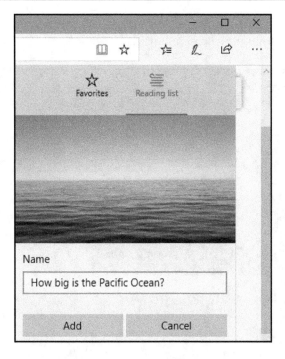

Figure 4.31. Adding articles on Microsoft Edge Reading list

Writing on the web

There may be many reasons why would you like to write on the web. However, if you have cultivated the habit of accentuating an important paragraph or underscoring a favorite quote for years, then that might be the main reason.

To write and highlight on the web using Microsoft Edge, complete the following steps:

1. Click the Start button.
2. Select Microsoft Edge from the pinned tile on the Start menu.
3. Select **Add notes** on the menu bar located at the top-right corner of the Microsoft Edge window.

4. Select any of the available tools on the menu to start writing on the web page (as shown in the following screenshot):

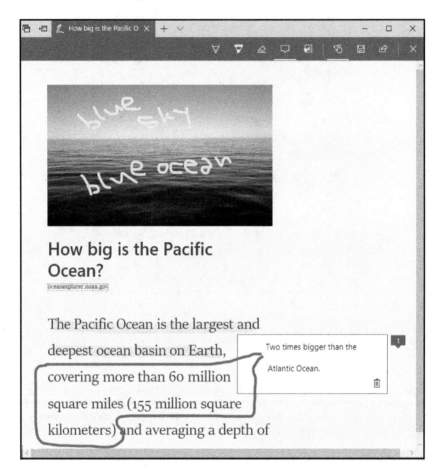

Figure 4.32. Microsoft Edge Add notes enables you to add notes on a web

5. When you are done, select **Save Web Note** from the menu.
6. Select **Exit** from the menu to exit the **Add notes** feature.

Managing tabs in Microsoft Edge

In the *Configuring Microsoft Edge* section of this chapter, it was said that Microsoft Edge offers a whole new way of working with the browser when compared to Internet Explorer. Such an approach is also expressed through tabs.

To show tab previews in Microsoft Edge, complete the following steps:

1. In the upper part of the Microsoft Edge window, locate the **Show tab previews** button next to the **New tabs** button.
2. Click the **Show tab previews** button and the tabs will be previewed, as shown in the following screenshot:

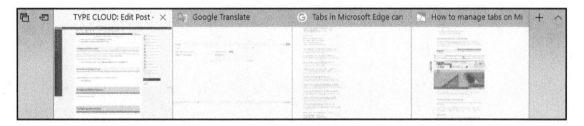

Figure 4.33. Showing tab previews in Microsoft Edge

To set tabs aside in Microsoft Edge, complete the following steps:

1. At the top-left corner of the Microsoft Edge window, locate the **Set these tabs aside** button next to the **Tabs you've set aside** button.
2. Click the **Set these tabs aside** button to set aside groups of tabs for later viewing.
3. To display the tabs that you have already set aside, click the **Tabs you've set aside** button on the far top-left corner of the browser.
4. Click on any thumbnail to individually restore that particular web page or you can click the **Restore tabs** link located above the thumbnails to restore all tabs, as shown in the following screenshot:

Figure 4.34. Restoring tabs in Microsoft Edge

Setting Microsoft Edge settings

Although they differ from the user interface perspective, when it comes to the settings in Microsoft Edge, you will encounter almost the same options and features as in Internet Explorer, except in the another way.

To access settings in Microsoft Edge, complete the following steps:

1. At the top-right corner of the Microsoft Edge window, locate the **Settings and more** button (the three horizontal dots).
2. Clicking on the **Settings and more** button. It opens a menu with **Settings** as the last item on it (see the following screenshot):

Figure 4.35. Settings option in Microsoft Edge

To choose a theme for Microsoft Edge, complete the following steps:

1. From within **Settings**, at the **Choose a theme** section, click the drop-down list to choose a theme for your Microsoft Edge, as shown in the following screenshot:

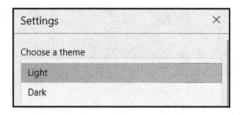

Figure 4.36. Choosing a theme for Microsoft Edge

To import favorites and other info in Microsoft Edge, complete the following steps:

1. From within **Settings**, at the **Import favorites and other info** section, click the **Import from another browser** button (see the following screenshot):

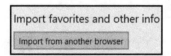

Figure 4.37. Importing favorites and other info into Microsoft Edge

To clear browsing data in Microsoft Edge, complete the following steps:

1. From within **Settings**, at the **Clear browsing data** section, click the **Choose what to clear** button (see the following screenshot):

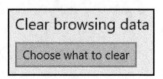

Figure 4.38. Clearing browsing data in Microsoft Edge

To view advanced settings in Microsoft Edge, complete the following steps:

1. From within **Settings**, at the **Advanced settings** section, click the **View advanced settings** button (see the following screenshot):

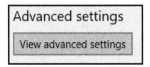

Figure 4.39. Viewing Advanced Settings in Microsoft Edge

To let Cortana assist you in Microsoft Edge, complete the following steps:

1. From within **Advanced settings**, at the **Privacy and services** section, turn on the **Have Cortana assist me in Microsoft Edge** option (see the following screenshot):

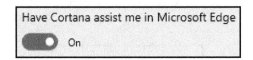

Figure 4.40. Letting Cortana assist you in Microsoft Edge

Configuring Internet Explorer

When talking about a browser that has resisted the times and the many changes in technology that are related to web access, then that certainly is Internet Explorer. Although recently, since the introduction of Windows 10 and Microsoft Edge, Internet Explorer seems to be abandoned by Microsoft, it continues to be the users' choice across the globe, though at a lower rate.

Running Internet Explorer

As you know, Internet Explorer, like Microsoft Edge, can run in several ways. That's because of the many alternatives that Windows 10 offers.

To run Internet Explorer using the Cortana's search box on the taskbar, complete the following steps:

1. Click the search box on the taskbar.

2. Enter `Internet Explorer` and instantly Cortana will list the **Best match**.

3. Select **Internet Explorer** from the **Best match** list (as shown in the following screenshot) and press *Enter*:

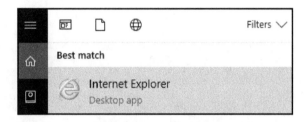

Figure 4.41. Internet Explorer on the **Best match** list

Setting Internet Explorer Internet options

Can you think of how many times you've accessed **Internet options** in Internet Explorer to configure the home page, the zone's security settings, pop-up blocker, LAN settings, add-ons, advanced settings, and so on. I think you will agree that **Internet options** is the most clickable thing after the Start button in any Windows version (except Windows 8).

To access **Internet options** in Internet Explorer, complete the following steps:

1. At the top-right corner of the Internet Explorer window, locate the **Tools** (*Alt +* X) button next to **Favorites** (*Alt + C*) button.

2. Clicking on the **Tools** button opens a menu with **Internet options** as the penultimate item on it (see the following screenshot):

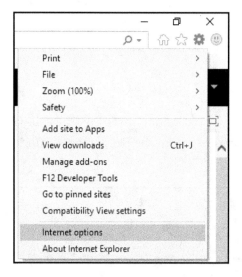

Figure 4.42. Accessing Internet options in Internet Explorer

To delete the browsing history when exiting Internet Explorer, complete the following steps:

1. From the **General** tab of the **Internet options** dialog box, locate the **Browsing history** section.
2. Check **Delete browsing history on exit** (see the following screenshot), and then click **OK** to close **Internet options**:

Figure 4.43. Deleting browsing history when exiting Internet Explorer

To manage **AutoComplete** in Internet Explorer, complete the following steps:

1. Click the **Content** tab in the **Internet options** dialog box.
2. Locate the **AutoComplete** section.
3. Click the **Settings** button, as shown in the following screenshot, and then review the options offered:

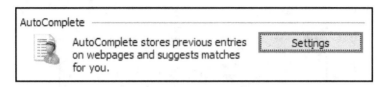

Figure 4.44. Managing **AutoComplete** in Internet Explorer

4. Click **OK** to close **AutoComplete Settings**, and again click **OK** to close **Internet options**.

To set the program that you want Internet Explorer to use for editing HTML files, complete the following steps:

1. Click the **Programs** tab in the **Internet options** dialog box.
2. Locate the **HTML editing** section.
3. Click the drop-down list, as in shown in the following screenshot, to select your favorite HTML editor:

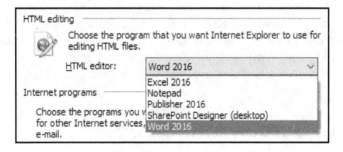

Figure 4.45. Choosing HTML editor in Internet Explorer

4. Click **OK** to close **Internet options**.

To reset Internet Explorer's settings to their default condition, complete the following steps:

1. Click **Advanced** tab in the **Internet options** dialog box.
2. Locate the **Reset Internet Explorer settings** section.
3. Click the **Reset** button, and then click **OK** to close the warning dialog box (see the following screenshot):

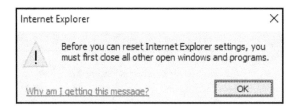

Figure 4.46. Resetting Internet Explorer settings

4. Click **OK** to close **Internet options**.

Configuring Power & sleep settings

You probably have experience with previous versions of Windows! If that's the case, then whatever you've done in previous versions of Windows to configure **Power & sleep**, you will be doing almost the same in Windows 10, except that you will be using Windows **Settings** as well as the old **Control Panel**. That being said, if you are using a desktop PC, then **Power & sleep** takes care of your monitor and the power in your computer when your computer is in an idle state. With a laptop, **Power & sleep**, as it does with a desktop, saves your laptop's battery power when you are not working with your laptop.

Configuring Screen and Sleep

Power & sleep in Windows **Settings** lets you choose when your screen turns off, both with the battery and when plugged in, and when your computer goes to sleep, both with the battery and when plugged in.

To configure screen settings in Windows 10, complete the following steps:

1. Click the Start button.
2. With the Start menu open, select **Settings**.

3. Select **System** from the Windows **Settings** window.
4. Select **Power & sleep** on the **System** setting's navigation menu.
5. From the **Screen** section (as shown in the following screenshot), you can set the screen settings for both the battery and when plugged in:

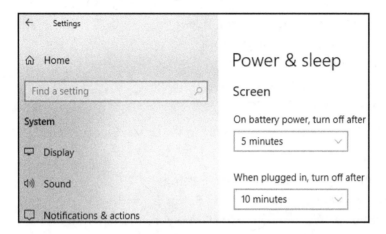

Figure 4.47. Configuring screen settings in Windows 10

To configure **Sleep** settings in Windows 10, complete the following steps:

1. Click the Start button.
2. With the Start menu open, select **Settings**.
3. Select **System** from the Windows **Settings** window.
4. Select **Power & sleep** on the **System** setting's navigation menu.
5. From the **Screen** section (as shown in the following screenshot), you can set the **Sleep** settings for both the battery and when plugged in:

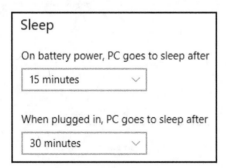

Figure 4.48. Configuring **Sleep** settings in Windows 10

Configuring advanced power settings

As mentioned earlier, Windows **Settings** in Windows 10, mainly through **Power & sleep**, enables you to set screen and power settings. However, if you want to configure advanced settings, such as the following, then you should use the old **Control Panel**:

- **Choose what the power button does**
- **Choose what closing the lid does**
- **Create a power plan**
- **Choose when to turn off the display**
- **Change when the computer sleeps**

With that in mind, to access **Power Options** in Windows 10, complete the following steps:

1. Click the Start button.
2. With the Start menu open, select **Settings**.
3. Select **System** from the Windows **Settings** window.
4. Select **Power & sleep** on the **System** setting's navigation menu.
5. From within **Power & sleep**, locate **Additional power settings** (see the following screenshot) on the right side of the screen:

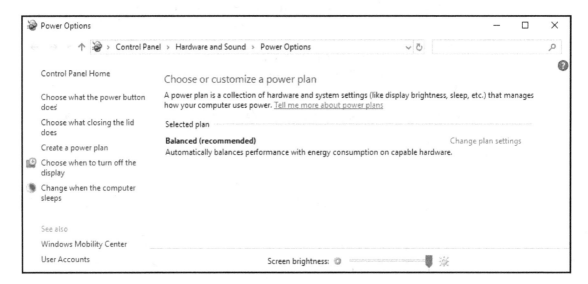

Figure 4.49. Control Panel's Power Options enables you to configure advanced power settings

Chapter lab – Turning off Internet Explorer

In this chapter lab, you will learn how to turn off Internet Explorer in Windows 10 using the **Windows Features** tool.

Disabling Internet Explorer in Windows 10

To turn off Internet Explorer in Windows 10, complete the following steps:

1. Click the search box on the taskbar and enter `Turn Windows features on or off`.
2. Click the **Best match**, which is **Turn Windows features on or off**.
3. On a **Windows Features** dialog box, locate and uncheck **Internet Explorer**.
4. Click **Yes** to close the warning dialog box.
5. Click **OK** to close the **Windows Features** dialog box (see the following screenshot):

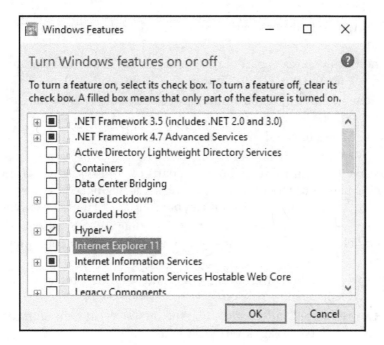

Figure 4.50. Disabling Internet Explorer in Windows 10

6. **Windows Features** will start to **Apply Changes**.
7. Once completed, **Windows Features** displays the message **Windows completed the requested changes**.
8. Click **Restart now** to close the **Windows Features** dialog box.

Summary

We can summarize the chapter with the following points:

- The Start menu in Windows 10 represents a combination of Windows Start menus (Windows 95 to Windows 7) and the Windows Start screen (Windows 8/8.1)
- On touch-enabled devices, Windows 10 automatically enables the **Tablet mode**, whereas on non-touch-enabled devices, it automatically enables the **Desktop mode**
- The Windows desktop, introduced in Windows 95, consists of the work area and the taskbar
- The Windows **Taskbar** is a ribbon that, by default, is located at the bottom of the screen
- The notification area is part of the Windows **Taskbar** and is located on the far right side next to the **Action Center**
- The network, battery level, volume level, and system clock status are referred to as system icons
- **Ease of Access** in Windows **Settings** enables Windows 10 to see, hear, use, and focus on tasks
- You can use **Magnifier** to zoom in on parts of your display, **Narrator** to control your device, **Audio** to allow your device to hear, **Speech** to make your device easier to use, and the **On-Screen Keyboard** to make it easier to type
- Cortana is a virtual personal assistant that comes with Windows 10, enabling you to find help, apps, files, settings, and other stuff on your computer and from the internet
- Cortana's search box offers you a quick and easy way to search for help whenever you need to
- The **Get Help** application offers you the option to get help with computer problems from Microsoft's Virtual Agent

- Microsoft Edge provides a completely new approach in finding stuff, reading and writing on the web, and getting help from Cortana from within the browser
- The browser that has resisted the times and changes in technology that are related to web access certainly is Internet Explorer
- If you are using a desktop PC, then **Power & sleep** takes care of your monitor and the power in your computer when your computer is in an idle state
- If you are using a laptop, **Power & sleep**, as it does with a desktop PC, saves your laptop's battery power when you are not working on it
- To configure advanced power setting in Windows 10, you should use the Control Panel's **Power Options**

Questions

1. Cortana is a virtual personal assistant that comes with Windows 10, enabling you to find help, apps, files, settings, and other stuff on your computer and from the internet.
   1. True
   2. False

2. _____ provides a completely new approach in finding stuff, reading and writing on the web, and getting help from Cortana from within the browser.

3. In which of the following modes can the Start menu be configured? (Choose two):
   1. Desktop mode
   2. Tablet mode
   3. Mobile mode
   4. Dynamic mode

4. To configure advanced power setting in Windows 10, you should use the Control Panel's **Appearance** and **Personalization**.
   1. True
   2. False

5. In laptops, the _____ saves your laptop's battery power when you are not working on it.

6. Which of the following combination keys makes Cortana listen to your commands?
    1. Windows key + C
    2. Windows key + E
    3. Windows key + I
    4. Windows key + X

7. Network, battery level, volume level, and system clock status are referred to as desktop icons.
    1. True
    2. False

8. Cortana's _____ offers you a quick and easy way to search for help whenever you need to.

9. Which of the following features does Microsoft Edge support? (Choose three)
    1. **Configuring network settings**
    2. **Hub**
    3. **Reading list**
    4. **Writing on the web**
    5. **Configuring Power & sleep**

10. The **Notification area** is part of the Windows **Taskbar** and is located on the far right side next to the **Action Center**.
    1. True
    2. False

11. You can use _____ to zoom in on parts of your display, _____ to control your device, _____ to allow your device to hear, _____ to make you device easier to use, and _____ to make it easier to type.

12. Which of the following advance power settings can be configured using the Control Panel's **Power Options**? (Choose two)
    1. **Change Windows To Go startup options**
    2. **Change default settings for media or devices**
    3. **Choose what closing the lid does**
    4. **Create a power plan**

Further reading

- **Accessibility Information for IT Professionals**: `https://docs.microsoft.com/en-us/windows/configuration/windows-10-accessibility-for-itpros`
- **Manage Windows 10 Start and taskbar layout**: `https://docs.microsoft.com/en-us/windows/configuration/windows-10-start-layout-options-and-policies`
- **Cortana integration in your business or enterprise**: `https://docs.microsoft.com/en-us/windows/configuration/cortana-at-work/cortana-at-work-overview`
- **Microsoft Edge Group Policy Configuration Options**: `https://docs.microsoft.com/en-us/microsoft-edge/deploy/index`
- **Internet Explorer 11 (IE11) - Deployment Guide for IT Pros**: `https://docs.microsoft.com/en-us/internet-explorer/ie11-deploy-guide/index`

5
Implement Windows in an Enterprise Environment

This chapter is designed to provide you with the necessary information on how Windows 10 deployment in organizations is undertaken. From the configuration of Windows 10 devices to the setting up GPOs to automate the Windows 10 activation process in the organizations, they all present the tools and methods available to implement Windows 10 in an enterprise environment. With that in mind, this chapter explains the importance of provisioning, as well as software licensing and activation, in a deployment process. As such, it requires a sound knowledge of how to use the **Windows Configuration Designer (WCD)** tool for provisioning, as well as the Microsoft Volume Licensing options such as **Active Directory-Based Activation (ADBA)**, and **Key Management Service (KMS)**. Likewise, this chapter covers the **Group Policies (GP)** too by listing the steps required to set up a logon script via GPO. Each topic is accompanied by step-by-step instructions driven by targeted, easy-to-understand screenshot. It concludes with a chapter lab on **User Account Control (UAC)**.

In this chapter, we will cover the following topics:

- Provisioning with the WCD tool
- Windows 10 software licensing and activation
- Implementing ADBA
- Implementing volume activation using a KMS
- Querying and configuring activation states using the command line
- Configuring Active Directory, including Group Policies
- Chapter lab—configuring and optimizing UAC

Technical requirements

In order to complete the labs for this chapter, you will need the following equipment:

- A PC with Windows 10 Enterprise, at least 8 GB of RAM, 500 GB of HDD, and access to the internet

Provisioning with the Windows Configuration Designer tool

The **Out-of-Box Experience** (**OOBE**) is the first-run setup experience that enables the configuration of Windows 10 devices purchased from the **Original Equipment Manufacturer** (**OEM**). Connecting to a network, joining a domain, and creating an account, are just some of the settings that need to be configured during the first-run setup experience. The grouping of these and many other tasks together is known as **provisioning**, which represents a task to configure end-user devices. In this way, Windows provisioning makes it easy for system administrators to specify desired configuration and settings, thereby configuring devices in a matter of minutes. A provisioning package, `.ppkg`, is a file that contains configuration settings. However, Windows provisioning does not remove the software pre-installed by the manufacturers that is commonly known as bloatware. Because of that, organizations frequently prefer to employ the **wipe and load** method, where Windows imaging plays an important role. Windows provisioning is best suited for small and medium-sized businesses.

Downloading and installing Windows Configuration Designer

The WCD tool, formerly known as **Windows Imaging and Configuration Designer** (**WICD**), can be downloaded from the Microsoft Store, as shown in *Figure 5.1*:

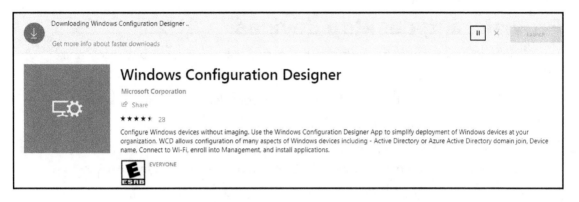

Figure 5.1: Downloading WCD from the Microsoft store

WCD can also be installed from the **Windows Assessment and Deployment Kit (Windows ADK)**, which can also be downloaded from the Microsoft website (see *Figure 5.2*):

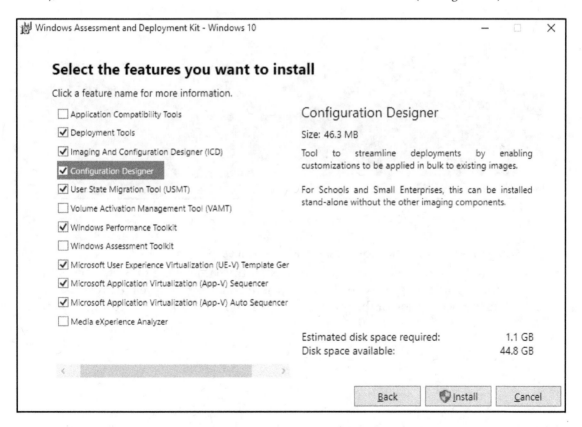

Figure 5.2: Installing the WCD tool from Windows ADK

Provisioning desktop devices

The WCD tool makes it easy to create provisioning packages, or set up devices to use within your organization.

To provision desktop devices using the WCD tool, complete the following steps:

1. Click the Start button to open the Start menu.
2. Click the WCD tool from the Start menu.
3. A short time thereafter, the WCD tool will open as shown in the following screenshot:

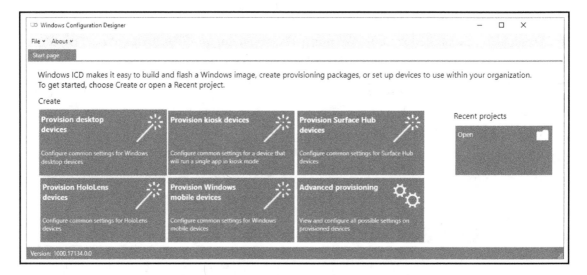

Figure. 5.3: WCD user interface

4. To get started, click **Provision desktop devices**.
5. Once the **New project** wizard opens, enter the name of the project, browse the project folder to specify the location where you want to store the project, and enter a description of the project, as shown in *Figure 5.4*. Click **Next** to continue:

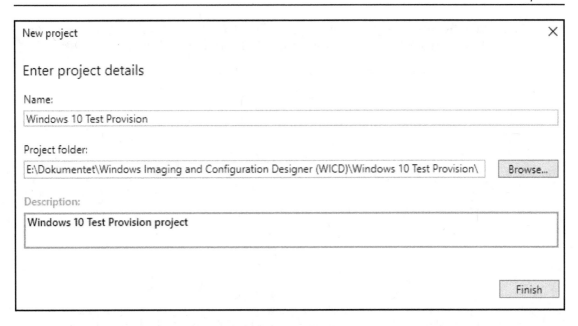

Figure 5.4: New project with WCD tool

6. On the **Set up device** page, enter the device name (see *Figure 5.5*), and then click **Next**:

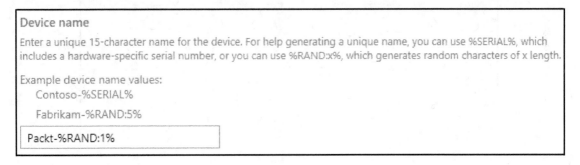

Figure 5.5: Entering device name

7. On the **Set up network** page, enter Wi-Fi network information such as **Network SSID**, **Network type**, and **Password**, as in *Figure 5.6*, and then click **Next**:

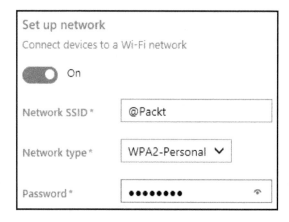

Figure 5.6: Entering Wi-Fi information

8. On the **Account Management** page, select the **Local admin** option, enter the **User name** and **Password**, as shown in *Figure 5.7*, and then click **Next**:

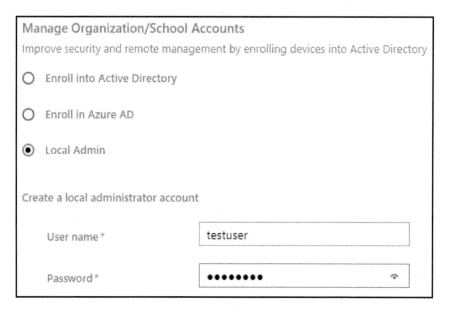

Figure 5.7: Creating local administrator account

9. On the **Add applications** page, click **Add an Application**, enter the **Application name**, specify the **Installer Path**, click the **Add** button (see *Figure 5.8*), and then click **Next**:

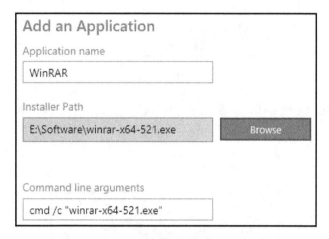

Figure 5.8: Adding an application

10. On the **Add certificates** page, click **Add a certificate**, enter the **Certificate name**, specify the **Certificate path**, click **Add** button, as in *Figure 5.9*, and then click **Next**:

Figure 5.9: Adding a certificate

11. On the **Finish** page, review the information presented in the **Summary** section, and then click the **Create** button, as shown in *Figure 5.10*:

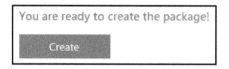

Figure 5.10: Creating a provision package

12. On the **Start** page, under **Recent projects**, you will notice your project (see *Figure 5.11*):

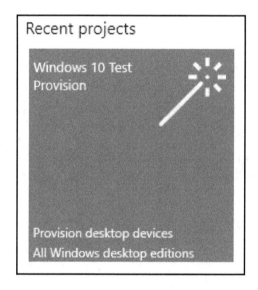

Figure 5.11: A recently created project

 Since Windows 10, version 1703, Microsoft has renamed WICD to WCD. However, it has removed the Windows imaging. Thus, in terms of customizing Windows 10 desktop devices, Microsoft recommends that you use the old **Windows System Image Manager** (**Windows SIM**), which is part of the Windows ADK.

Windows 10 software licensing and activation

In the 20-year history (from Windows 95 to Windows 10) of Microsoft Windows, there was no version of it that was offered free of charge, except for Windows 10. And that is because, in its first year of the launch (from August, 2015, to July, 2016), Microsoft offered a free upgrade to Windows 10 for all users who owned a PC running a genuine copy of Windows 7, and 8/8.1. The nice aspect of this unusual offer from Microsoft was that following such an upgrade, Windows 10 was **activated** and, just like that, the user already had a new **licensed** OS on his computer. That itself highlights the question of what a software license is? A **software license** is a legal agreement between an end user and the owner of the software that governs the use and redistribution of its software. Another aspect associated with the software license is **software activation**, which represents a process that ensures that the end user is using a **genuine software copy**. Back to Windows 10, the **product key** you own represents a software license, whereas the software activation verifies the product key that you have used to install the OS. Once activated, your product key has been legitimately licensed in compliance with the software's **End User License Agreement** (**EULA**).

Windows 10 activation methods

When talking about Windows 10 activation, there are three main methods:

- **Retail activation** is any Windows 10 version (including product key) purchased at a retail store.
- **OEM activation** is any computer system with any Windows 10 version (including the product key) that is built by OEM, and purchased either from OEM or at a retail store.
- **Microsoft Volume Licensing activation**, known also as **volume activation**, is a software licensing program that is tailored to the needs of organizations. It uses ADBA, KMS, and **multiple activation key** (**MAK**) models to assist with activation tasks.

Historically, Microsoft is a company that has been maximally devoted to what is called **intellectual property protection**. And that has been achieved by taking adequate measures in licensing the software. Like that, almost every version of the Windows OS is accompanied by the relevant licensing technology. However, since Windows Vista, Microsoft has enhanced its anti-piracy technologies by establishing the so-called **Software Protection Platform (SPP)**. **Windows Product Activation (WPA)** and **Windows Genuine Advantage Validation** are the two main components of SPP for retail users.

Implementing Active Directory-based activation (ADBA)

If an organization needs to deploy 1,000 computers, do you think that they should also buy 1,000 Windows 10 licenses (including 1,000 installation media)? Technically, it is possible to purchase this number of Windows 10 licenses. However, from an administrative point of view, that would cause overhead. To avoid such situations, Microsoft has introduced **Microsoft Volume Licensing**, which enables a single Windows 10 license to be used on multiple computers at the same time.

What is Active Directory-based activation?

ADBA, introduced with Windows 8 and Windows Server 2012, is a **graphical user interface (GUI)**-based activation method that automatically activates computers with Windows 10 generic **Volume License Key (VLK)** editions once they join the organization's domain. To simplify the maintenance of volume activation services for an organization network, you can use ADBA. ADBA is a role service in Windows Server 2016 that you set up to your organization's activation server by adding the **Volume Activation Services** role. It is a forest-wide network service that only works with Windows 8/8.1, Windows Server 2012/2012 R2, Windows 10, and Windows Server 2016. If your organization needs to activate Windows 7, Windows Server 2008 R2, and earlier versions of Windows, both desktop and server, then you need the **Key Management Service (KMS)** (see the next section: *Implementing volume activation using a KMS*). With ADBA, to maintain the active status of activation, client computers must remain members of the organization's domain. Activation lasts for 180 days, and after that, the client computers will query AD for the Activation Object. ADBA utilizes **Lightweight Directory Access Protocol (LDAP)** to maintain communication between the **Active Directory (AD)** and client computers.

Activation takes place without user intervention, and largely depends on the licensing service. Once the licensing service starts, computers with Windows 10 connect to AD automatically so they can get object activation and, with that, get activated:

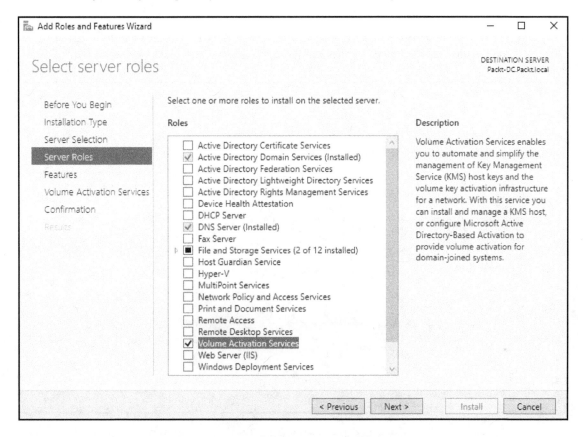

Figure 5.12: Adding the volume activation services role to Windows Server 2016

Configuring ADBA

To configure ADBA in an organization's activation server (running Windows Server 2016), complete the following steps:

1. The system administrator needs to install the ADBA role service on a domain controller, as shown in *Figure 5.12*, including the KMS host key (see *Figure 5.13*):

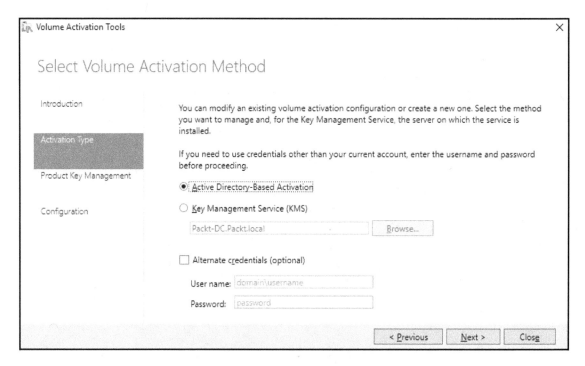

Figure 5.13: Configuring ADBA in Windows Server 2016

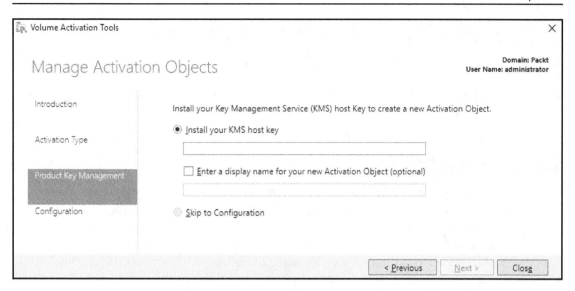

Figure 5.14: Installing the KMS host key

2. The system administrator needs to activate the KMS host key with **Microsoft-hosted activation services** using the **Volume Activation Management Tool (VAMT)**.

3. Once the domain member computers that are running Windows 10 (excluding Home edition) are powered up, the licensing service on such computers automatically queries the AD for licensing information.

4. Actually, the client computer queries **Active Directory Domain Services (ADDS)** for activation information.

5. If the licensing service on the client computers finds a valid activation object on a domain controller, the activation takes place silently without any user intervention.

6. If the licensing service on the client computers **does not** find a valid activation object on a domain controller, the client computers look for a **KMS host** in order to attempt activation.

 ADBA simplifies the volume activation process by activating clients that are running Windows 8, Windows 8.1, Windows 10, Windows Server 2012, Windows Server 2012 R2, Windows Server 2016, or Windows Server 2019. It requires extending the AD schema by running `adprep.exe`.

Implementing volume activation using a KMS

As opposed to ADBA, KMS is a legacy method of automatically activating Windows (both desktop and server) and Office editions based on volume licensing.

What is KMS?

To understand KMS better and, with this, to explain the process of how KMS works, it will be compared with ADBA. Unlike ADBA which is GUI-based, KMS is **command-line interface (CLI)** based. KMS is a network service that can also activate the newest versions of Windows, such as Windows 10, and Windows Server 2016. However, KMS is primarily used by organizations to activate earlier versions of both desktop and server Windows, such as Windows Vista, Windows 7, and Windows Server 2008/2008 R2, as well as MS Office 2010 and later. Like ADBA, KMS is configured (as shown in *Figure 5.15*) by adding a **Volume Activation Services** role to your organization's activation server. The KMS service can coexist on a server that provides other services too, thereby not requiring a dedicated server. In this way, organizations can benefit from that KMS flexibility by saving a physical or virtual server:

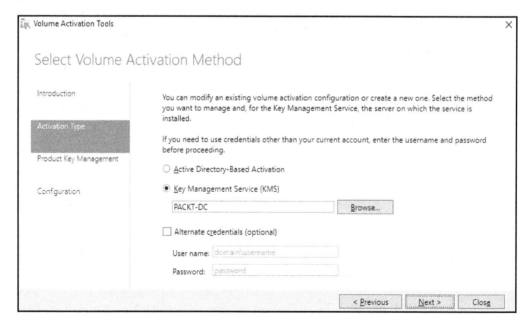

Figure 5.15: Configuring a KMS service in Windows Server 2016

How does KMS work?

Similar to ADBA, KMS also requires the installation of a KMS host key (see *Figure 5.16*) to enable KMS functionality. With a dynamic DNS enabled, the KMS activation server automatically creates a service record (SRV) in DNS. Then, KMS clients over the RPC 1688 TCP port use the resource records in DNS to locate the KMS host and request activation. As with ADBA, activation over KMS requires no action from users either. Unlike ADBA, where activation lasts 180 days and client computers are bound to being a member of the domain, in KMS, where activation also lasts for 180 days, the reactivation of client computers is effected via attempts to renew with the KMS host every seven days by default. Since there is no such thing with ADBA, in KMS, there is something called **threshold**, which represents the minimum activation requirements. The threshold applies to both physical and virtual client machines and servers:

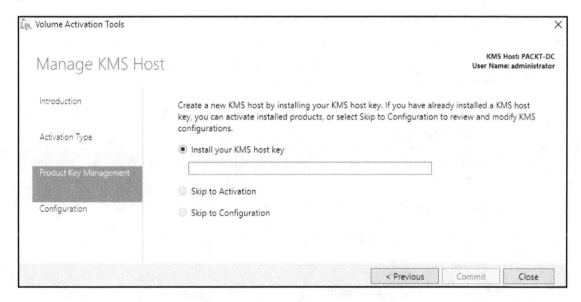

Figure 5.16: Installing a KMS host key while configuring a KMS activation server

 The KMS threshold is an essential requirement where more than 25 physical or virtual Windows client OSes, or five MS Office clients, or five Windows Server KMS licenses, need to be in an organization's networking environment before system administrators can begin activating any computer over KMS.

Querying and configuring activation states using the command line

As explained in the section entitled *Implementing volume activation using a KMS*, the installation of a KMS host key is required in order to enable KMS service functionality. The KMS host key can then either be activated over the phone in the region where you are located, or using an online Microsoft's web service. Knowing that KMS is a CLI-based service, the following section lists some of the most frequently used slmgr.vbs commands. It is Microsoft command-line licensing tool, and it stands for **Windows Software Licensing Management Tool**.

slmgr.vbs commands

This section describes how and when to use the slmgr.vbs commands. Open Command Prompt in elevated mode, and begin entering the commands according to requirements and circumstances.

- Enter the following command to display the current license information:

  ```
  slmgr.vbs -dli
  ```

- Enter the following command to display the current license with more detailed information:

  ```
  slmgr.vbs -dlv
  ```

- Enter the following command to display the installation ID:

  ```
  slmgr.vbs -dti
  ```

- Enter the following command to display the expiration date of the current license:

  ```
  slmgr.vbs -xpr
  ```

- Enter the following command to enter a new product key or change the existing one:

  ```
  slmgr.vbs -ipk <product key>
  ```

- Enter the following command to activate the current product key:

  ```
  slmgr.vbs -ato
  ```

- Enter the following command to uninstall the currently installed product key:

  ```
  slmgr.vbs -upk
  ```

- Enter the following command to reset the evaluation period:

  ```
  slmgr.vbs -rearm
  ```

- Enter the following command to set the KMS server and the port:

  ```
  slmgr.vbs -skms <activationservername:port>
  ```

- Enter the following command to learn more about the slmgr.vbs options:

  ```
  slmgr.vbs -?
  ```

 You can learn more about the slmgr.vbs commands from http://blog.pemato.de/2017/01/24/windows-activation-kms-and-slmgr-exe/.

Configuring Active Directory, including Group Policies

As you know, the Windows Server-based domain is a centralized environment. Everything revolves around the ADDS role, which, when installed and configured, establishes a hierarchical database known as **AD** that consists of objects. Typically, **AD objects** represent users, computers, peripheral devices, and network services. From the administration point of view, domain is a complex environment that requires additional tools that will help manage AD objects. One such option is **Group Policy** which enables limit restrictions to be established, both at a computer level and a user level. In general, group policies are preconfigured templates that control user behavior on computers, peripheral devices, and network applications across the organization's network. By default, group policies are stored in C:\Windows\SYSVOL\sysvol\domain\Policies on a domain controller.

Setting up a logon script via GPO

Group policies do not activate KMS clients, but they can enable the execution of scripts that are aimed at activating KMS clients. So, first things first: a script needs to be compiled and then a GPO set up that will execute that script once the user logs in to the domain.

Writing an activation script

To create an activation script using Notepad, complete the following steps:

1. Click the search box on a taskbar, and enter `Notepad`.
2. From the **Best match** list, click on **Notepad**.
3. In the **Notepad** window, enter the following commands:

```
slmgr.vbs -ipk <product key>
slmgr.vbs -skms <activationservername:port>
```

4. Instead of `<product key>`, enter the Windows 10 generic VLK.
5. Instead of `<activationservername:port>`, enter the name of the KMS host and the TCP port.
6. Save the file with the `.bat` extension.
7. Create a shared folder and assign **Read** permissions for **Everyone,** as in *Figure 5.17*:

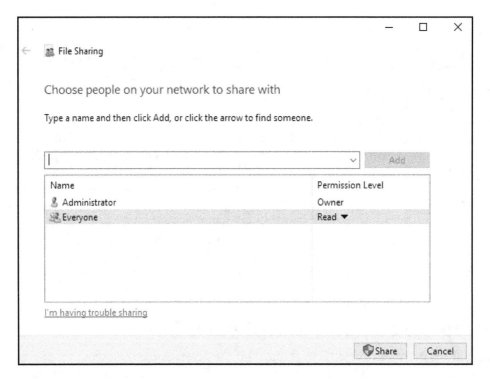

Figure 5.17: Creating a shared folder, and assigning read permission to everyone

Setting up the logon script GPO

To set up the logon script GPO, complete the following steps in **domain controller** (DC):

1. Click the Start button on the taskbar, and select **Server Manager** from the Start menu.
2. From the **Tools** menu, select **Group Policy Management**.
3. In the **Group Policy Management** console, right-click the domain and select **Create a GPO in this domain, and Link it here...,** as shown in *Figure 5.18*:

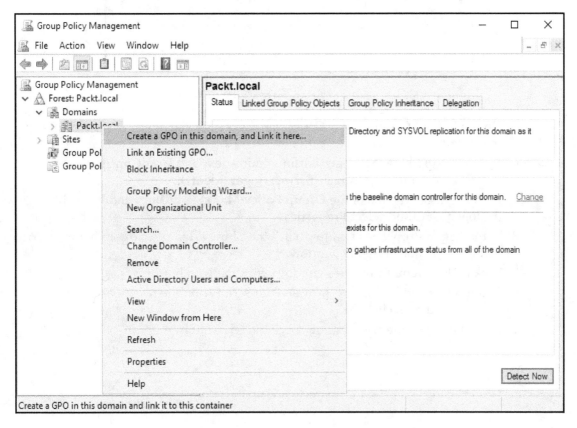

Figure 5.18: Setting up a logon script GPO via the GPM console in Windows Server 2016

4. In the **New GPO** window, enter the name for the GPO and click **OK** (see *Figure 5.19*):

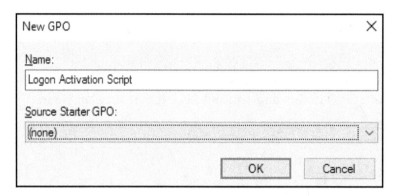

Figure 5.19: Naming the logon script GPO

5. On the **Linked Group Policy Object** tab, right-click the newly created GPO and select **Edit**.
6. In the **Group Policy Manager Editor** window, expand **User Configuration | Policies | Windows Settings | Scripts (logon/logoff)**.
7. In the right-hand pane of the **Group Policy Manager Editor** window, right-click the logon GPO and select **Properties**.
8. In the **Logon Properties** window, click the **Show Files** button, copy your script to that location, and close the window.
9. Back to the **Logon Properties** window, click the **Add** button.
10. In the **Add a script** window, browse your script from the recently copied location, and then click **OK**.
11. In the **Logon Properties** window, click the **OK** button.

12. Close the **Group Policy Manager Editor** window.

13. On the **Linked Group Policy Object** tab in the **Group Policy Management** console, right-click the newly created GPO and select **Enforced**, as in *Figure 5.20*:

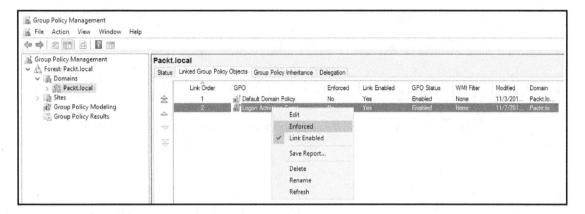

Figure 5.20: Enforcing the newly created logon script GPO

14. Click **OK** when asked **Do you want to change the Enforced setting for this GPO Link(s)**.

15. On one of the computers that are part of the domain, log on, and then test the newly created activation script.

> You can learn more about Windows 10 and Windows Server 2016 Group Policies from `https://getadmx.com/?Category=Windows_10_2016`.

Chapter lab – configuring and optimizing UAC

In this chapter lab, you will learn the following:

- Configuring and optimizing UAC

Configuring UAC

To **configure UAC** on your Windows 10 computer using **Control Panel**, complete the following steps:

1. Click the search box on the taskbar.
2. With Cortana open, enter uac.
3. Select **Change User Account Control settings** from the **Best match** list, as in *Figure 5.21*:

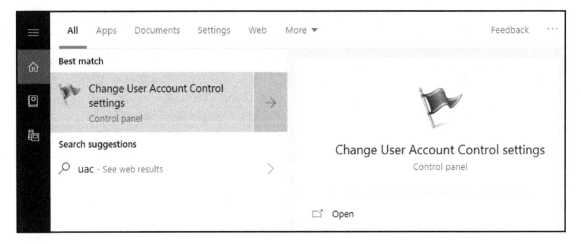

Figure 5.21: User account control settings on the **Best match** list

4. In the **User Account Control Settings** window, **Notify me only when apps try to make changes to my computer** is a default configuration (see *Figure 5.22*):

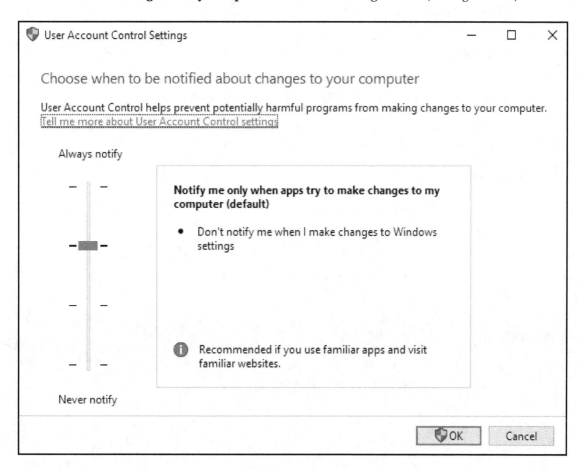

Figure 5.22: Default configuration in UAC

5. In the **User Account Control Settings** window, move the UAC slider to the bottom level where the **Never notify** option is located, as shown in *Figure 5.23*. This will disable the UAC settings:

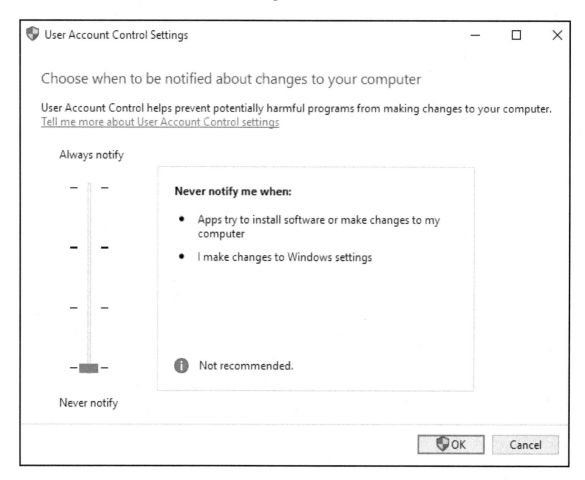

Figure 5.23: Disabling UAC in Windows 10

6. In the **User Account Control Settings** window, move the UAC slider to the top level where the **Always notify** option is located, as shown in *Figure 5.24*:

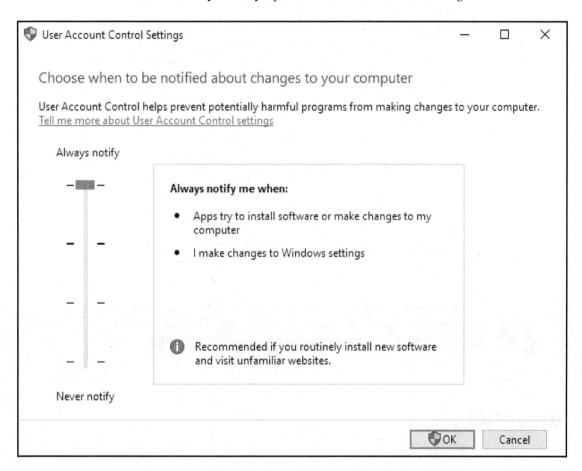

Figure 5.24: Always notifying option in UAC

7. Depending on any option you have selected, click **OK** to apply the configuration.
8. When asked **Do you want to allow this app to make changes to your device?**, click the **Yes** button (see *Figure 5.25*):

Figure 5.25: Approving changes to a Windows 10 computer

 Introduced in Windows Vista, UAC, although highly discussed, has accompanied every version of Windows up to Windows 10, and has taken care to prevent unauthorized changes to the operating system.

Summary

We can summarize this chapter as follows:

- The **Out of Box Experience (OOBE)** is the first-run setup experience that facilitates the configuration of Windows 10 devices purchased from the **Original Equipment Manufacturer (OEM)**
- Provisioning represents a task to configure end-user devices
- The **Windows Configuration Designer (WCD)** is a tool that helps to configure Windows 10 devices
- A software license is a legal agreement between an end user and the owner of the software that governs the use and redistribution of the software

- The software activation represents a process that ensures that the end user is using a genuine copy of the software
- The product key represents a software license, whereas the software activation verifies the product key that is used to install the Windows OS
- Microsoft Volume Licensing enables a single Windows 10 license to be used on multiple computers at the same time
- ADBA is a GUI-based activation method that automatically activates computers with Windows 10 generic VLK editions once they join the organization's domain
- KMS is a legacy method of automatically activating Windows (both desktop and server) and Office editions based on volume licensing
- A KMS host key enables KMS functionality
- `slmgr.vbs` is Microsoft's command-line licensing tool that stands for Windows Software Licensing Management Tool
- Active Directory objects represent users, computers, peripheral devices, and network services
- Group Policies are pre-configured templates that control user behavior on computers, peripheral devices, and network applications across the organization's network

Questions

1. Active Directory objects represent users, computers, peripheral devices, and network services.
    1. True
    2. False

2. _____ are preconfigured templates that control user behavior on computers, peripheral devices, and network applications across the organization's network.

3. Which of the following are Windows 10 activation methods?
    1. Retail activation
    2. OEM activation
    3. Microsoft Volume Licensing activation
    4. All of the above

4. A **Key Management Service** (**KMS**) host key enables KMS functionality.
   1. True
   2. False

5. _____ prevents unauthorized changes to the operating system.

6. Which of the following are Microsoft Volume Licensing activation options?
   1. **Active Directory-based activation** (**ADBA**)
   2. **Key Management Service** (**KMS**)
   3. **Multiple Activation Key** (**MAK**)
   4. All of the above

7. Since Windows 10, version 1809, Microsoft has renamed **Windows Imaging and Configuration Designer** (**WICD**) to **Windows Configuration Designer** (**WCD**).
   1. True
   2. False

8. The _____ is an essential requirement where more than 25 physical or virtual Windows client OSes, or five MS Office clients, or five Windows Server KMS licenses, need to be in an organization's networking environment before system administrators can begin activating any computer over KMS.

9. Which of the following are essential components of the Windows OS activation process? (Choose two)
   1. Internet connection
   2. Software license
   3. Software activation
   4. Installation media

10. The product key represents a software license, whereas the software activation verifies the product key that is used to install the Windows OS.
    1. True
    2. False

11. The _____ represents a process that ensures that the end user is using a genuine copy of the software.

12. Which of the following tools enables Windows 10 provisioning?
    1. **Windows Configuration Designer** (**WCD**)
    2. **Out-of-Box-Experience** (**OOBE**)
    3. **Original Equipment Manufacturer** (**OEM**)
    4. **Windows Assessment and Deployment Kit** (**Windows ADK**)

Further reading

- **Deploy Windows 10 with the Microsoft Deployment Toolkit**: `https://docs.microsoft.com/en-us/windows/deployment/deploy-windows-mdt/deploy-windows-10-with-the-microsoft-deployment-toolkit`
- **Overview of Windows Autopilot**: `https://docs.microsoft.com/en-us/windows/deployment/windows-autopilot/windows-10-autopilot`
- **Activate using Active Directory-based activation**: `https://docs.microsoft.com/en-us/windows/deployment/volume-activation/activate-using-active-directory-based-activation-client`
- **Activate using Key Management Service**: `https://docs.microsoft.com/en-us/windows/deployment/volume-activation/activate-using-key-management-service-vamt`
- **How User Account Control works**: `https://docs.microsoft.com/en-us/windows/security/identity-protection/user-account-control/how-user-account-control-works`

6
Configuring Networking

This chapter is designed to provide you with the detailed instructions regarding network configuration in Windows 10. Tasks such as configuring IP network settings and name resolution are necessary to connect the computer to the network. Configuring network locations, Windows Defender Firewall, and network discovery will enable your computer to communicate securely with peers on the network. In addition, this chapter also explains technologies such as **virtual private network** (**VPN**), DirectAccess, and **Internet Protocol Security** (**IPsec**) that will enable your computer to communicate securely with remote computers and networks over public networks, such as the internet. Likewise, Wi-Fi settings and Wi-Fi Direct can enable your computer to communicate on wireless networks. You're likely to encounter different networking problems, hence troubleshooting is also part of this chapter. Each topic is accompanied with step-by-step instructions driven by targeted, easy-to-understand screenshots. This chapter concludes with a chapter lab about DirectAccess.

In this chapter, we'll cover the following topics:

- Configuring and supporting IPv4 and IPv6 network settings
- Configuring name resolution
- Connecting to a network
- Configuring network locations
- Configuring Windows Defender Firewall
- Configuring Windows Defender Firewall with Advanced Security
- Configuring network discovery
- Configuring Wi-Fi settings
- Configuring Wi-Fi Direct
- Troubleshooting network issues
- Configuring a VPN
- Configuring IPsec
- Chapter lab—configuring DirectAccess

Technical requirements

In order to complete the labs for this chapter, you'll need the following equipment:

- PC with Windows 10 Pro, at least 4 GB of RAM, 500 GB of HDD, and access to the internet

Configuring and supporting IPv4 and IPv6 network settings

As you may know, for a computer to be able to communicate in a computer network, it requires two logical elements. They are a **computer name** and an **IP address**. Unlike the computer name, which is alphanumeric, the IP address is all numeric. A computer name in Windows 10 can be of two types: hostname and NetBIOS name. The IP address can be of version v4 (IPv4) or version v6 (IPv6). Just as your computer gets a default name while installing Windows 10, similarly the network interface of your computer receives an IP address, either from the DHCP server or an APIPA. These and many other tasks related to the network represent the common administrative tasks of the help desk member. That necessarily implies that help desk staff are required to know how to configure and troubleshoot network connections in order to be able to perform common tasks in the organization's infrastructure.

IPv4 network addresses

As specified in the **Internet Engineering Task Force** (**IETF**) publication, *RCF 791*, the label v4 represents the **fourth version** of IP addressing (that is, IPv4). The IPv4, usually known as an **IP address**, is a logical element that consists of 32 bits and is organized into four octets (eight bits each), separated by a period. An IPv4 address has a size of **four bytes**, where each octet represents one byte. The total number of IPv4 addresses is 4,294,967,296. If each person in the world is assigned an IPv4 address, then it's apparent that there are more than 3 billion IPv4 addresses missing. That's why IPv6 network addresses were introduced.

IPv6 network addresses

As mentioned earlier, if it weren't for the lack of IPv4 address space, most probably there wouldn't have been IPv6! Like IPv4, IPv6 too is a logical element that identifies a device on a computer network. The label v6 represents the sixth version of IP addressing (that is, IPv6), as specified in the IETF publication, *RFC 2460*. Unlike IPv4, IPv6 is a 128-bit network address that is organized into eight hextets (16 bits each), separated by a colon. The total number of IPv6 addresses is $2128 = 340,282,366,920,938,463,463,374,607,431,768,211,456$, meaning that there are plenty of IPv6 addresses available for every resident on planet Earth!

Configuring IPv4 network settings

As you may know, Windows 10 provides a number of tools to configure **IPv4** network settings on your computer.

To configure IPv4 network settings in your Windows 10 computer using Windows **Settings**, complete the following steps:

1. Click the Start button and select **Settings** on the Start menu.
2. Select **Network & Internet** on the Windows **Settings** window.
3. Select **Ethernet** on the **Network & Internet** navigation menu.
4. Select **Change adapter options**.
5. Right-click your computer's Ethernet adapter, and then select the **Properties** option.
6. In **This connection uses the following items,** select **Internet Protocol Version 4 (TCP/IPv4)**, and then click the **Properties** button.
7. On the **Internet Protocol Version 4 (TCP/IPv4) Properties** window, you can configure IPv4 network settings **automatically** or **manually**.

8. Enter the **IP address**, **Subnet mask**, and **Default gateway** (see the following screenshot):

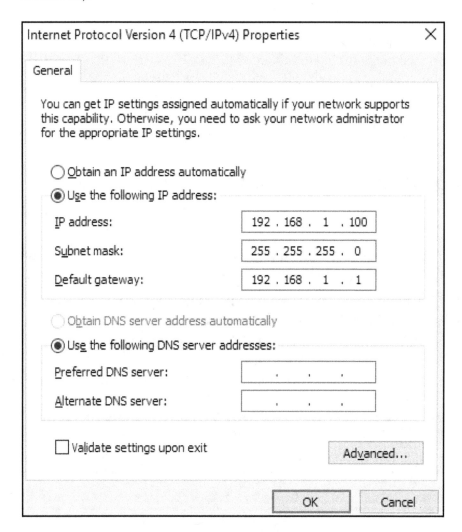

Figure 6.1. Configuring IPv4 network settings in Windows 10

9. Click **OK** to close the **Internet Protocol Version 4 (TCP/IPv4) Properties** window and then **OK** to close the **Ethernet's network adapter properties** window.

Configuring IPv6 network settings

More than half a decade has passed since the official launch of IPv6 in 2012, but ironically, IPv4 continues to deliver the majority of the internet traffic.

To configure IPv6 network settings in your Windows 10 computer using Windows **Settings**, complete the following steps:

1. Click the Start button and select **Settings** on the Start menu.
2. Select **Network & Internet** on the Windows **Settings** window.
3. Select **Ethernet** on the **Network & Internet** navigation menu.
4. Select **Change adapter options**.
5. Right-click your computer's Ethernet adapter, and then select the **Properties** option.
6. In **This connection uses the following items**, select **Internet Protocol Version 6 (TCP/IPv6)**, and then click the **Properties** button.
7. On the **Internet Protocol Version 6 (TCP/IPv6) Properties** window, you can configure IPv6 network settings **automatically** or **manually**.

8. Enter the **IPv6 address**, **Subnet prefix length**, and **Default gateway**, as shown in the following screenshot:

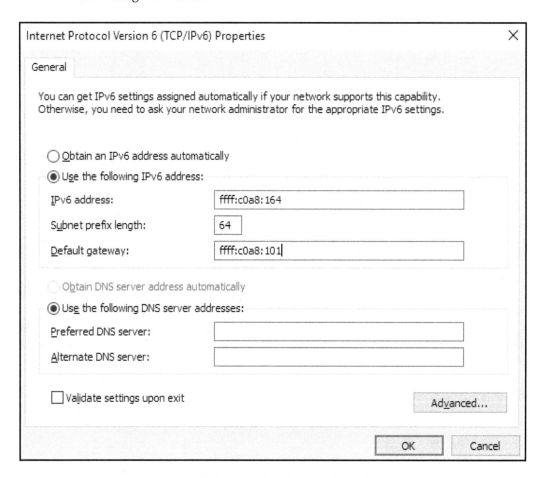

Figure 6.2. Configuring IPv6 network settings in Windows 10

9. Click **OK** to close the **Internet Protocol Version 6 (TCP/IPv6) Properties** window and then **OK** to close the **Ethernet's network adapter properties** window.

Configuring name resolution

The **name resolution** process is governed by the protocol known as the **Domain Name System** (**DNS**). As you know, DNS translates domain names into IP addresses. As a concept, DNS has been available since the ARPANET era. However, as a standard, the first DNS specifications, known as **Requests for Comments** (**RFC**) documents, were published at the beginning of the 1980s. In its architecture, DNS is hierarchical and consists of three main components: domain name, domain namespace, and name server. The **domain name** represents the website and consists of one or more parts called labels that are separated by a period (for example, `PacktPub.com`). The **domain namespace** is the hierarchical naming scheme of the DNS database organized into zones, where each zone represents a root domain, top-level domains, second level domains, subdomains, and hostnames. The **name server** is a network server responsible for responding to queries against a directory service by mapping the domain name into the correct IP address.

Configuring IPv4 DNS server settings

To configure IPv4 DNS server settings in your Windows 10 computer using Windows **Settings**, complete the following steps:

1. Repeat *step 1* to *step 8* from the *Configuring IPv4 network settings* section.
2. Enter the **Preferred DNS server**, as demonstrated in the following screenshot:

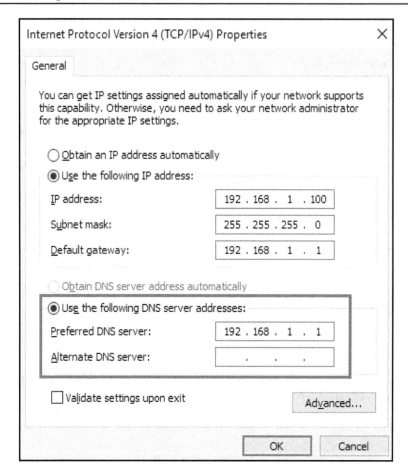

Figure 6.3. Configuring IPv4 DNS server settings in Windows 10

3. Click **OK** to close the **Internet Protocol Version 4 (TCP/IPv4) Properties** window and then **OK** to close the **Ethernet's network adapter properties** window.

 If you're running more than one DNS server in a network, then you may want to enter the **Alternate DNS server** IP address so you can have redundancy in the naming resolution.

Configuring IPv6 DNS server settings

To configure IPv6 DNS server settings using Windows **Settings** in your Windows 10 computer, complete the following steps:

1. Repeat *step 1* to *step 8* from the *Configuring IPv6 network settings* section.
2. Enter the **Preferred DNS server**, as shown in the following screenshot:

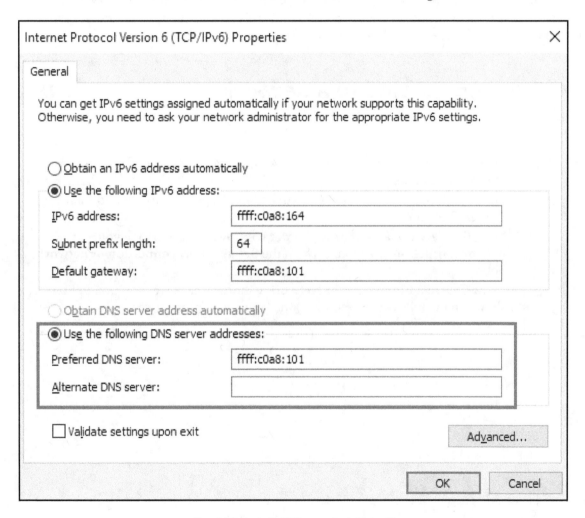

Figure 6.4. Configuring IPv6 DNS server settings in Windows 10

3. Click **OK** to close the **Internet Protocol Version 6 (TCP/IPv6) Properties** window and then **OK** to close the **Ethernet's network adapter properties** window.

Connecting to a network

Assuming that your computer has a network interface, both wired and wireless, then it can be said that Windows 10 offers many options and tools to connect your computer easily and quickly to these networks and others.

Getting connected to a network

To connect your Windows 10 computer to a network using Windows **Settings**, complete the following steps:

1. Press the Windows key + *X*, and then select **Network Connections** from the administrator's menu.
2. The penultimate option in the **Network Status** page is **Network and Sharing Center**. Click on that.
3. From the **Network and Sharing Center** window, in the **Change your networking settings** section, click on the **Set up a new connection or network** option.
4. In the **Set Up a Connection or Network** window, select a connection option (as shown in the following screenshot) that suits your preferences:

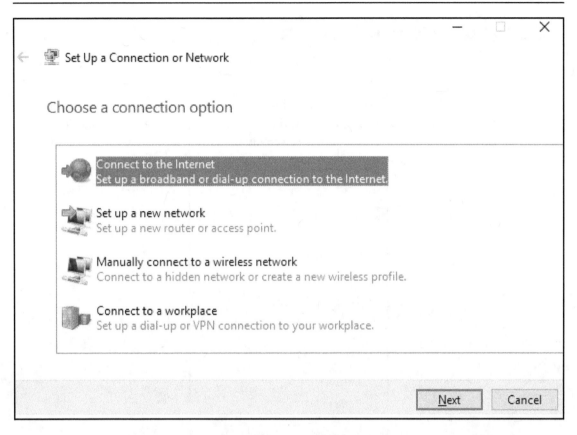

Figure 6.5. Connecting to a network in Windows 10

Configuring network locations

Initially introduced in Windows Vista and then improved in the following versions of Windows, **network locations** come in Windows 10 as an easy option to implement and as a good way to manage network connections and network sharing.

Adding a network location

To a configure network location in your Windows 10 computer, complete the following steps:

1. Press the Windows key + *E* to open **File Explorer**.
2. Right-click over **This PC** and, from the context menu, select **Add a network location**, as shown in the following screenshot:

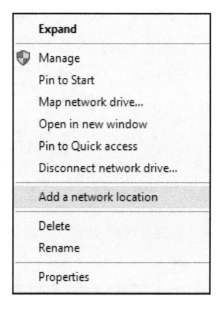

Expand

Manage

Pin to Start

Map network drive...

Open in new window

Pin to Quick access

Disconnect network drive...

Add a network location

Delete

Rename

Properties

Figure 6.6. Adding a network location in Windows 10

3. After you've read the first page of the **Add Network Location Wizard**, click **Next**.
4. Select **Choose a custom network location**, and then click **Next**.
5. On the **Specify the location of your website** page, enter the website address FTP site or browse to a network share. Then, click **Next** to continue.

6. On the **Completing the Add Network Location Wizard** page, click **Finish** to close the wizard (see the following screenshot):

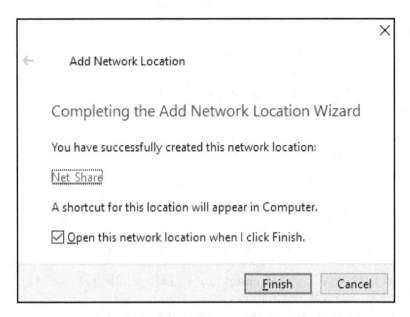

Figure 6.7. Completing the Add Network Location Wizard in Windows 10

Configuring Windows Defender Firewall

As you know, a **firewall** is a network device that protects your computer and network from malware and security breaches based on **preconfigured security rules**. A firewall, which may be hardware-or-software based, corresponds to the security officer at the gate of the company, who allows entrance for employees with an entrance permit and denies entrance to those who don't have one.

Turning Windows Defender Firewall on or off

To **turn on/off** the Windows Defender Firewall in your Windows 10 computer, complete the following steps:

1. Click the **search box** on the taskbar.
2. With Cortana open, enter `firewall`.
3. Select **Windows Defender Firewall** from the **Best match** list, as shown in the following screenshot:

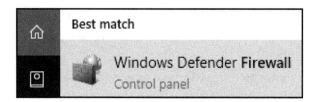

Figure 6.8. Windows Defender Firewall on the Best match list

4. Select **Turn Windows Defender Firewall On or Off** from the **Windows Defender Firewall** navigation menu.
5. **Turn on/off Windows Defender Firewall** for the domain, private, and public networks, as shown in the following screenshot:

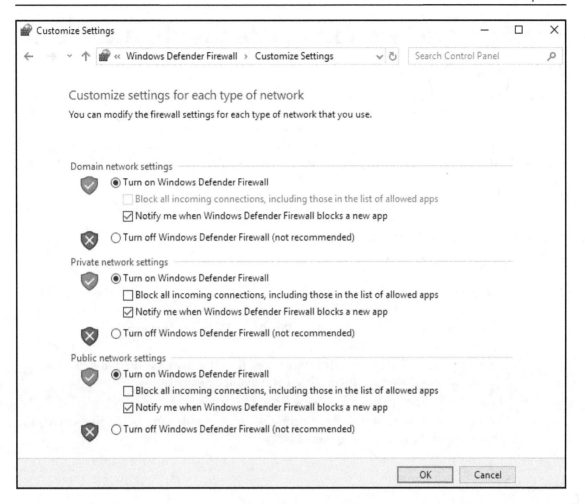

Figure 6.9. Turning on/off Windows Defender Firewall

6. Click **OK** to close the **Customize Settings** window.

Configuring Windows Defender Firewall with Advanced Security

If you need to block unauthorized network traffic from entering or exiting your computer, then you can use Windows Defender Firewall with **Advanced Security**. That applies to the network traffic that you want to permit to enter or exit your computer. By providing host-based security for your computer, Windows Defender Firewall with Advanced Security proves to be an important part of an overall layered security model that Windows 10 relies on.

Creating firewall rules

To create firewall rules in Windows Defender Firewall, complete the following steps:

1. **Repeat step 1 to step 3** from the *Turning Windows Defender Firewall On or Off* section.
2. Select **Advanced settings** from the **Windows Defender Firewall** navigation menu.
3. Select **Inbound Rules** or **Outbound Rules** from the **Navigation** pane of the **Windows Defender Firewall with Advance Security** window.
4. From the **Actions** pane, select **New Rule.**
5. You may want to continue by selecting the type of rule you would like to create, as shown in the following screenshot:

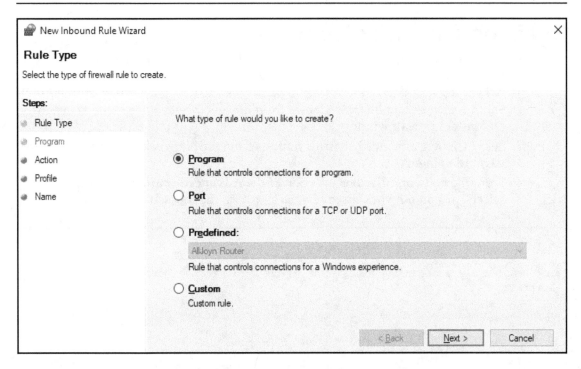

Figure 6.10. Creating firewall rules in Windows 10

 To learn how to create firewall rules, you may want to explore the content in the following URL: `https://docs.microsoft.com/en-us/windows/security/threat-protection/windows-firewall/procedures-used-in-this-guide`.

Configuring network discovery

In Windows 10, **network discovery** is the network setting that enables your computer to find computers and other devices on the network. That also applies to computers and other network devices to find your computer. This indicates that network discovery is reciprocal. In addition, network discovery, by default, is blocked by Windows Defender Firewall. So, if you plan using it, then you must enable it.

Enabling network discovery

To enable network discovery in your Windows 10 computer, complete the following steps:

1. Repeat *step 1* to *step 3* from the *Turning Windows Defender Firewall on or off* section.
2. Select **Network and Sharing Center** from the lower-left corner of the **Windows Defender Firewall** window.
3. Select **Change advanced sharing settings** from the **Network and Sharing Center** navigation menu.
4. From the **Network discovery** section of the **Advanced sharing settings** window, select **Turn on network discovery**, as shown in the following screenshot:

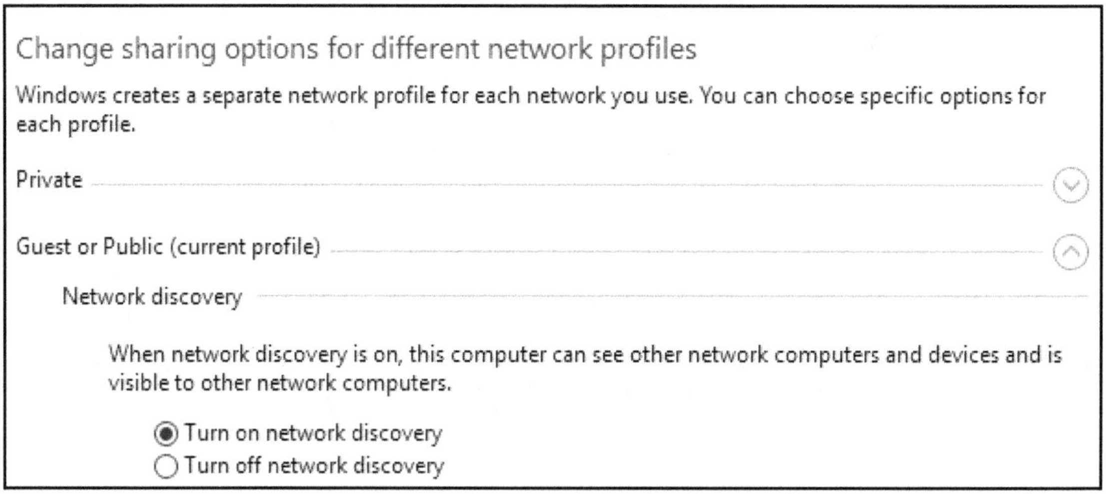

Change sharing options for different network profiles

Windows creates a separate network profile for each network you use. You can choose specific options for each profile.

Private ⌄

Guest or Public (current profile) ⌃

Network discovery

When network discovery is on, this computer can see other network computers and devices and is visible to other network computers.

◉ Turn on network discovery
○ Turn off network discovery

Figure 6.11. Turning on network discovery in Windows 10

Configuring Wi-Fi settings

As you may know, **Wi-Fi**, short for **Wireless Fidelity**, is a networking technology that uses radio waves as a communication medium. Wi-Fi utilizes a networking device known as an **access point** that enables you to create a **Wireless Local Area Network** (**WLAN**). WLANs enable network services to be accessed in an on-the-go format, hence enabling organizations to deploy new networking trends, such as **Bring Your Own Devices** (**BYOD**).

Connecting to a Wi-Fi network

To connect to a **Wi-Fi network** from your Windows 10 computer, complete the following steps:

1. Click the Start button and select **Settings** on the Start menu.
2. Select **Network & Internet** on the Windows **Settings** window.
3. Select **Wi-Fi** from the **Network & Internet** navigation menu.
4. From the **Wi-Fi** section, select **Show available networks** to display the available Wi-Fi networks (see the following screenshot):

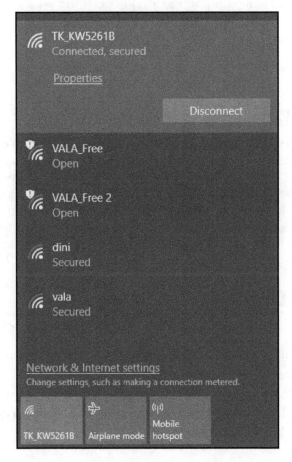

Figure 6.12. The list of available Wi-Fi networks

5. Select the Wi-Fi network that you want your computer to get connected to, and then click the **Connect** button.

6. Enter the network security key if that Wi-Fi network happens to be protected, and then click **Next**.

7. When asked **Do you want to allow your PC to be discoverable by other PCs and devices on this network?**, select **Yes** if it's a work or private network, or select **No** if it's a public network.

8. Shortly, after the authentication completes, your computer gets connected to the Wi-Fi network.

 To connect your computer to a Wi-Fi network, your computer must be equipped with a **Wi-Fi Network Interface Card (Wi-Fi NIC)**.

Configuring Wi-Fi Direct

If you want to connect your computer with other wireless devices over radio waves without the need for an access point, then you can use **Wi-Fi Direct**, which is supported by Windows 10. As stated, Wi-Fi Direct, also known as **Wi-Fi P2P (Peer-to-Peer)**, is a proprietary standard set by **Wi-Fi Alliance** that operates on the basis of two services known as *Wi-Fi Direct Device Discovery* and *Service Discovery*. It doesn't need access points because the devices in such wireless network are directly connected to each other, hence creating a well-known legacy network known as the **ad-hoc wireless network**.

Using Wi-Fi Direct

To use **Wi-Fi Direct** on your Windows 10 computer, complete the following steps:

1. Click the Start button and select the **Settings** on the Start menu.
2. Select **Devices** on the Windows **Settings** window.
3. Select **Bluetooth & other devices** from the **Devices** navigation menu.
4. Click **Add Bluetooth and other devices** and click the **Everything else** option from the **Add a device** window.

5. On your smartphone, navigate to the Wi-Fi networks and tap **Wi-Fi Direct**.
6. Soon both your computer and smartphone will list each other.
7. On your computer, from the **Add a device** window, click on your listed smartphone to connect with it (see the following screenshot):

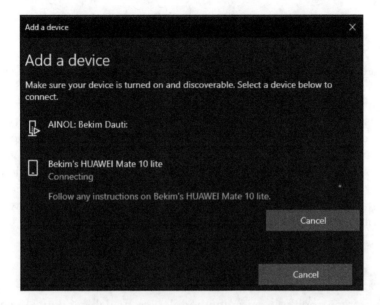

Figure 6.13. Connecting a computer with a smartphone over Wi-Fi Direct

8. At this point, on your smartphone, you should **enable the connection** with your computer.
9. Both on your computer (as shown in the following screenshot) and smartphone, you will notice the **connected** status:

Figure 6.14. Successfully connected computer with a smartphone over Wi-Fi Direct

To be able to use the Wi-Fi Direct feature on your Windows 10 computer, you need to make sure that your computer's wireless NIC is Wi-Fi Direct compatible. The same applies to your smartphone, too.

Troubleshooting network issues

If you've ever been involved in network problem solving in particular, and computer systems in general, then you will know that you've been involved in an activity that is called **troubleshooting**. As you know, in information technology, troubleshooting is a process that consists of certain steps and each step is characterized by a certain activity. From the perspective of an IT professional, troubleshooting is a skill that, no matter how hard you try, simply requires time in order to master it. Every time you solve a certain technical problem, it helps you to gain self-confidence, become more experienced, and with that, establish a knowledge base. That being said, learning about and practicing troubleshooting are **reciprocal activities**. That's because, while learning how to troubleshoot, you practice troubleshooting at the same time.

Troubleshooting steps

There may be different troubleshooting methodologies available today. However, best practice recognizes the six-step troubleshooting model. The steps are as follows:

1. Identify the problem by gathering as much technical information as possible
2. Establish a theory of probable cause by asking questions to determine whether any hardware, software, or network changes have been made recently
3. Test your theories to determine the cause of the problem by isolating the problem through removing or disabling hardware or software components
4. Establish a plan of action to resolve the problem through testing solutions and, at the same time, implement the solution, ensuring that you have a plan B too
5. Verify full functionality by checking results and, if the problem has not been solved, go back to *step 3*
6. Document your applied actions and received outcomes while troubleshooting the problem

Running the troubleshooter

To run the **troubleshooter** on your Windows 10 computer using Windows **Settings**, complete the following steps:

1. Click the Start button and select **Settings** on the Start menu.
2. Select **Update & Security** on the Windows **Settings** window.
3. Select **Troubleshoot** from the **Update & Security** navigation menu.
4. From the **Find and fix other problems** section, select **Network Adapter** to find and fix problems with wireless and other network adapters, as shown in the following screenshot:

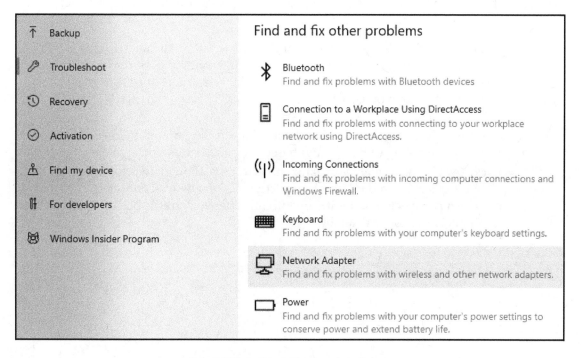

Figure 6.15. Selecting Network Adapter to run the troubleshooter

5. Click the **Run the Troubleshooter** button.
6. You may want to continue with the **Network Adapter** wizard by selecting the right options and clicking the **Next** button.

Configuring the VPN

As you may know, a **virtual private network** (**VPN**) is a logical connection on the internet for transmitting data securely. As its name suggests, a VPN creates a virtual point-to-point link between two computers on the WAN (that is, internet). That way, by utilizing tunneling protocols and data encryption algorithms, the VPN enables remote users to get connected to an organization's network over the internet infrastructure. This kind of network is usually implemented in two ways: **remote access VPN** and **site-to-site VPN**. In the remote access VPN, remote users (telecommuters) are connected with the server on their organization's private network, whereas the site-to-site VPN enables organizations to connect two separate networks over the internet. We all know that Windows 10 enables setting up the VPN connection. More than that, Windows 10 also offers advanced VPN profile features. Here are some of them:

- **App-triggered VPN**: It enables organizations to automatically trigger the VPN connection by simply launching a certain app. From the user's perspective, you do not have to worry about clicking on the **VPN-connect** button, as that's done by the application you've selected.
- **Traffic filter VPN**: It enables organizations to filter the in/out traffic. From the user's perspective, you have the option of controlling the traffic that's coming and going to/from your computer based on policies that you create.
- **Lockdown VPN**: It enables organizations to only allow network traffic over the VPN interface. From the user's perspective, it's an always-connected VPN that can't be disconnected and with an outbound network traffic being blocked when no VPN connection is available.

Setting up a VPN connection

To set up a **VPN connection** on your Windows 10 computer using Windows **Settings**, complete the following steps:

1. Click the Start button and select **Settings** on the Start menu.
2. Select the **Network & Internet** on the **Windows Settings** window.
3. Select **VPN** from the **Network & Internet** navigation menu.
4. From the **VPN** section, click on **Add a VPN connection** to set up a VPN connection (see the following screenshot):

Figure 6.16. Adding a VPN connection in Windows 10

5. In the **Add a VPN connection** form, select **VPN provider**, enter **Connection name**, enter **Server name or address**, select **VPN type**, select **Type of sign-in info**, enter **User name** and **Password** if required, and make sure to check the **Remember my sign-in info** checkbox (see the following screenshot):

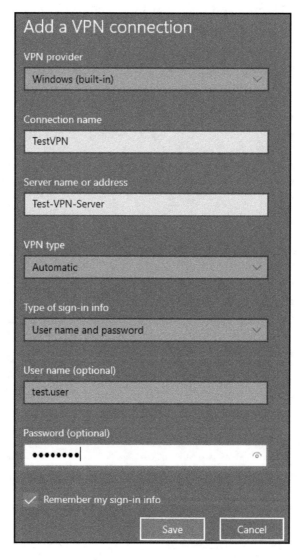

Figure 6.17. Setting up a VPN connection in Windows 10

6. Click the **Save** button.

 To be able to set up a VPN connection, it's necessary to have a **VPN server**. In Windows Server 2016, the **Remote Access** role enables setting up the VPN server.

Configuring IPsec

Internet Protocol Security (**IPsec**) is a suite of protocols that enables secure network services on IP packet-switched networks. IPsec is a standard (RFC 2401-2412) that has been developed under the supervision of the **Internet Engineering Task Force** (**IETF**) organization to allow authentication, integrity, access control, and confidentiality on network services. That being said, the authentication is achieved using the **Internet Key Exchange** (**IKE**) protocol, integrity is achieved using hashing algorithms, and confidentiality is achieved using encryption. **Authentication Header** (**AH**) and **Encapsulation Security Protocol** (**ESP**) are protocols that are utilized by IPsec. These features, and many more, enable IPsec to define how a VPN can be secured across all IP networks.

Securing a VPN connection using IPsec

To secure a VPN connection on your Windows 10 computer using IPsec, complete the following steps:

1. Repeat *step 1* to *step 5* from the *Setting up a VPN connection* section.

2. In the **Add a VPN connection** form, select **VPN provider**, enter **Connection name**, enter **Server name or address**, select **L2TP/IPsec with pre-shared key** as **VPN type**, enter **Pre-shared key**, select **Type of sign-in info**, enter **User name** and **Password** if required, and make sure to check the **Remember my sign-in info** checkbox (see the following screenshot):

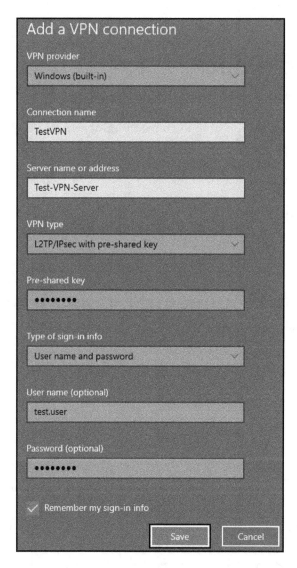

Figure 6.18. Securing a VPN connection using IPsec in Windows 10

3. Click the **Save** button.

Chapter lab – Configuring DirectAccess

In this chapter lab, you will learn how to enable DirectAccess on a client computer.

Enabling DirectAccess on a client computer

To enable and verify **DirectAccess configuration** on your Windows 10 computer, complete the following steps:

1. Sign in with a user account that has administrator rights.
2. Open **Command Prompt** with elevated privileges, and enter gpupdate /force, as shown in the following screenshot:

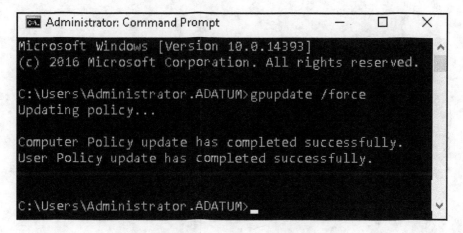

Figure 6.19. Refreshing Windows computer policies in Windows 10

3. To verify that the **DirectAccess Client Settings GPO** is applied to the computer settings, enter `gpresult /R` (see the following screenshot):

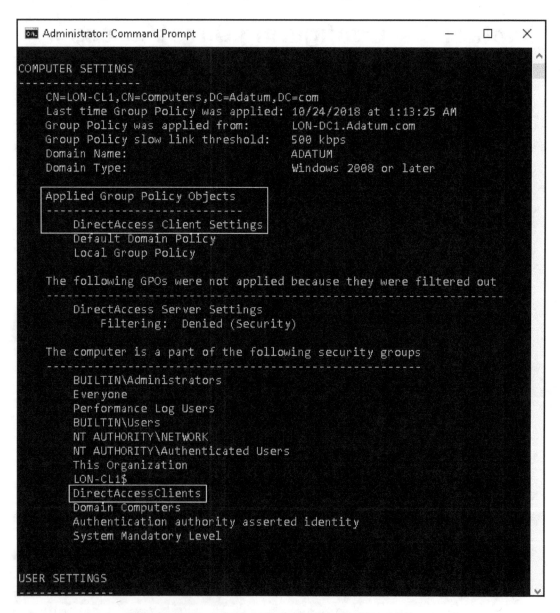

Figure 6.20. Verifying that the DirectAccess Client Settings GPO is applied to the computer settings

4. To display the actual **Name Resolution Policy Table (NRPT) entries** that are currently active on the DirectAccess client, enter the `netsh name show effectivepolicy` command, as shown in the following screenshot:

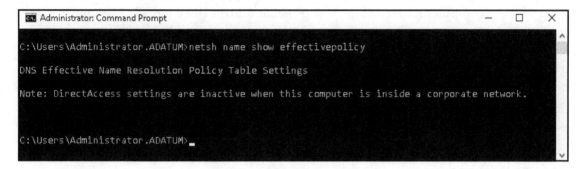

Figure 6.21. Displaying NRPT entries in Windows 10

5. Click the Start button and select the **Settings** on the Start menu.
6. Select **Network & Internet** on the Windows **Settings** window.
7. Select **DirectAccess** from the **Network & Internet** navigation menu.
8. From the **DirectAccess** section, click on the recently configured **DirectAccess connection,** as shown in the following screenshot:

Figure 6.22. Verifying that DirectAccess is enabled in Windows 10 computer

As you may know, **DirectAccess**, known also as Unified Remote Access, is a feature in Windows Server-based network services that enables remote access to intranet resources. Introduced in Windows Server 2008 R2, unlike a VPN, DirectAccess is connected automatically once the computer has access to the internet. It utilizes IPsec tunnels to establish secure connections between *DirectAccess clients* and the *DirectAccess server*, and IPv6 traffic for accessing intranet over the internet. With the DirectAccess server, you may want to use any of the Windows Server versions from 2008 R2 to 2019. For your DirectAccess clients, you must use domain-joined computers that run only the Enterprise edition of the Windows OS versions from 7 to 10, including 8/8.1 too.

Summary

We can summarize this chapter with the following points:

- For a computer to be able to communicate in a computer network, it requires two logical elements: a computer name and an IP address
- The IPv4 address is a logical element that consists of 32 bits and is organized into four octets (each octet has eight bits), separated by a period
- IPv6 is a 128-bit network address that's organized into eight hextets (each hextet has 16 bits each), separated by a colon
- The **Domain Name System** (**DNS**) translates domain names into IP addresses
- The network locations in Windows 10 is easy to implement and a good way to manage network connections and network sharing
- The firewall is a network device that protects your computer and network from malware and security breaches based on preconfigured security rules
- If you need to block unauthorized network traffic from entering or exiting your computer, then use Windows Defender Firewall with Advanced Security
- Network discovery is the network setting that enables your computer to find computers and other devices on the network
- Wi-Fi is a networking technology that uses radio waves as a communication medium
- If you want to connect your computer with other wireless devices over radio waves without the need for an access point, then you can use Wi-Fi-Direct

- Troubleshooting is a process that consists of certain steps and each step is characterized by a certain activity
- The **virtual private network** (**VPN**) is a logical connection on the internet for transmitting data securely
- The **Internet Protocol Security** (**IPsec**) is a suite of protocols that enables secure network services on IP packet-switched networks

Questions

1. The IPv4 address is a logical element that consists of 32 bits and is organized into four octets (each octet has eight bits), separated by a period.
    1. True
    2. False

2. For a computer to be able to communicate in a computer network requires two logical elements: _____ and an _____.

3. Which of the following are advanced VPN profile features? (Choose two)
    1. App-triggered VPN
    2. Lockdown VPN
    3. Remote access VPN
    4. Site-to-site VPN

4. The firewall is a computer that protects your computer and network from malware and security breaches based on preconfigured security rules.
    1. True
    2. False

5. The _____ is a logical connection on the internet for transmitting data securely.

6. Which of the following are steps in the troubleshooting process?
    1. Identify the problem
    2. Test your theories
    3. Verify full functionality
    4. All of the above

7. Wi-Fi is a networking technology that uses a coaxial cable as a communication medium.
    1. True
    2. False

8. The _____ is a suite of protocols that enables secure network services on IP packet-switched networks.

9. Which of the following logical elements identify a computer on a network? (Choose two)
    1. Computer name
    2. Domain name
    3. IP address
    4. MAC address

10. Network discovery is the network setting that enables your computer to find computers and other devices on the network.
    1. True
    2. False

11. The _____ translates domain names into IP addresses.

12. Which of the following protocol dynamically assigns an IP address?
    1. **Address Resolution Protocol (ARP)**
    2. **Automatic Private IP Addressing (APIPA)**
    3. **Reverse Address Resolution Protocol (RARP)**
    4. **Dynamic Host Configuration Protocol (DHCP)**

Further reading

- **Networking**: https://docs.microsoft.com/en-us/windows-server/ networking/networking
- **Windows 10 VPN Technical Guide**: https://docs.microsoft.com/en-us/ windows/security/identity-protection/vpn/vpn-guide
- **DirectAccess**: https://docs.microsoft.com/en-us/windows-server/remote/re mote-access/directaccess/directaccess
- **Windows Defender Advanced Threat Protection**: https://docs.microsoft. com/en-us/windows/security/threat-protection/windows-defender-atp/ windows-defender-advanced-threat-protection
- **Top Support Solutions for Windows 10**: https://docs.microsoft.com/en-us/ windows/client-management/windows-10-support-solutions

Configuring Storage 7

This chapter is designed to provide you with hands-on instructions for configuring disks, volumes, and filesystems by using both Disk Management and Windows PowerShell. In addition to fixed devices, the chapter also focuses on removable devices. Another thing in this chapter is that it covers Storage Spaces, which is a feature in Windows 10 that enables you to create software-defined storage by grouping disks into storage pools. It includes hands-on instructions for creating and configuring storage spaces. This chapter also addresses the troubleshooting of storage and removable device issues. Here, you will get to know some of the most common hardware and software problems that you may encounter in storage and removable devices, as well as troubleshooting tips to overcome both hardware and software problems. Each topic is accompanied by step-by-step instructions driven by targeted, easy-to-understand screenshot. The chapter concludes with a chapter lab on creating and configuring VHDs.

In this chapter, we will cover the following topics:

- Configuring disks, volumes, and filesystem options using Disk Management and Windows PowerShell
- Configuring removable devices
- Creating and configuring storage spaces
- Troubleshooting storage and removable devices issues
- Chapter lab—creating and configuring VHDs

Technical requirements

In order to complete the labs for this chapter, you will need the following equipment:

- A PC with Windows 10 Pro, at least 4 GB of RAM, 500 GB of HDD, and access to the internet

Configuring disks, volumes, and filesystem options using Disk Management and Windows PowerShell

I guess you have noticed what happens to the disk during the Windows 10 installation process? Disk partitioning and formatting are two of the processes that are required to install Windows 10. If these can be regarded as Disk Management activities at the pre-installation phase of Windows 10, then there are also disk management activities at the post-installation phase. Some of these post-installation disk management activities include initializing disks, creating volumes, formatting volumes, moving disks between computers, changing disks between basic and dynamic types, and changing the disk's partition scheme. So, in the following sections, you will become familiar with Disk Management and Windows PowerShell as two old tools that continue to be available in Windows 10, too, for managing disks.

Managing storage with Disk Management

As you know, **Disk Management** (`diskmgmt.msc`) is a snap-in of the **Microsoft Management Console** (**MMC**) that is used for, as the name indicates, managing disks, and volumes. Introduced in Windows 2000 as a joint project between Microsoft and Veritas, Disk Management (see *Figure 7.1.*) offers a full-featured graphical interface and, as such, enables the management of basic and dynamic disks too, both on local and remote computers. Apart from the activities mentioned here and in the previous section, Disk Management enables you to quickly confirm the health of each volume as well.

In Windows 10, you can access Disk Management in the following ways:

1. Right-click the **Start** button
2. Select **Disk Management**

Or:

1. Press the Windows key + *R* to open the **Run** window.
2. Enter `diskmgmt.msc` and hit *Enter*:

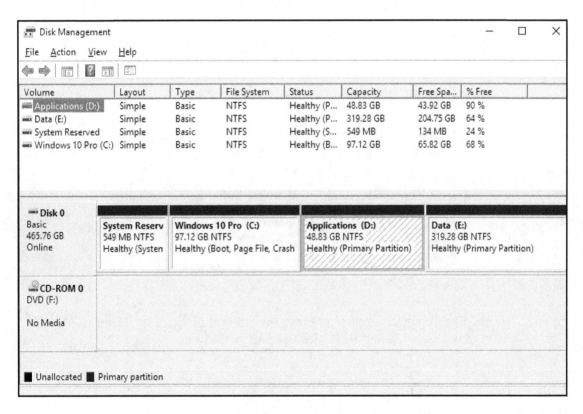

Figure 7.1: Managing storage with a Disk Management snap-in

Shrinking the volume

To **shrink** the existing volume so as to create a new volume in Windows 10 using Disk Management, complete the following steps:

1. Right-click the volume you want to **shrink**.
2. From the **Context** menu, select **Shrink Volume...**, as in *Figure 7.2*:

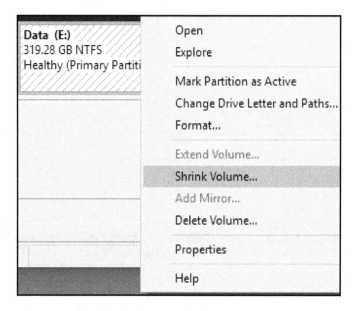

Figure 7.2: Shrinking volume in Windows 10

3. In the **Shrink** window, click on **Enter the amount of space to shrink in MB:**, as shown in *Figure 7.3*, and then click the **Shrink** button:

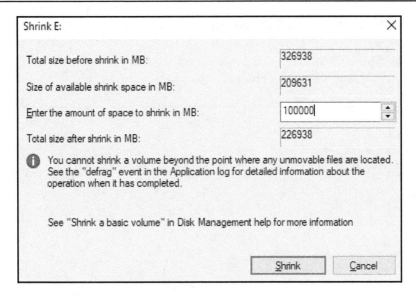

Figure 7.3: Specifying the amount of space to shrink

Creating and formatting the volume

To create a new volume in Windows 10 using Disk Management, complete the following steps:

1. Right-click **Unallocated** space.
2. From the **Context** menu, select **Create New Simple Volume...**, as shown in *Figure 7.4*:

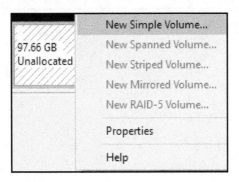

Figure 7.4. Creating a new simple volume in Windows 10

3. In the **New Simple Volume wizard**, click **Next** to begin creating a simple volume on a disk.

4. In the **Specify Volume Size** page, accept the **Simple volume size in MB:** (see *Figure 7.5*), and then click **Next**:

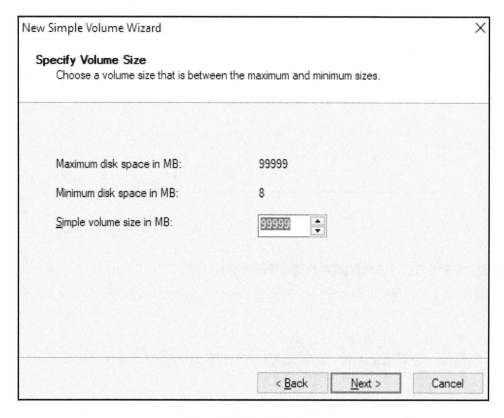

Figure 7.5: Specifying the volume size

5. In the **Assign Drive Letter or Path** page, ensure that the **Assign the following drive letter:** option is selected, as in *Figure 7.6*, and then click **Next**:

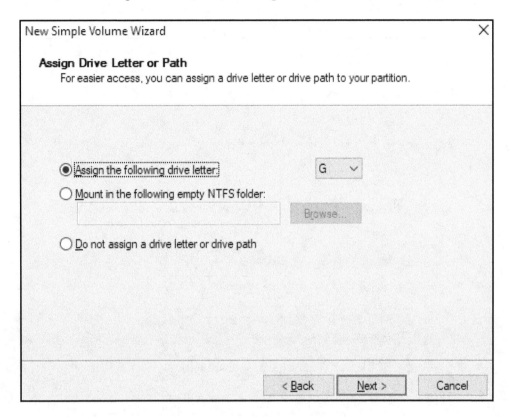

Figure 7.6: Assigning a drive letter or path

6. In the **Format Partition** page, choose the **Format this volume with the following settings:** option to format the newly created volume, as shown in *Figure 7.7*, and then click **Next:**

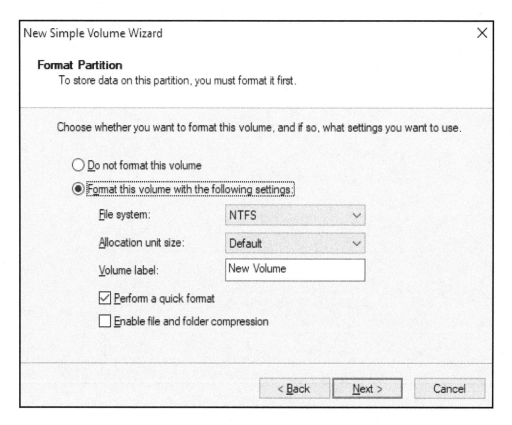

Figure 7.7: Formatting the partition

7. Click **Finish** to close the **New Simple Volume Wizard**.

Extending the volume

To extend a volume in Windows 10 using Disk Management, complete the following steps:

1. Right-click the volume you want to extend.
2. From the **Context** menu, select **Extend Volume...**, as in *Figure 7.8*:

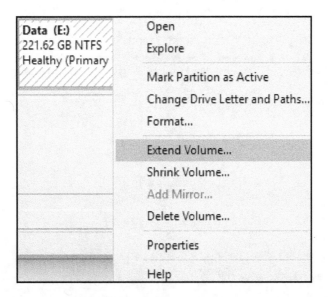

Figure 7.8: Extending the volume in Windows 10

3. In the **Extend Volume Wizard**, click **Next** to begin increasing the size of a simple and spanned volume.

4. In the **Select Disks** page, select the available disk space, click the **Add** button (see *Figure 7.9*), and then click **Next**:

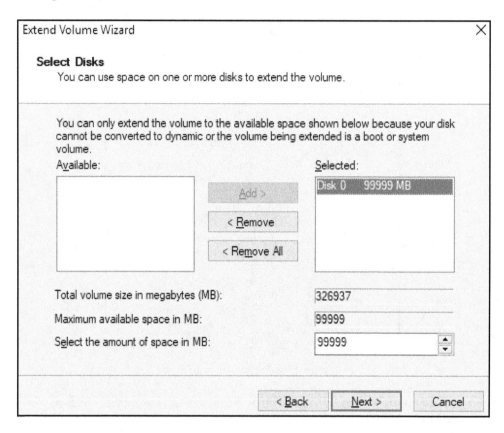

Figure 7.9: Selecting the available disk space

5. Click **Finish** to close the **Extend Volume Wizard**.

Converting the basic disk to dynamic

To convert the basic disk to dynamic in Windows 10 using **Disk Management**, complete the following steps:

1. Right-click the basic disk you want to convert to dynamic.

2. From the **Context** menu, select **Convert to Dynamic Disk...**, as in *Figure 7.10*:

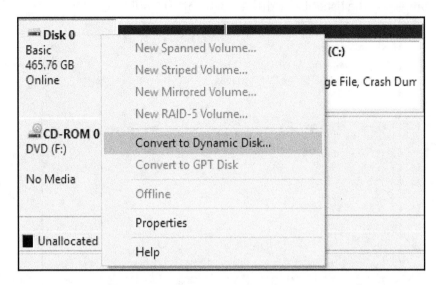

Figure 7.10: Converting basic to dynamic disks in Windows 10

3. In the **Convert to Dynamic Disk** window, select the basic disk you want to convert to dynamic (see *Figure 7.11*), and then click **OK**:

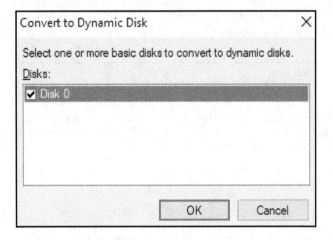

Figure 7.11: Selecting the basic disk to convert to a dynamic disk

4. Click the **Convert** button in the **Disks to Convert** window in order to begin converting the listed basic disk to dynamic, as in *Figure 7.12*:

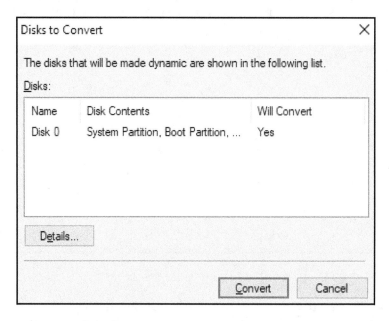

Figure 7.12: Listing the disk that will be made dynamic

5. In the **Disk Management** dialog box, click **Yes**, as shown in *Figure 7.13*, to continue converting the basic disk to dynamic:

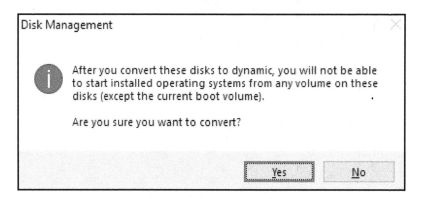

Figure 7.13: Clicking on the **Yes** button converts the basic disk to dynamic

6. Shortly thereafter, the converted disk contains the **Dynamic** status.

Managing storage with Windows PowerShell

Other than **Disk Manager**, you can manage storage in Windows 10 with Windows PowerShell (`powershell.exe`) too, as shown in *Figure 7.14*. Introduced in Windows Vista, because of its command-line shell and associated scripting language, Windows PowerShell is among the most popular system administrator tools for task automation and configuration.

In Windows 10, you can access Windows PowerShell in the following ways:

1. Right-click the **Start** button
2. Select **Windows PowerShell (Admin)**

Or:

1. Press the Windows key + *R* to open the **Run** window.
2. Enter `powershell.exe` and hit *Enter*:

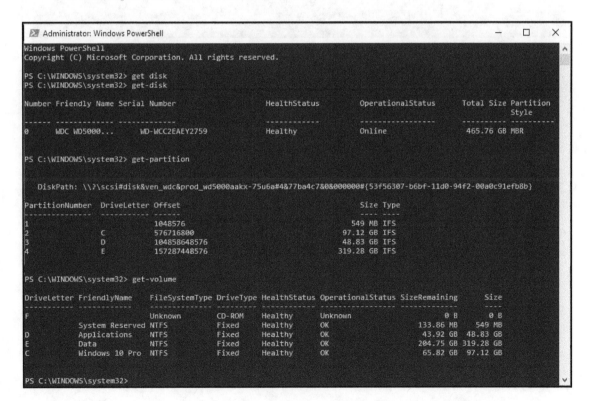

Figure 7.14: Managing storage with Windows PowerShell

Windows PowerShell commands for managing storage

This section describes the Windows PowerShell commands for managing storage. Open Windows PowerShell in elevated mode, and begin entering the commands according to requirements and circumstances:

- Enter the following command to list (see *Figure 7.15*) all disks in the system information:

    Get-Disk

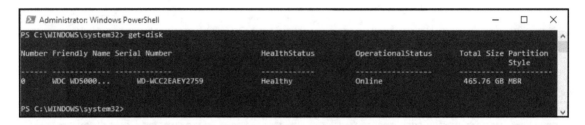

Figure 7.15: Listing all disks in the system information

- Enter the following command to clean a disk by removing all partition information:

    Clear-Disk

- Enter the following command to prepare a disk for use:

    Initialize-Disk

- Enter the following command to update a physical disk with the specified attributes:

    Set-Disk

- Enter the following command to return information on all filesystem volumes:

    `Get-Volume`

- Enter the following command to format existing volumes or a new volume:

    `Format-Volume`

- Enter the following command to return a list of all partitions:

    `Get-Partition`

 You can learn more about storage concepts in general from Chapter 8, *Storing Data in Windows Server*, from the *Windows Server 2016 Administration Fundamentals* book published by *Packt Publishing*, available at `https://www.packtpub.com/virtualization-and-cloud/windows-server-Fundamentals-2016 administration`.

Configuring removable devices

As you know, computer systems, in addition to fixed storage technology such as **hard disk drives (HDDs)**, also contain removable disks, such as external HDDs, USB flash drives, and **Secure Digital High-Capacity (SDHC)** memory cards. All these storage technologies, except HDDs, are common since they can offer tremendous portability benefits. However, such benefits also entail disadvantages associated with the security and loss of data. That being said, this section teaches you how to prepare removable devices for use, data encryption in case they are lost or stolen, and how to enable access restrictions.

Formatting the removable devices

To format removable devices, you can use **Disk Management**, as well as Windows PowerShell. As to which tool you are going to use, it all depends on your own preferences. In **Disk Management** (see *Figure 7.16*), in the same way as fixed disks appear, the removable disks will appear:

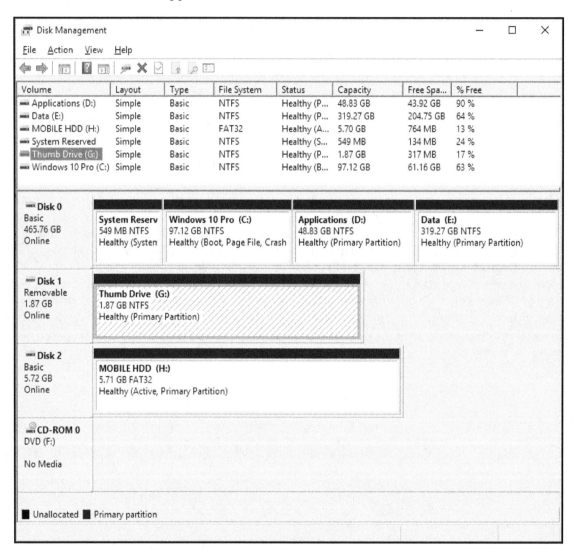

Figure 7.16: The Disk 1 and Disk 2 removable disks are listed in Disk Management

To format a removable disk in Windows 10 using **Disk Management**, complete the following steps:

1. In the **Disk Management** window, locate and right-click on the removable disk and, from the **Context** menu (see *Figure 7.17*), select **Format...**:

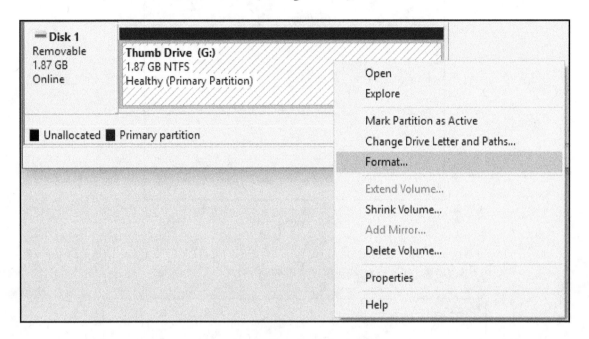

Figure 7.17: Selecting the **Format...** option from the context menu

2. In the **Format** window, as in *Figure 7.18*, after entering the **Volume label**, and specifying **File system** and **Allocation unit size**, click **OK**:

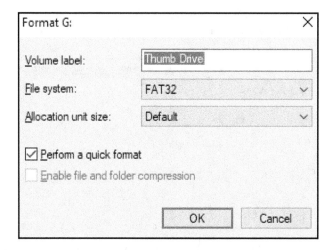

Figure 7.18: Formatting settings

3. In the **Format** dialog box, as shown in *Figure 7.19*, click **OK** again to continue with the formatting of the removable disk:

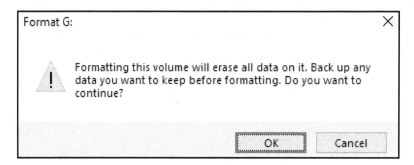

Figure 7.19: Warning dialog box

4. Shortly thereafter, Disk Management completes the removable disk formatting.

To format a removable disk in Windows 10 using Windows PowerShell (*Figure 7.20*), enter the following command:

```
format-volume <driveletter>
```

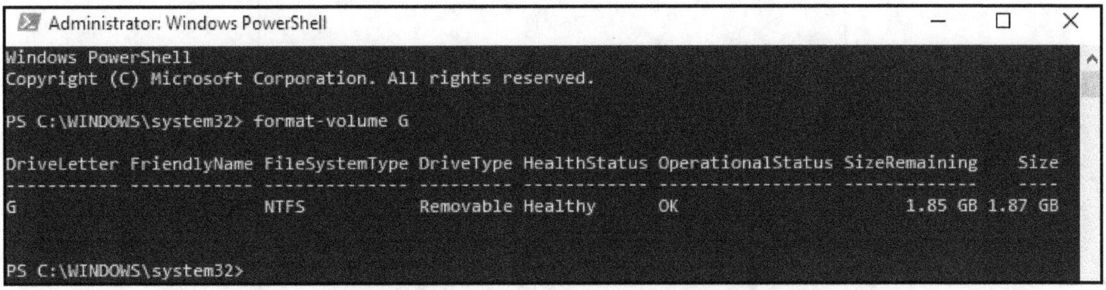

Figure 7.20: Formatting the removable disk using Windows PowerShell

Encrypting the removable devices

To encrypt a removable disk in your Windows 10 using BitLocker, complete the following steps:

1. Press the Windows key + *E* to open File Explorer.

2. Locate the removable disk, right-click on it, and, from the context menu, select **Turn on BitLocker** (see *Figure 7.21*):

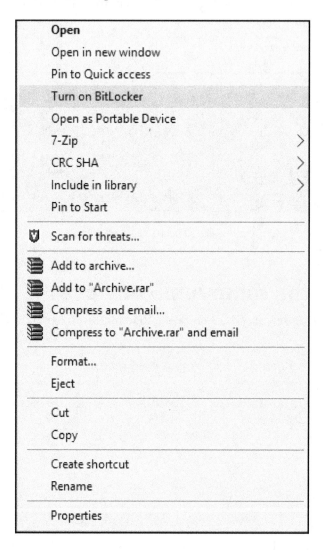

Open

Open in new window

Pin to Quick access

Turn on BitLocker

Open as Portable Device

7-Zip   >

CRC SHA   >

Include in library   >

Pin to Start

Scan for threats...

Add to archive...

Add to "Archive.rar"

Compress and email...

Compress to "Archive.rar" and email

Format...

Eject

Cut

Copy

Create shortcut

Rename

Properties

Figure 7.21: Enabling BitLocker on a removable device

3. In the **Choose how you want to unlock this drive** page, select your preferred option between **password** and **smart card**, or you may want to select both options, as in *Figure 7.22*, and then click **Next**:

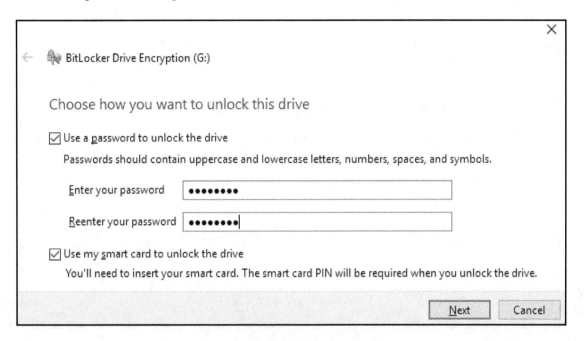

×

BitLocker Drive Encryption (G:)

Choose how you want to unlock this drive

☑ Use a password to unlock the drive

Passwords should contain uppercase and lowercase letters, numbers, spaces, and symbols.

Enter your password   ●●●●●●●●

Reenter your password   ●●●●●●●●|

☑ Use my smart card to unlock the drive

You'll need to insert your smart card. The smart card PIN will be required when you unlock the drive.

Next   Cancel

Figure 7.22: Unlocking the removable device using a password

4. In the **How do you want to back up your recovery key?** page, select your preferred option between **Save to a file** or **Print the recovery key** (see *Figure 7.23*), and then click **Next**:

Figure 7.23: Backing up the recovery key

5. In the **Choose how much of your drive to encrypt** page, select your preferred option and then click **Next**.
6. In the **Choose which encryption mode to use** page, select **Compatible mode** for removable devices, and then click **Next**.
7. In the **Are you ready to encrypt this drive?** page, click **Start encrypting**.
8. Once the removable drive gets encrypted, the dialog box is displayed to confirm this, as demonstrated in *Figure 7.24*:

Figure 7.24: Encryption of a removable device is complete

9. The next time you want to access the removable drive, you will be asked to first unlock the drive (see *Figure 7.25*):

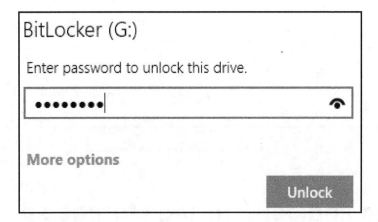

Figure 7.25: Unlocking the BitLocker locked removable drive

Restricting access to removable disks

To restrict access to removable disks in your Windows 10 computer using **Group Policy (GP)**, complete the following steps:

1. Click the search box on the taskbar.
2. Enter gpedit.msc to open **Local Group Policy Editor**.
3. Navigate to the following path: **Computer Configuration | Administrative Templates | System | Removable Storage Access**.

4. Enable the following policy settings: **Removable Disk: Deny execute access**, **Removable Disk: Deny read access**, and **Removable Disk: Deny write access** (see *Figure 7.26*):

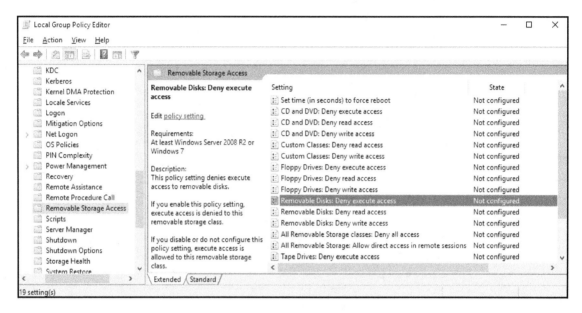

Figure 7.26: Using GP to enable restriction on removable disks

Creating and configuring storage spaces

Storage Spaces is a feature on Windows 10 that enables you to create software-defined storage by grouping disks into storage pools. Other than extending your computer's storage, Storage Spaces helps to protect your data from drive failures too. That is possible by storing your data on two or more drives. In addition, Storage Spaces enables you to easily add drives in case your computer runs out of storage capacity.

Creating a new storage pool

To **create** a new storage pool in your Windows 10 computer using Manage Storage Spaces, complete the following steps:

1. Click the Search box on the taskbar.
2. Enter `storage spaces`, and select **Manage Storage Spaces** from the **Best match** list (see *Figure 7.27*):

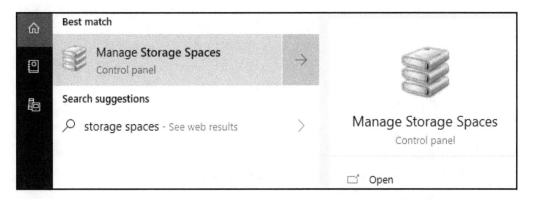

Figure 7.27: Accessing the Manage Storage Spaces option in Windows 10

3. In the **Storage Spaces** window, click **Create a new pool and storage space**.
4. Click **Yes** when asked **Do you want to allow this app to make changes to your device?**

5. From the list of drives, choose **Select drives to create a storage pool**, and then click the **Create pool** button as in *Figure 7.28*:

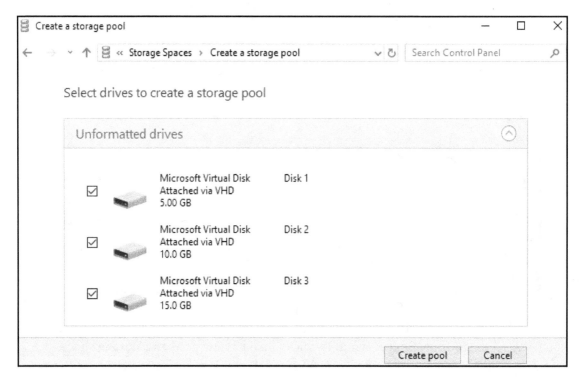

Figure 7.28: Creating a new storage pool

Creating a storage space

Continuing on from the *Creating a new storage pool* section, complete the following steps to create a storage space in your Windows 10 computer using **Managing Storage Spaces**:

1. In the **Create a storage space** window, change the default name, **Storage space**, to a meaningful name for you, and, after reviewing the default settings, click the **Create storage space** button (see *Figure 7.29*):

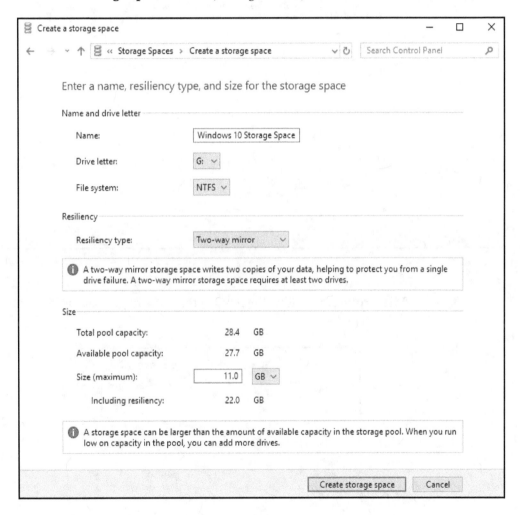

Figure 7.29: Creating a storage space in Windows 10

2. In due course, the **Storage Spaces** window displays the newly created **Storage pool** that contains the newly created **Storage space**, as shown in *Figure 7.30*:

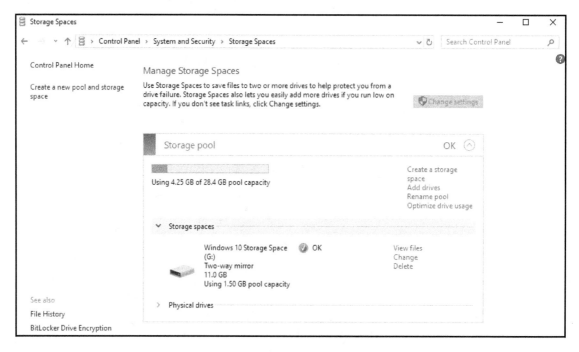

Figure 7.30: Viewing the storage pool and the storage spaces within it

3. In the **File Explorer** window, the newly created storage space is visible too (see *Figure 7.31*):

Figure 7.31: Newly created storage space is available in File Explorer

Troubleshooting storage and removable devices issues

I am sure the same thing has happened to you, too, such as when you have started your computer and the screen has come on, but the operating system did not? Of course, knowing that the OS is resident on the hard drive, we will instantly think that there is something wrong with the disk. To further reinforce our thinking, it is the **Power-On Self-Test (POST)** that displays an error message on the monitor that refers to a non-system disk, disk error, or missing a boot device. Although such a problem does not necessarily mean that the disk, as a physical component, is not functional, because it may be that the OS system files are corrupted. However, there is a general opinion that such a problem is categorized as a computer storage issue. Therefore, problems of that type and many others that relate to computer storage, whether fixed or removable devices, will be discussed in this section.

Hardware and software problems

As you may know, problems with storage and removable devices are categorized into **hardware** and **software problems**. That is due to the physical nature of both fixed storage and removable devices, and, at the same time, being an important component of the so-called computer system when it comes to storing data. In the case of hardware issues, standard practices suggest that you do not deal with such problems if you are not a specialist, or if you do not possess professional knowledge. Whereas, in the case of software issues, the fact that you are learning to become certified in Windows 10 constitutes a good chance to become familiar with software problems associated with fixed storage and removable devices, as well as gaining experience in troubleshooting issues on such devices.

The following lists some of the most common hardware and software problems that you may encounter in fixed storage and removable devices:

- **Hardware problems**: These problems include, but will not be limited to, the following: faulty IDE/ATA/SATA connectors and cables, loose or missing power to the disk, an incorrect BIOS configuration, an incorrect hardware configuration, a missing or wrong jumper, bad sectors, bad read/write head, a crashed hard drive, an inability to format the disk, an inability to partition the disk, an unsupported disk, the flash drive has burned out, an inability to read optical media, and a frequently occurring **Blue Screen of Death (BSOD)**.

- **Software problems**: These problems include, but will not be limited to, the following: data access, share and NTFS permissions, excessively slow running, drive becomes read-only, data recovery, BitLocker encrypted drives, missing device drivers, devices not showing up in Windows 10, USB devices not recognized on Windows 10, a device that is unrecognized by BIOS/UEFI/firmware, the problem of not ejecting when using the **Safely Remove Hardware** option, scanning the drive now and fixing it, and setting issues in the Registry.

Troubleshooting tips

As you know, when installing a new or used storage device on your computer, best practices suggest that you need to prepare it for use. There are different types of storage devices that come in different shapes and sizes, as well as with different types of connectors and cables. That being said, a hard disk drive, a CD/DVD drive, an SSD, a USB flash drive, and so on, all constitute storage technologies. Apart from the fact that storage technologies can be fixed or removable, another consideration has to do with whether they are internal or external devices. For an internal device, you need to open the case in order to mount the drive in one of the drive bays, whereas, for an external device, all you need to do is to connect the cable to the right connector and, if needed, to supply it with power.

As regards hardware problems, if not every time, in most cases, you will need to turn off the computer so that you can access your computer's internal devices. Another thing to consider is that visual inspection plays an important role, since fixed storage and removable devices contain indicators that show statuses such as a power LED or data transfer. In a situation where the device that you are examining for the hardware problem is a laptop and not a desktop PC, then make sure to remove the battery if possible.

As far as software problems are concerned, the troubleshooting recommendation suggests that you restart the computer in Safe Mode. Knowing that Safe Mode operates with only Windows generic drivers, it is a good way to find out if the software problem is causing your computer to malfunction. Another good practice for both avoiding and troubleshooting software problems is to make sure that the operating system, applications, and device drivers are updated regularly. The recommended utilities also include the disk utility software that facilitates an assessment of the health status of the filesystem installed on that storage device. However, it sometimes transpires that even though you have tried several testing solutions, you may not get the expected result. In that case, you will need to consider resetting the PC (reinstalling Windows).

If you are experiencing issues with a USB device connected to your desktop PC, laptop, or tablet, then you may want to consider downloading Windows **USB Troubleshooter** from Microsoft, named as `WinUSB.diagcab` (`https://support.microsoft.com/en-us/help/17614/automatically-diagnose-and-fix-windows-usb-problems`).

Chapter labs – creating, configuring, and mounting VHDs

In these chapter labs, you will learn the following:

- Creating, configuring, and mounting VHDs

Creating and configuring VHDs

To create and configure VHDs on your Windows 10 computer using **Hyper-V Manager**, complete the following steps:

1. Click the **Search** box on the taskbar, and enter **Hyper-V.**
2. From the **Best match** list, select **Hyper-V Manager.**

3. In the **Actions** pane, click **New**, and then click **Hard Disk,** as shown in *Figure 7.32*:

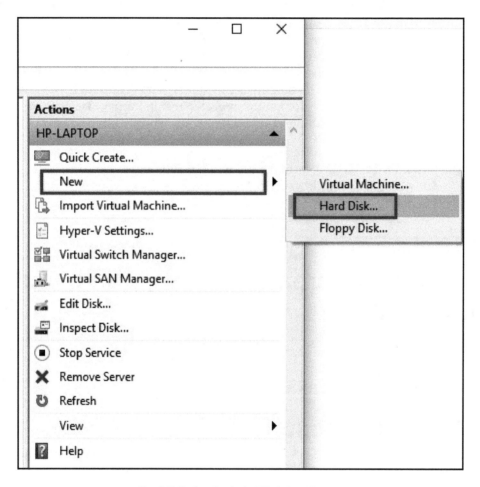

Figure 7.32: Creating and configuring VHDs in Hyper-V Manager

4. Click **Next** in the **Before You Begin** page (see *Figure 7.33*) of the **New Virtual Hard Disk** wizard in order to begin creating your VHD:

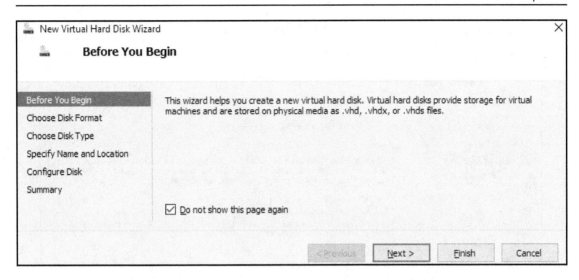

Figure 7.33: The Before You Begin page of New VHD wizard provides information about VHDs

5. Choose the disk format of the VHD, and then click **Next**:

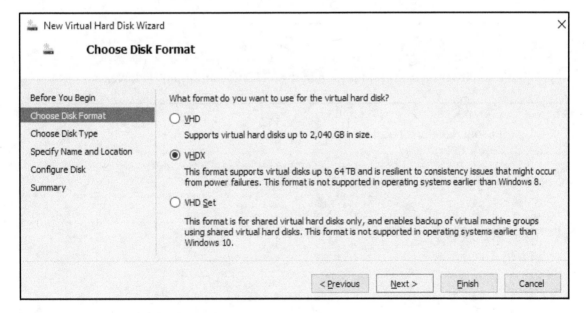

Figure 7.34: Choosing the disk format

6. Choose the disk type of the VHD, and then click **Next**:

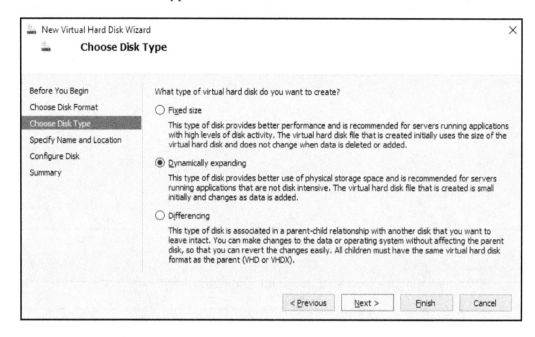

Figure 7.35: Choosing the disk type

7. Specify the name and location of the VHD file, and then click **Next**:

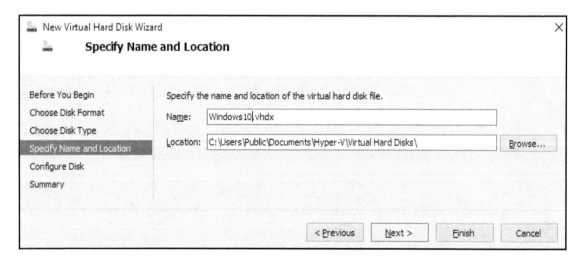

Figure 7.36: Specifying the name and location

8. Choose one of the three options available to configure the VHD disk, and then click **Next**:

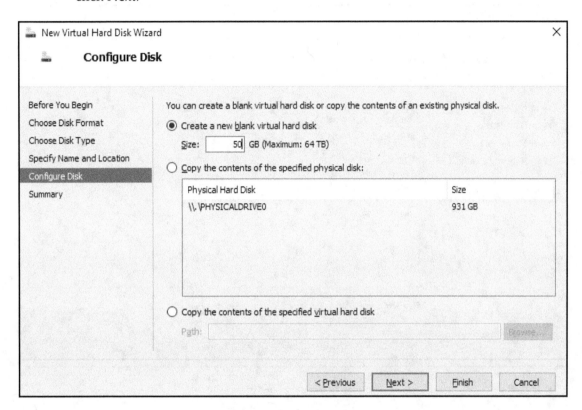

Figure 7.37: Configuring a disk

9. Click **Finish** to create the VHD and close the wizard:

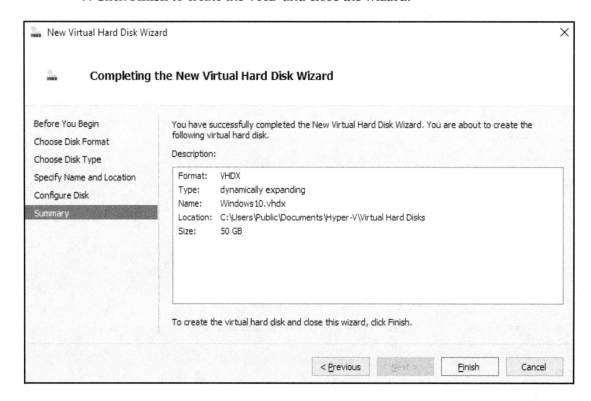

Figure 7.38: Completing the process of creating a VHD

See `Chapter 2`, *Installing Windows 10*, specifically, the section entitled *Installing additional Windows 10 features*, to install Hyper-V on your Windows 10 computer. However, make sure that you are using one of the following versions of Windows 10:

- Windows 10 Pro
- Windows 10 Education
- Windows 10 Enterprise

Mounting VHDs

To mount VHDs on your Windows 10 computer using Disk Management, complete the following steps:

1. Right-click the **Start** button to open the Administrator's menu.
2. Select **Disk Management.**
3. In the **Disk Management** window, click the **Action** menu, and select **Attach VHD** (see *Figure 7.39*):

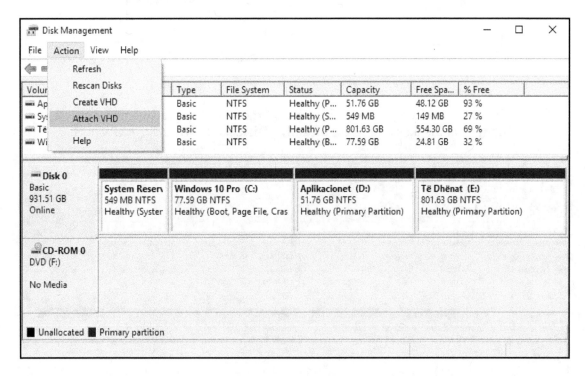

Figure 7.39: Attaching the VHD

4. In the **Attach Virtual Hard Disk** window, browse to the location where your VHD is stored, and then click **OK** (as in *Figure 7.40*):

Figure 7.40: Browsing the existing VHD

5. Once the attached VHD disk becomes part of the Disk Management console, right-click the disk and select **Initialize Disk**, as shown in *Figure 7.41*:

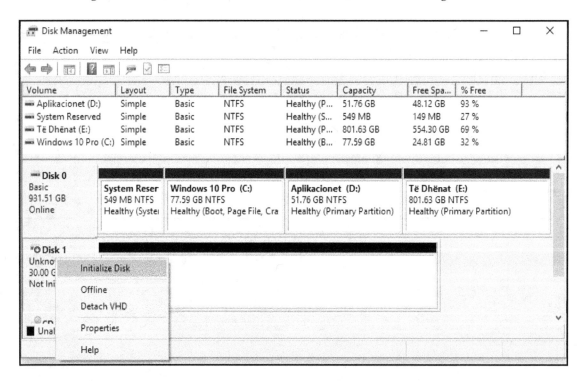

Figure 7.41: Initializing the newly attached VHD

6. In the **Initialize Disk** window, select the disk and choose the partition style (as in *Figure 7.42*), and then click **OK**:

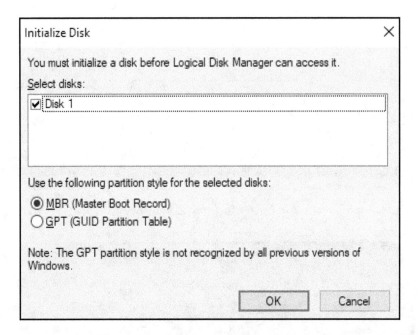

Figure 7.42: Selecting the disk and specifying the partition style

7. Once the disk becomes online, right-click on the disk and select **New Simple Volume**, as shown in *Figure 7.43*:

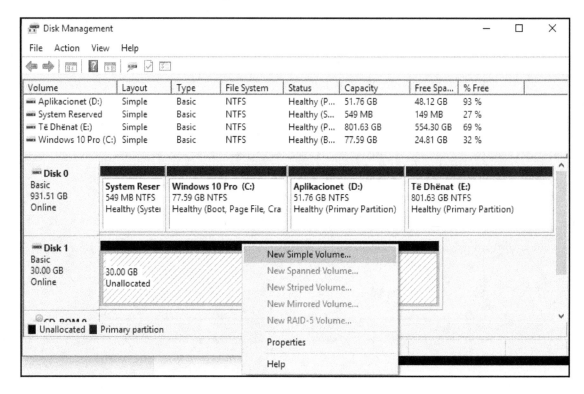

Figure 7.43: Creating a new simple volume

8. The **New Simple Volume** wizard is self-explanatory, so walk through it by clicking **Next** until you reach the **Finish** button (see *Figure 7.44*):

Figure 7.44: Completing the New Simple Volume wizard

9. The newly mounted VHD becomes part of your Windows 10 computer's storage, as demonstrated in *Figure 7.45*:

Figure 7.45: The newly mounted VHD

Summary

We can summarize this chapter as follows:

- Disk partitioning and formatting are two of the processes that are required to install Windows 10
- Disk Management is a snap-in of the **Microsoft Management Console** (**MMC**) that is used for managing disks and volumes
- Windows PowerShell is among the most popular system administrator tools for task automation and configuration
- A computer system, in addition to fixed storage technology such as a **hard disk drive** (**HDD**), also contains removable disks, including removable HDDs, USB flash drives, and **Secure Digital High-Capacity** (**SDHC**) memory cards
- Storage Spaces is a feature in Windows 10 that enables you to create software-defined storage by grouping disks into storage pools
- Problems with storage and removable devices are categorized into hardware and software problems
- Standard practice suggests that you do not deal with hardware problems if you are not a specialist, or if you do not possess professional knowledge
- The fact that you are learning to become certified in Windows 10 represents a good opportunity to become familiar with software problems of storage and removable devices, as well as gaining experience in troubleshooting issues on such devices
- Apart from the fact that storage technologies can be fixed or removable, another consideration has to do with whether they are internal or external devices
- For hardware problems, if not every time, in most cases, you will need to turn off the computer so that you can access your computer's internal devices
- As far as the software problems are concerned, the troubleshooting recommendation suggests that you restart the computer in Safe Mode

Questions

1. Windows PowerShell is among the most popular system administrator tools for task automation and configuration.
    1. True
    2. False

2. _____ and _____ are two of the processes that are required to install Windows 10.

3. How are problems in storage technologies categorized? (Choose two)
    1. Operating system problems
    2. Application problems
    3. Hardware problems
    4. Software problems

4. As far as software problems are concerned, the troubleshooting recommendation suggests that you restart the computer in Safe Mode.
    1. True
    2. False

5. For hardware problems, if not every time, in most cases, you will need to _____ the computer so that you can access your computer's internal devices.

6. In addition to being fixed and mobile, storage technologies can also be? (Choose two)
    1. Internal devices
    2. External devices
    3. Integrated devices
    4. Networking devices

7. Standard practice suggests that you do deal with hardware problems if you are not a specialist, or if you do not possess professional knowledge.
    1. True
    2. False

8. _____ is a feature in Windows 10 that enables you to create software-defined storage by grouping disks into storage pools.

9. Which of the following tools are used to manage disks and volumes? (Choose two)
    1. Device Manager
    2. Event Viewer
    3. Disk Management
    4. Windows PowerShell

Further reading

- **Fast Guide to Storage Technologies**: `https://whatis.techtarget.com/reference/Fast-Guide-to-Storage-Technologies`
- **10 Network Storage Technologies You Need To Know**: `https://www.crn.com/slide-shows/storage/229000257/10-network-storage-technologies-you-need-to-know.htm/1`
- **Storage Technologies and their Devices**: `https://medium.com/computing-technology-with-it-fundamentals/storage-technologies-and-their-devices-1594293868f0`

8
Configuring Data Access and Usage

This chapter is designed to provide you with hands-on instructions for configuring file and printer sharing, folder shares, public folders, and OneDrive. To ensure who has been permitted access and who has been denied access, we will study filesystem permissions in this chapter. Another aspect of this chapter is OneDrive, which is free cloud-based storage. It includes **Files On-Demand**, which is a new feature that enables users to access their files from the cloud using File Explorer with no need to sync them directly. This chapter also addresses troubleshooting data access and usage. There, you will get to learn how to troubleshoot data access, troubleshoot share and NTFS permissions, troubleshoot data recovery, and recover BitLocker encrypted drives. Each topic is accompanied by step-by-step instructions driven by targeted, easy-to-understand graphics. The chapter concludes with a chapter lab on data access and usage.

In this chapter, we will cover the following topics:

- Configuring file and printer sharing
- Configuring folder shares, public folders, and OneDrive
- Configuring filesystem permissions
- Configuring OneDrive usage including Files On-Demand
- Chapter lab: Troubleshooting data access and usage

Technical requirements

In order to complete the labs for this chapter, you will need the following equipment:

- A PC with Windows 10 Pro, at least 4 GB of RAM, 500 GB of HDD, and access to the internet

Configuring file and printer sharing

You may have heard the slogan *anytime, anywhere,* which today is used by most technology companies. Given the flexibility offered by Windows 10, which has to do with accessing your data from the HomeGroup at home, the LAN at work, and on the go from the internet, it can be said that Windows 10 has been built to enable data access **anytime from anywhere**. In the following sections of this chapter, you will get acquainted with the different ways you can configure sharing of files and printers, as well as how you can set permissions on your shared files and printers so you can control access to your data and printers.

File and print services

The **file and print services** are as old as the computer networks themselves! I say that because computer networks were born out of the need to share resources. Thus, file and print services were among the pioneering services in computer networks. Nowadays, these two services have been transformed into essential services, whether at home or in business networks. That is because, these days, every OS on the market is capable of supporting file and print services, including Windows 10.

Configuring file sharing

To share a file in your Windows 10 computer using **Share**, complete the following steps:

1. Press Windows key + *E* to open **File Explorer**.
2. Browse the *folder where your files reside* and **select one or multiple files**.
3. Click the **Share** tab, and then click the **Share** icon.
4. In the **Share** dialog box, select sharing your file(s) over email, nearby sharing, or the Microsoft Store app, as shown in *Figure 8.1*:

Figure 8.1. Sharing files in Windows 10 through Share tool

5. Depending on what you have selected, continue with the onscreen directions to share the file(s).

To **share** a file in your Windows 10 computer using basic sharing, complete the following steps:

1. Press Windows key + *E* to open **File Explorer**.
2. Locate the **folder where your files reside** and right-click over it.
3. From the context menu, select **Give access to** | **Specific people**.

4. In the **Choose people to share with** page, type a name and then click **Add** (see *Figure 8.2*):

Figure 8.2. Choosing everyone to share the folder with

5. Once **Everyone** is part of the **Name** list, set the **Permission Level** to **Read** or **Read/Write** and click **Share**, as shown in *Figure 8.3*:

Figure 8.3. Setting the Permission Level for Everyone

6. Shortly after, you will receive a confirmation that your folder has been shared; then click **Done** to close the **File Sharing Wizard**.

 The **File Sharing Wizard** gives you the option of emailing the links to the shared items to someone, or copying and pasting the links into another application.

To share a file in your Windows 10 computer using **Advanced Sharing...**, complete the following steps:

1. **Repeat step 1 and step 2** from the previous example.
2. From the context menu, select **Properties**.
3. In the *Properties* dialog box, select **Sharing** tab.
4. Within the **Advance Sharing** section, click the **Advanced Sharing...** button as shown in *Figure 8.4*:

Figure 8.4. Advanced Sharing in Windows 10

5. In the **Advanced Sharing** dialog box, check the box for **Share this folder.**
6. In the **Share name** text box, enter the share name for your share (see *Figure 8.5*):

Figure 8.5. Advanced Sharing enables you to set other advanced sharing options

7. Click **OK** to close the **Advanced Sharing** dialog box.
8. Click **Close** to close the **Properties** dialog box.

 Not every user has the right to share files or folders. To do so, you must be a member of the administrators group. In case you are not, but still want to share files or folders across the network in Windows 10, then you will be asked to provide UAC credentials for an administrator.

Configuring printer sharing

To **share** a printer in your Windows 10 computer using **Windows Settings**, complete the following steps:

1. Press Windows key + *I* to open **Windows Settings**.

2. Click on **Devices** as shown in *Figure 8.6*:

Figure 8.6. Devices in Windows Settings

3. In the **Devices** navigation menu, click **Printers & scanners** as shown in *Figure 8.7*:

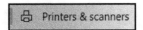

Figure 8.7. Printers & scanners in Devices navigation menu

4. Within the **Printers & scanners** section, select the printer you want to share and click **Manage** (see *Figure 8.8*):

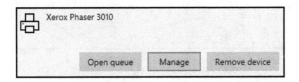

Figure 8.8. Managing the printer in Windows 10

5. On the printer's page, within the **Manage your device** section, select **Printer properties**.
6. In the printer's properties dialog box, select the **Sharing** tab.

7. Check the **Share this printer** option, and then, in the **Share name** text box, enter a descriptive name, as shown in Figure 8.9:

Figure 8.9. Sharing tab in the printer's properties dialog box

8. Click **Apply**, and then click the **OK** button to close the printer's properties dialog box.

Introduced initially in Windows Vista, HomeGroup has been an easy, fast, and user-friendly tool for sharing files and printers on your network. However, since version 1803, Microsoft has removed HomeGroup from Windows 10 (`https://support.microsoft.com/en-us/help/4091368/ windows-10-homegroup-removed`) in order to open up the way for new sharing tools such as Share, Nearby sharing, and OneDrive. Even so, according to Microsoft, you will continue to encounter HomeGroup in Windows 10 version 1803 or later when you right-click a folder in File Explorer and then point to **Give Access to**. However, Microsoft suggests that you select **Specific people** from the same shortcut menu instead.

Configuring folder shares, public folders, and OneDrive

When talking about folder shares, public folders, and OneDrive, all of these tools, share a common purpose, and that is the **resource sharing**. Applications, corporate data, and private data represent some of the resources that users can connect to and access their contents. For that reason, it is very important to pay attention to whom you give **access** when creating a **network share**. That way, you will ensure that you have permitted access to a user or group of users who should have access, and at the same time denied those who should not have access. In that regard, with every network share every group is given read access by default. As an IT specialist, you need to take care to change that setting for network shares if a group should not be on the access list. Usually, in a corporate network there is a **file server** that hosts the shared and public folders. However, in a **small office/home office** (**SOHO**) environment, a Windows 10 computer with **network attached storage** (**NAS**) can act as a solid file server. However, you should keep in mind the fact that regardless of which device is hosting the file service, it always needs to be on.

Configuring folder shares

To **share** a folder in your Windows 10 computer using **Microsoft Management Console** (**MMC**), complete the following steps:

1. Right-click the **Start** button, and select **Computer Management**.

2. In the **Computer Management** window, expand the **Shared Folders** and then click **Shares**, as shown in *Figure 8.10*:

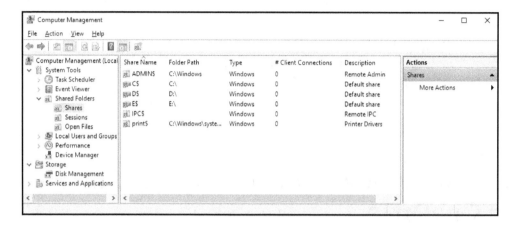

Figure 8.10. Shared Folders in Microsoft Management Console (MMC)

3. Right-click anywhere in the middle pane and select **New Share...** (see *Figure 8.11*):

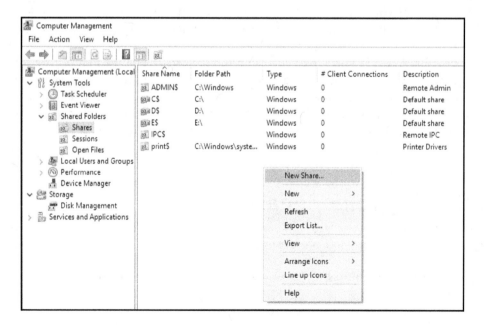

Figure 8.11. Creating new share within Shared Folders in MMC

4. In the **Create A Shared Folder Wizard**, click **Next** to continue.
5. On the **Folder Path** page, browse to **Folder path** and click **Next**.
6. On the **Name**, **Description**, and **Settings** page, take care for the **Share name**, **Description**, and **Offline setting**, and then click **Next**.
7. On the **Shared Folder Permissions** page, set the kinds of permissions you want for the shared folder, and then click **Next**.
8. On the **Sharing was Successful** page, click **Finish** to close the wizard.

You can launch the **Create A Shared Folder Wizard** from the **Run** dialog box by entering `Shrpubw.exe`.

To share a folder in your Windows 10 computer using the `net share` command in Command Prompt, complete the following steps:

1. Click the Search box in the *taskbar* and enter `cmd`.
2. Select **Run as administrator** on the right of the **Best match** list (see *Figure 8.12*):

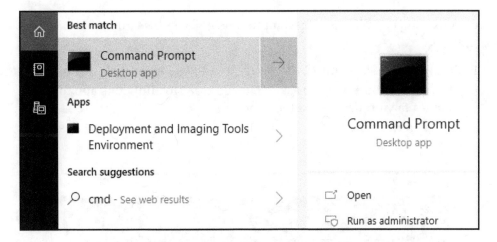

Figure 8.12. Running Command Prompt with elevated privileges

3. Click the **Yes** button when asked **Do you want to allow this app to make changes to your device**.

4. At the prompt, enter `net share Windows10Share=E:\` and press *Enter*, as shown in *Figure 8.13*:

Figure 8.13. Sharing files or folders using the net share command

 To access the `net share` command help, and, with it, learn more about its syntax, enter `net share ?` at the Command Prompt.

To **share** a folder in your Windows 10 computer using Windows PowerShell, complete the following steps:

1. *Right-click* the Start button, and select **Windows PowerShell (Admin)**.
2. Click the `Yes` button when asked **Do you want to allow this app to make changes to your device?** on the window.
3. At the prompt, enter `New-SmbShare -Name Windows10Share -Path E:\` and press *Enter*, as shown in *Figure 8.14*:

Figure 8.14. Sharing files or folders using Windows PowerShell

Windows PowerShell share cmdlets

Here are some of the most commonly used cmdlets for sharing folders:

- Enter the following cmdlet to **list** the existing shares on the computer:

  `Get-SmbShare`

- Enter the following cmdlet to **list** the current share permissions for a share:

  `Get-SmbShareAccess`

- Enter the following cmdlet to **set** the share permissions on an existing share:

  `Grant-SmbShareAccess`

- Enter the following cmdlet to **delete** an existing share:

  `Remove-SmbShare`

Configuring public folders

To **turn on** sharing in Windows 10 so anyone with network access can read and write files in public folders, complete the following steps:

1. Press Windows key + *I* to open **Windows Settings**.
2. Click **Network & Internet** as shown in *Figure 8.15*:

Figure 8.15. Network & Internet in Windows Settings

3. Within the **Change your network settings** section, select **Network and Sharing Center**.

4. In the **Network and Sharing Center** window, select **Change advanced sharing settings** (see *Figure 8.16*):

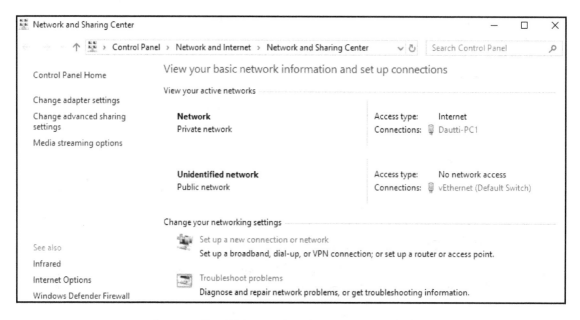

Figure 8.16. Network and Sharing Center in Windows 10

5. In the **Advanced sharing settings** window, expand **All Networks** (if it is not expanded).

6. Within the **Public folder sharing** section, select **Turn on sharing so anyone with network access can read and write files in Public folders**, as shown in *Figure 8.17*:

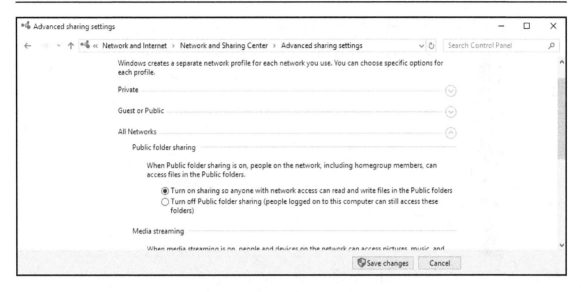

Figure 8.17. Turning on the Public folders via Advanced sharing settings

7. Click the **Save changes** button to close the **Advanced sharing settings** window.
8. Close the **Network and Sharing Center** window too.

> To simplify sharing, Microsoft continues to provide support for public folders in Windows 10. However, this feature is not enabled by default, so you need to enable it in order to benefit from it. Once public folders are enabled, by default the everyone system group is granted full permissions to the following folders: Public Documents, Public Downloads, Public Music, Public Pictures, and Public Videos. The Public folders can be navigated via File Explorer in the following path: `%systemdrive%\Users\Public`.

Configuring OneDrive

To **configure** OneDrive in your Windows 10 computer using a desktop app so you can store and synchronize files, complete the following steps:

1. Click the Search box in the taskbar and enter `onedrive`.

2. Select Open on the right of the Best match list (see *Figure 8.18*):

Figure 8.18. Opening the OneDrive desktop app in Windows 10

3. In the **Microsoft OneDrive** window, enter your email address and click the **Sign in** button as shown in *Figure 8.19*:

Figure 8.19. Sign in to the OneDrive desktop app

4. Enter your password and press *Enter*.

5. If you want to change the default path to your OneDrive folder, `C:\Users\Username\OneDrive`, click **Change location**.

6. Once you set your preferred location, click **Next** to continue.

7. Once you have reviewed OneDrive's desktop app features, click **Open my OneDrive folder** to sync your files (see *Figure 8.20*):

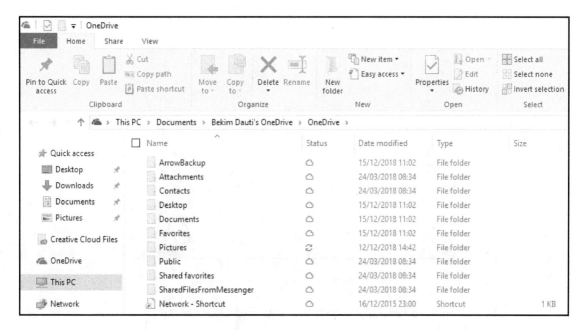

Figure 8.20. Opening my OneDrive folder in Windows 10

In todays internet era, cloud storage services have become the norm in our day-to-day lives. One of these services is OneDrive, designed to store and sync files. To have OneDrive, you need to set up a Microsoft account at Outlook.com. By doing that, you will receive 5 GB of free cloud storage for personal use. The service can be accessed from both a computer and a smartphone. In case you need more space, then you can upgrade to an Office 365 Home subscription with 1 TB of OneDrive storage space.

To download the OneDrive app in your Windows 10 computer using Microsoft Store, complete the following steps:

1. Click the **Microsoft Store** icon on the taskbar.
2. In the **Microsoft Store** window, click search and enter `onedrive` as shown in *Figure 8.21*:

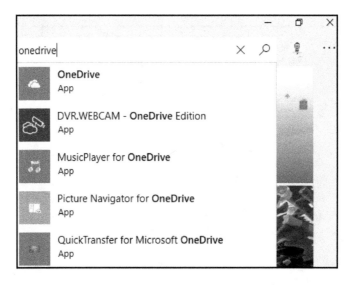

Figure 8.21. Searching for the OneDrive app in Microsoft Store

3. Click **OneDrive** from the search list, and then click **Install**.
4. Once OneDrive app gets installed, launch the app.
5. You will be signed automatically into your OneDrive app, if you are signed on your computer with your **Microsoft account**.
6. Click **Yes** if you want the OneDrive app to access your contacts.
7. Once you review the OneDrive app'd features, click **Start using OneDrive** to access your files as shown in *Figure 8.22*:

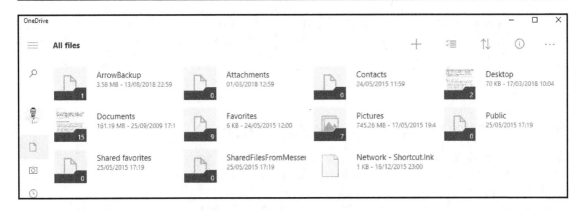

Figure 8.22. Accessing files via the OneDrive app

 Unlike OneDrive, which works with a Microsoft account, OneDrive for Business works with your work or school account. It is a Microsoft cloud service based on Microsoft SharePoint and enables you to access all your business files. OneDrive for Business isn't a free service; instead, several plans are available as a subscription with Office 365 Business or Enterprise.

Configuring filesystem permissions

As you know, Windows 10 is an operating system in which it is very easy to store, organize, and manage files and folders using **File Explorer**. That is the result of the filesystem that Windows is using. So, let's look at some of the filesystems that historically have been associated with the Windows OS:

- **File Allocation Table (FAT)**: This is the earliest filesystem and was used by both MS-DOS and Windows. It uses a table that contains a map of clusters, where a cluster represents a logical storage unit. FAT32 is the latest version of FAT.
- **Extended File Allocation Table (exFAT)**: This is a new version of FAT that is primarily used in USB flash drives and SD cards. exFAT is platform-independent, enabling drives to work on Apple Mac computers too.
- **New Technology File System (NTFS)**: This was introduced with Windows NT 3.1, and is still in use in both Windows 10 and Windows Server 2019. NTFS is a feature-rich OS; disk quotas, **Encrypting File System** (**EFS**), journaling, and **Volume Shadow Copy Service** (**VSS**) are some of the features available.

- **Resilient File System (ReFS)**: This has been introduced in Windows Server 2012 with the primary goal of superseding NTFS. Like NTFS, ReFS is a feature-rich OS too. Resiliency, performance, and scalability are a few of the significant features of ReFS.

NTFS versus share permissions

As mentioned earlier in this chapter, one of the main concerns of the network share is permissions management, which defines who has been permitted access and who has been denied access. In regard to permissions management, it is actually the filesystem's responsibility for providing the right utilities. Therefore, often in the network share we encounter something like **NTFS and share permissions**.

NTFS permissions are used to manage access to the files and folders that are stored in the NTFS filesystem. The following lists the NTFS permissions:

- **Full control**: It allows users to read, write, modify, execute, change attributes and permissions, and delete files and subfolders
- **Modify**: It allows users to view, modify, add, and delete files and subfolders
- **Read & execute**: It allows users to run and execute files
- **List folder contents**: It allows users to view data files and a list of a folder's contents
- **Read**: It allows users to view files and file properties
- **Write**: It allows users to write in a file
- **Special permissions**: It provides users with advanced permissions

Unlike NTFS permissions, **share permissions** determine the type of access others have to the network shares. The following lists the share permissions:

- **Full control**: It allows users to read, modify, edit permissions, and take ownership.
- **Change**: It allows users to read, execute, write, and delete files and subfolders.
- **Read**: It allows users to list and view the contents.

Configuring NTFS permissions

To **configure** NTFS permissions in your Windows 10 computer, complete the following steps:

1. Right-click the shared folder and select **Properties** from the context menu.
2. In the **Properties** dialog box, select the **Security** tab.
3. In the **Group or user names** section, select the group or user as shown in *Figure 8.23*:

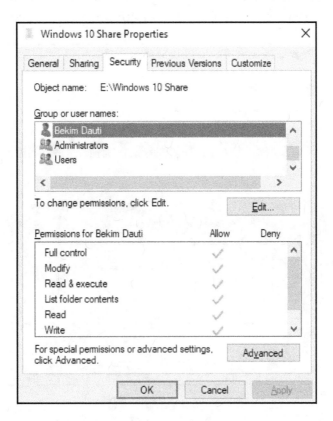

Figure 8.23. NTFS permissions in Windows 10

4. To change permissions, click **Edit**.
5. In the **Permissions for the selected user** section, select the appropriate permissions and click **OK**.
6. Click Close again to close the **Properties** dialog box.

Configuring share permissions

To configure share permissions in your Windows 10 computer, complete the following steps:

1. *Right-click* the shared folder and select **Properties** from the context menu.
2. In the **Properties** dialog box, select the **Sharing** tab.
3. In the **Advanced Sharing** section, click the **Advanced Sharing...** button.
4. In the **Advanced Sharing** dialog box, click the **Permissions** button.
5. In the **Permissions** dialog box, select the group or user as shown in *Figure 8.24*:

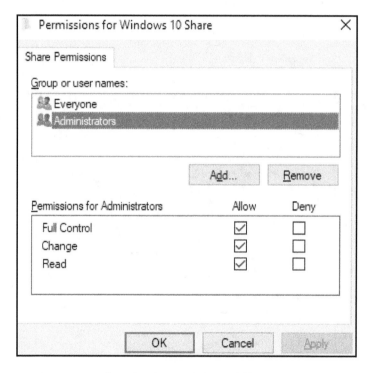

Figure 8.24. Share permissions in Windows 10

6. In the **Permissions for the selected user** section, select the appropriate permissions and click **OK**.
7. Click **OK** to close the **Advanced Sharing** dialog box.
8. Click Close to close the **Properties** dialog box.

Configuring OneDrive usage including Files On-Demand

Introduced in Windows 10 version 1709, OneDrive's **Files On-Demand** is a new feature that enables users to access their files from the cloud using File Explorer with no need to sync them directly. Besides the fact that this feature provides a more convenient way of accessing files from the cloud, additionally, it enables users to save storage space on their computers.

Enabling Files On-Demand

To enable Files On-Demand in your Windows 10 computer using OneDrive, complete the following steps:

1. Press Windows key + *E* to open **File Explorer**.
2. Locate the OneDrive icon, and right-click on it.
3. From the context menu, select **Settings** as shown in *Figure 8.25*:

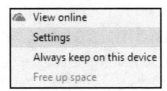

Figure 8.25. OneDrive settings

4. Within the **Files On-Demand** section, check the **Save space and download files as you use them** option (see *Figure 8.26*):

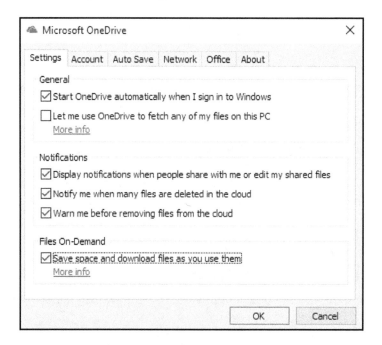

Figure 8.26. Enabling Files On-Demand in Microsoft OneDrive

5. Click **OK** to close the **Microsoft OneDrive** dialog box.

Statuses of files and folders

After enabling the Files On-Demand feature, the **File Explorer** displays the statuses in the bottom-left corner of the files and folders. These statuses (as shown in *Figure 8.27*) allow users to know that their files and folders are available online only, or offline.

As soon as you enable OneDrive's Files On-Demand, then the following statuses show up next to your files and folders:

- **Always available** files have an icon of solid green with white check mark. These files have been marked as Always keep on this device, and as such they reside in your computer's storage. You need not be connected to the internet to access these files.

- **Locally available** files have a white icon with green borders and a check mark. These files have been opened by you at least once, and as such they have become available locally. These files take computer storage space, and can be accessed without an internet connection. Right-click the file and select **Free up space** if you want to remove it from your computer's storage.
- **Online-only** files have an icon of a white cloud with blue borders. These files are only available online, and as such they reside on the cloud. These files do not take computer storage space, and you need an internet connection to access them. When you open the file, it is downloaded from the cloud and opened locally:

Figure 8.27. File and folder statuses in File Explorer

Chapter labs – troubleshooting data access and usage

In these chapter labs, you will learn how to do the following:

- Troubleshoot data access
- Troubleshoot share and NTFS permissions
- Troubleshoot data recovery
- Recover BitLocker encrypted drives

Troubleshooting data access

To **troubleshoot data access** in your Windows 10 computer using Group Policy, complete the following steps:

1. Right-click the Start button, and select **Run**.

2. In the **Run** dialog box, enter `gpedit.msc` and press *Enter*.

3. In the **Local Group Policy Editor** window, navigate to **Computer Configuration | Windows Settings | Security Settings | Local Policies | User Rights Assignment** as shown in *Figure 8.28*:

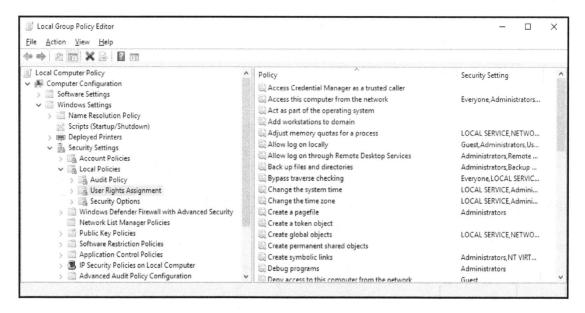

Figure 8.28. User Rights Assignment GPs in Windows 10

Troubleshooting share and NTFS permissions

To **reset permissions** in your Windows 10 computer using *ICACLS*, complete the following steps:

1. Sign in to your computer with a user account that has administrator rights.
2. Press Windows key + *E* to open **File Explorer**.
3. Navigate and select the folder that has issues.

4. Click the **File** menu and select **Open Windows PowerShell | Open Windows PowerShell as administrator** (see *Figure 8.29*):

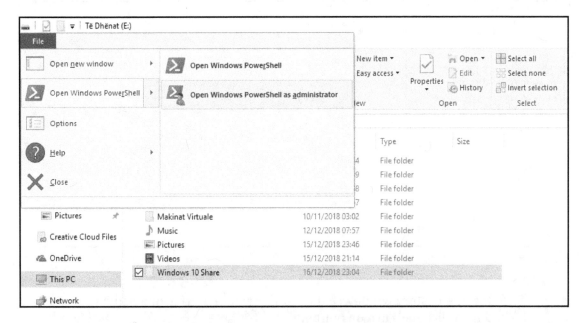

Figure 8.29. Opening Windows PowerShell in File Explorer

5. Click the **Yes** button when asked **Do you want to allow this app to make changes to your device?**.
6. Enter `icacls * /RESET /T /C /Q` and press *Enter*.
7. Close the **Windows PowerShell** window.

Troubleshooting data recovery

To turn on **File History** in your Windows 10 computer, complete the following steps:

1. Click the search box in the taskbar and enter `control panel`.
2. Select **Open** on the right of the **Best match** list.
3. In the **Control Panel** window, select **System and Security**.

4. In the **System and Security** window, select **File History** as shown in *Figure 8.30*:

Figure 8.30. File History in Windows 10

5. In the **File History** window, either add an **external drive or a network location**, and then click the **Turn on** button.
6. Close the **File History** window.

Recovering BitLocker encrypted drives

To **recover** BitLocker encrypted keys in your Windows 10 computer using OneDrive, complete the following steps:

1. Click the Start button to open the Start menu.
2. From the Start menu, select **Microsoft Edge.**
3. In the address bar of your browser,
   enter `https://onedrive.live.com/recoverykey` and press *Enter*.

Summary

We can summarize the chapter with the following points:

- Windows 10 has been built to enable data access anytime from anywhere.
- Computer networks were born from the need to share resources.
- To be able to share files or folders, you must be a member of the administrator's group.
- HomeGroup is an easy, fast, and user-friendly tool for sharing files and printers on your network.
- It is very important to pay attention to whom you give access when creating a network share.
- In a corporate network, there is a file server that hosts the shared and public folders.
- You can launch the **Create A Shared Folder Wizard** from the **Run** dialog box by entering Shrpubw.exe.
- The public folders can be navigated via File Explorer in the following path: %systemdrive%\Users\Public.
- To have OneDrive, you need to set up a Microsoft account at Outlook.com.
- OneDrive for Business is the Microsoft cloud service that is based on Microsoft SharePoint and enables you to access all your business files.
- The filesystems that historically have been associated with Windows OS are the following:
    - **File Allocation Table (FAT)**
    - **Extended File Allocation Table (exFAT)**
    - **New Technology File System (NTFS)**
    - **Resilient File System (ReFS)**
- One of the main concerns of the network share is permissions management, which defines who has been permitted access and who has been denied access.
- NTFS permissions are used to manage access to the files and folders that are stored in the NTFS filesystem.
- Share permissions determine the type of access others have to network shares.
- OneDrive's Files On-Demand is a new feature that enables users to access their files from the cloud using File Explorer with no need to sync them directly.
- Always available files have an icon of solid green with a white check mark.
- Locally available files have a white icon with green borders and a check mark.
- Online-only files have an icon of a white cloud with blue borders.

Questions

1. Windows 10 has been built to enable data access anytime from anywhere.
    1. True
    2. False

2. _____ are used to manage access to the files and folders that are stored in the NTFS filesystem.

3. Which of the following are OneDrive's statuses for files and folders?
    1. Always available files
    2. Locally available files
    3. Online-only files
    4. All of the above

4. OneDrive for Business is the Microsoft cloud service that is based on Microsoft SharePoint and enables you to access all your business files.
    1. True
    2. False

5. In a corporate network, there is a _____ that hosts the shared and public folders.

6. Which of the following are Windows OS filesystems? (Choose two)
    1. File Allocation Table (FAT)
    2. New Technology File System (NTFS)
    3. Microsoft SharePoint
    4. OneDrive for Business

7. HomeGroup is an easy, fast, and a user-friendly tool for sharing files and printers on your network.
    1. True
    2. False

8. The Public folders can be navigated via File Explorer at the following path: _____ .

9. In the network share, we encounter something like? (Choose two)
    1. NTFS permissions
    2. share permissions
    3. HomeGroup
    4. Public Folders

10. OneDrive's Files On-Demand is a new feature that enables users to access their files from the cloud using File Explorer with no need to sync them directly.
    1. True
    2. False

11. _____ determine the type of access others have to network shares.

12. Which of the following are NTFS permissions? (Choose three)
    1. Modify
    2. Read and Execute
    3. Write
    4. Change

Further reading

- **Windows file sharing**: https://docs.microsoft.com/en-us/windows/iot-core/manage-your-device/windowsfilesharing
- **How to share files and printers without HomeGroup on Windows 10**: https://www.windowscentral.com/how-share-files-and-printers-without-homegroup-windows-10
- **Beginner's guide to Microsoft OneDrive on Windows 10**: https://www.windowscentral.com/how-get-started-onedrive-windows-10
- **How to use Public folder to share files with other people on Windows 10**: https://pureinfotech.com/public-folder-share-files-windows-10/
- **How to use OneDrive Files On-Demand on Windows 10**: https://www.windowscentral.com/how-use-onedrive-files-demand-windows-10

9
Implementing Apps

This chapter is designed to provide you with information about the types of apps that can run on Windows 10. So, you will learn how you can implement desktop apps and Microsoft Store apps. Then, you will get acquainted with the so-called **fast startup** feature, as well as how applications impact Windows startup. This chapter also addresses the implementation of Microsoft Store for Business, respectively Microsoft Store for Education. While Microsoft Store for Business enables IT decision makers and system administrators to find, acquire, manage, and distribute free and paid apps, Microsoft Store for Education offers cloud services and tools to implement a full IT cloud solution for your school. Each topic is accompanied with step-by-step instructions driven by targeted, easy-to-understand graphics. The chapter concludes with a chapter lab on configuring Microsoft Store.

In this chapter, we will cover the following topics:

- Configuring desktop apps
- Configuring startup options
- Implementing Microsoft Store apps
- Implementing Microsoft Store for Business
- Implementing Microsoft Store for Education
- Chapter lab—configuring Microsoft Store

Technical requirements

In order to complete the labs for this chapter, you will need the following equipment:

- A PC with Windows 10 Pro, at least 4 GB of RAM, 500 GB of HDD, and access to the internet

Configuring desktop apps

You may have heard the term **general-purpose computer,** which refers to a device with adequate applications that is capable of performing most computer work. This definition makes us understand the importance of applications on personal computers, making them very useful devices. Because of that, it is vital to know how to install, configure, and manage apps on Windows 10 devices. In this section, the installation of desktop apps is covered.

Installing desktop apps

In regard to Windows 10 apps, since Windows 8, two types of apps are supported: **desktop apps** and **Microsoft Store apps**. The two types of apps are installed and managed entirely differently. In contrast to Microsoft Store apps, desktop apps are larger and more complex, and there are multipurpose programs designed for desktops, laptops, and tablets.

Installing desktop apps manually

To **install** a desktop app **manually** in your Windows 10 computer using a `.msi` file, complete the following steps:

1. Press the Windows key + *E* to open **File Explorer.**
2. In the **File Explorer** window, navigate to the `.msi` file of your desktop app and double-click on it.
3. Click the **Yes** button when asked **Do you want to allow this app to make changes to your device?**
4. In the **Setup** dialog box, depending on the application requirements, click **Next** to begin the installation, as shown in *Figure 9.1*:

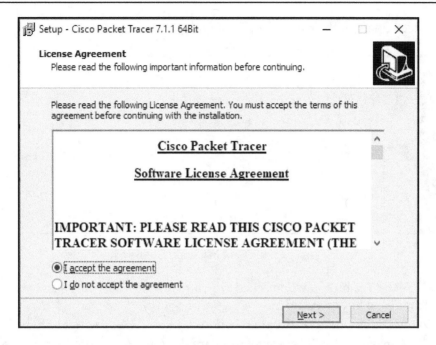

Figure 9.1 Installing desktop on Windows 10

5. Since the dialog box is self-explanatory with desktop apps, you may want to **continue installation** by following the instructions in the dialog box itself.

Usually, when installing an application manually (involves user interaction) in Windows 10, you will end up executing a file with the .exe or .msi extension either downloaded from the internet, located on disk, or supplied via DVD. However, such activity requires you to have local administrator privileges.

Installing desktop apps automatically

To **install** a desktop app **automatically** on your Windows 10 computer using **Microsoft Deployment Toolkit (MDT)**, complete the following steps:

1. Click the search box on the taskbar and enter deployment workbench.

2. Select **Open** on the right of the **Best match** list; see *Figure 9.2*:

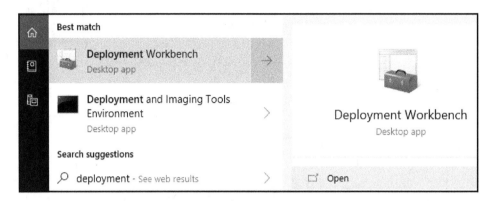

Figure 9.2 Opening the Microsoft Deployment Toolkit (MDT)

3. Click the **Yes** button when asked **Do you want to allow this app to make changes to your device?**.
4. In the **DeploymentWorkbench** window, expand **Deployment Shares**.
5. Then, expand **MDT Deployment Share** (in your case, it might be named differently).
6. Right-click **Applications** and select **New Application,** as shown in *Figure 9.3*:

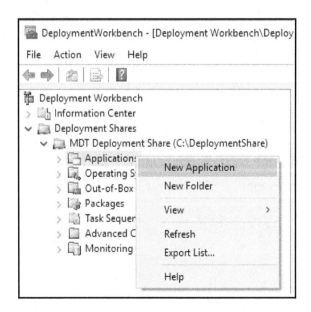

Figure 9.3 Deploying a new application using MDT

7. On the **Application Type** page, select **Application with source files** as the type of application to add, and click **Next**.

8. On the **Details** page, enter the **Application Name** (see *Figure 9.4*), since that is required, and click **Next**:

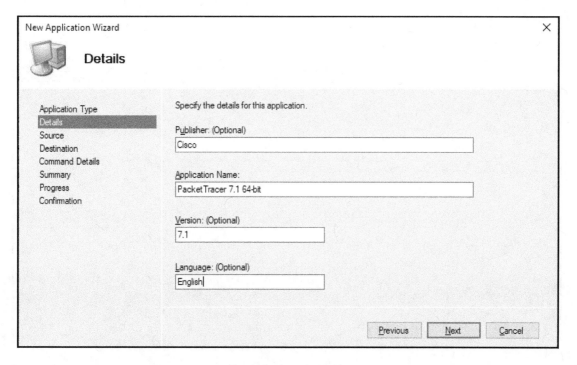

Figure 9.4 Entering Application Name

9. On the **Source** page, browse the **location** of your application and then click **Next**.

10. On the **Destination** page, specify the **name of the directory** that should be created and then click **Next**.

11. On the **Command Details** page, specify the **quite install command line** needed to install the application and then click **Next**.

12. On the **Summary** page, review all the details entered so far and then click **Next**.

13. On the **Confirmation** page, once the **process completes successfully** click **Finish,**
as shown in *Figure 9.5*:

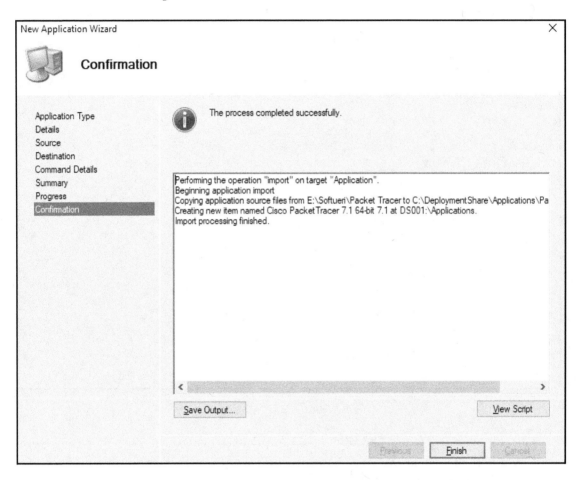

Figure 9.5 The app import has been completed successfully

14. Once an application has been added to MDT, the expanded **Applications** folder displays the imported app, as shown in *Figure 9.6*:

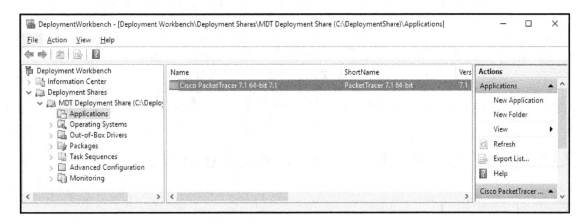

Figure 9.6 The Applications folder displays the imported app

15. If you try to navigate to the **Deployment Shares** folder, you will notice that the **Applications** folder contains the imported app; see *Figure 9.7* :

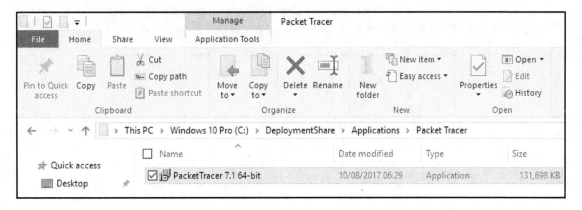

Figure 9.7 The imported app is contained in Deployment Shares

In addition to MDT, another way of implementing apps automatically is by using **Group Policy Objects** (**GPOs**). This works in a way that in container objects, such as site, domain, and **organization unit** (**OU**) of your domain environment, you target the app deployment. Usually, there are two methods of implementing apps through a GPO: assign and publish. The apps can be assigned to both users and computers, and will get installed once the user signs in or the computer starts. Also, the apps can be published to users that are installed from **Control Panel** in **Programs And Features** and cannot be published to computers.

Uninstalling or changing a desktop app

To **uninstall** a desktop app on your Windows 10 computer using **Control Panel**, complete the following steps:

1. Click the search box on the taskbar and enter `control panel`.
2. Select **Open** on the right of the **Best match** list.
3. In the **Control Panel** window, select **Uninstall a program** in the **Programs** section.
4. In the **Programs and Features** window, select the program you want to uninstall and click the **Uninstall** button, as shown in *Figure 9.8*:

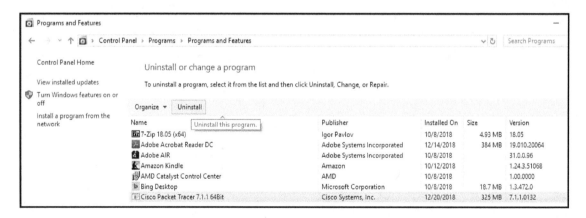

Figure 9.8 Uninstalling a desktop app via Control Panel

5. Click the **Yes** button when asked **Do you want to allow this app to make changes to your device?**
6. Click the **Yes** button on the dialog box to begin uninstalling your desktop app.

7. Click **OK** to close the dialog box once the uninstall completes.

 To uninstall a desktop app, open **Control Panel** and then click **Programs and Features**. Right-click the desktop app that you want to uninstall, and then select **Uninstall** from the context menu.

To **change** a desktop app in your Windows 10 computer using **Control Panel**, complete the following steps:

1. Repeat **step 1 to step 3** from the previous section.
2. In the **Programs and Features** window, select the program you want to change and click the **Change** button as shown in *Figure 9.9*:

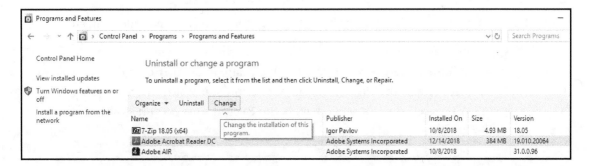

Figure 9.9 Changing a desktop app via Control Panel

3. Depending on the application, the setup dialog box also changes so choose the preferred option and then click **Continue**, **Next,** or **OK**.
4. Since the dialog box is self-explanatory, you may want to **continue changing** your desktop app by following the instructions in the dialog box itself.

 To change a desktop app, open **Control Panel** and then click **Programs and Features**. Right-click the desktop app that you want to change, and then select change from the context menu.

Configuring startup options

In the past, among many users complaints, there have been concerns that Windows is slow during startup. Microsoft responded to these complaints by introducing fast startup in Windows 8. So what is fast startup? The first answer is that it enables Windows to start faster than before. But how does fast startup work? Fast startup is also known as a **hybrid shutdown** because it is a state between hibernate and shutdown. Hence, fast startup is the best of both worlds by signing off the user and then saving the kernel session to hard disk. It is clear that this approach affects how fast Windows 10 can start. And that is obviously important to many users.

Configuring Windows 10 fast startup

To **configure** fast startup in your Windows 10 computer, complete the following steps:

1. Click the Start button and then **Settings** from the Start menu.
2. In the **Windows Settings** window, click **Update & Security**.
3. Select **Recovery** from the navigation menu on the left side of the screen.
4. In the **Advanced startup** section, click the **Restart now** button as shown *Figure 9.10*:

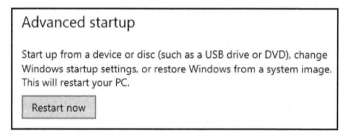

Figure 9.10 Restarting Windows 10 in advanced startup

5. hortly after, options including **Continue**, **Troubleshoot**, and **Turn off your PC** will show up.
6. Click **Troubleshoot** to access **Advanced options**.
7. On the **Advanced options** page, select **UEFI Firmware Settings** and then click **Restart**.

8. Based on your computer's UEFI manufacturer, look for and enable fast boot (or fast startup).
9. Save the UEFI settings and then exit.

9. Once the computer restarts and you are able to sign in, click the Start button and then **Settings** from the Start menu.
10. In the **Windows Settings** window, click **System**.
11. Select **Power & sleep** from the navigation menu on the left side of the screen.
12. On the right of the screen, in **Related settings**, select **Additional power settings** (see *Figure 9.11*):

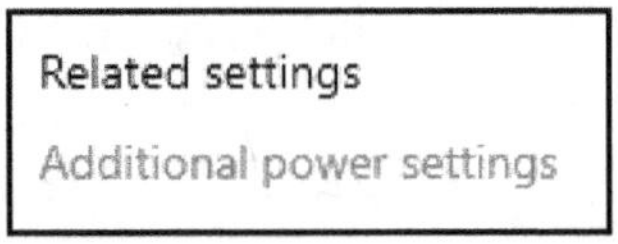

Related settings

Additional power settings

Figure 9.11 Accessing Additional power settings from Windows Settings

13. In the **Power Options** windows, select **Choose what the power button does**.
14. In the **System** setting's window, select **Change settings that are currently unavailable**.
15. In the **Shutdown settings** section, select the **Turn on fast startup (recommended)** checkbox as shown in *Figure 9.12*:

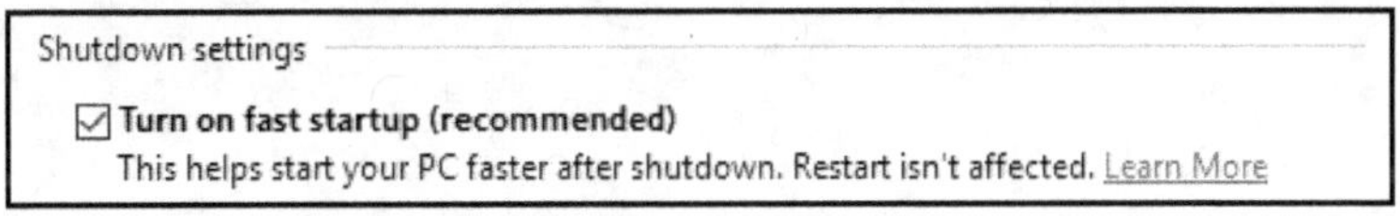

Shutdown settings

☑ **Turn on fast startup (recommended)**
This helps start your PC faster after shutdown. Restart isn't affected. Learn More

Figure 9.12 Enabling fast startup in Windows 10

Configuring app startup behavior

To **configure** app startup behavior in your Windows 10 computer using **Task Manager**, complete the following steps:

1. Press the Windows key + R to open the **Run** dialog box.

2. Enter `taskmgr.exe` (see *Figure 9.13*) and press *Enter*:

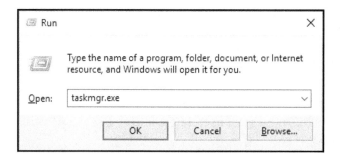

Figure 9.13 Running Task Manager

3. Click the **Startup** tab to see the impact on a system of each app that is running in the background.
4. Notice that each app has a **Startup impact** reported as **Not measured**, **Low**, **Medium**, or **High**.
5. If an app's impact is too high, right-click the app and then select **Disable** as shown in *Figure 9.14*:

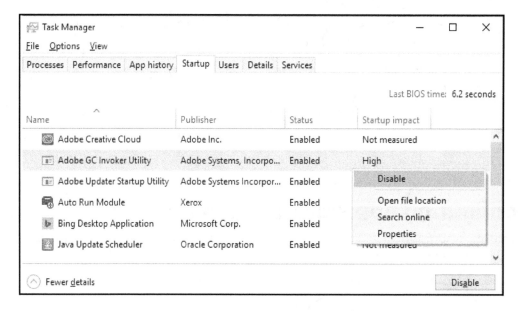

Figure 9.14 Disabling the apps with the high impact on a system's startup

6. That prevents the app from running at startup.

 Another way to control the running apps at system startup is by using a system registry. Open the **Registry Editor** by pressing Windows key + *R*, enter regedit.exe, and press *Enter*. In the **Registry Editor** window, navigate to the following two registry keys: HKEY_CURRENT_USER\SOFTWARE\Microsoft\Windows\CurrentVersion\Run and HKEY_LOCAL_MACHINE\SOFTWARE\Microsoft\Windows\CurrentVersion\Run, to control the apps configured to start for a particular signed-in user and the apps configured to start for any signed-in user, respectively.

Implementing Microsoft Store apps

Introduced first in Windows 8 and Windows Server 2012, **Microsoft Store** serves as a digital platform for distributing Windows apps. Microsoft Store apps are designed to be used across **multiple platforms** such as desktops, laptops, smartphones, and tablets. Mostly, these apps are focused on performing a certain task, though there are also apps that can perform a small subset of tasks. Despite the great benefits that Microsoft Store offers to individual users, for IT support staff it raises challenges because users in a corporate network want to be able install and use these apps across all of their devices. For that reason, it is very important for organizations to put in place appropriate **policies** that will enable configuring and managing Windows 10 devices in order to support the use of these new apps properly in a business environment.

Installing apps

To **install** an app in your Windows 10 computer using Microsoft Store, complete the following steps:

1. Click on the Microsoft Store icon in the taskbar to open it.
2. In the **Microsoft Store** window, click **Apps** on the menu.
3. Click the **Top apps** tile.
4. On the **Top apps** page, identify the app that you want to install and then click on it.

5. Depending on the availability of the application as **Free**, **Trial**, or with a price, click on the **Get** button, receptively install (see *Figure 9.15*):

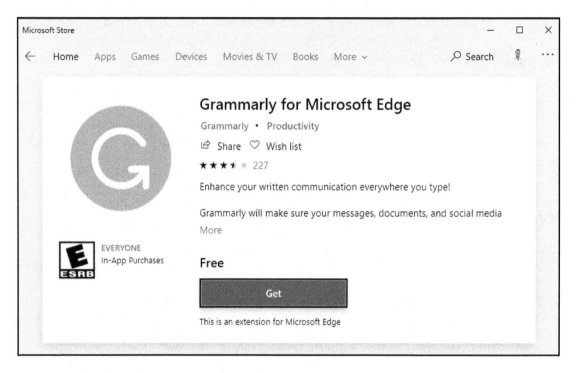

Figure 9.15 Installing an app from Microsoft Store

6. Shortly after (depending on your internet connection), the app is **installed** and its tile is listed in **All Apps**.

 To uninstall a Microsoft Store app, simply right-click on the app and then from the context menu, select uninstall. Another way of uninstalling Microsoft Store apps is through **Windows Settings**, **Apps & Features**.

Configuring Microsoft Store app settings

To access the Microsoft Store apps settings in your Windows 10 computer, complete the following steps:

1. **Repeat step 1 and step 2** from the previous section.

2. From the displayed menu, select Settings (see *Figure 9.16*):

Figure 9.16 Accessing Microsoft Store Settings in Windows 10

3. On the **Settings** page, there are a number of **settings** that you can use to customize Microsoft Store.

To configure the default file save location for Microsoft Store apps, complete the following steps:

1. Press Windows key + *I* to open the Windows settings
2. Click on **System**, and then select **Storage**
3. In **More storage settings**, select **Change where new content is saved**
4. On the **Change where new content is saved** page, select **New apps will save to:** and set the appropriate location

Blocking Microsoft Store apps

To **block** Microsoft Store apps in your Windows 10 computer using GPOs, complete the following steps:

1. Press the Windows key + *R* to open the **Run** dialog box.
2. Enter gpedit.msc and press *Enter*.
3. In the **Local Group Policy Editor** window, navigate to the following GPO: User Configuration\Administrative Templates\Windows Components\Store.
4. In the Store folder, double-click **Turn off the Store application**.
5. In the **Turn off the Store application** window, select **Enabled** (see *Figure 9.17*) and then click **OK**:

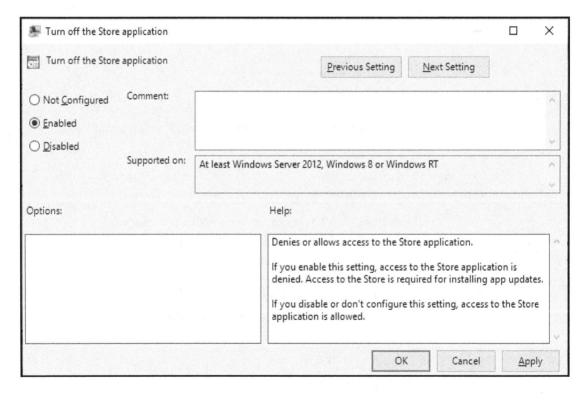

Figure 9.17 Configuring GPO Turn off the Store application

In the Windows Server-based domain corporate network, it is recommended to use **Group Policy Management** (**GPM**) to create and link a GPO to the domain. In that case, the GPO that turns off the store application that is located in the `User Configuration\Policies\Administrative Templates\Windows Components\Store` path must be enabled.

Implementing Microsoft Store for Business

Microsoft Store for Business, as its name indicates, is solely designed for organizations. It enables IT decision makers and system administrators to find, acquire, manage, and distribute free and paid apps. In that way, Microsoft Store apps along with line-of-business apps can be managed in one **inventory**. On top of that, system administrators can assign and reuse licenses as needed. Thus, Microsoft Store for Business helps to choose the best **distribution** method for the organization.

The following prerequisites are required when using Microsoft Store for Business:

- **A compatible browser** running on PCs or mobile devices
- **At least Windows 10, version 1511** running on PCs or mobile devices
- **Azure AD or Office 365 accounts** are needed for system administrators
- Employees need **Azure AD accounts** to access Microsoft Store for Business content

Setting up Microsoft Store for Business

To set up Microsoft Store for Business, complete the following steps:

1. Create a **Microsoft Azure account** by going to `https://account.windowsazure.com/SignUp`.
2. `Configure` **custom domain** `on Azure Portal`.
3. Configure Azure **Active Directory (AD) Connect/Active Directory Federation Services (ADFS)** in order to integrate your on-premises identities with Azure AD.
4. Create an **Azure Global Administrator**.

5. Set up the **Microsoft Store for Business** by going to `https://businessstore.microsoft.com`, and then selecting **Sign in**.

6. Accept the **agreement**, begin **configuring** your business store, and **add apps** to your inventory.

Implementing Microsoft Store for Education

Unlike Microsoft Store for Business, **Microsoft Store for Education** offers cloud services and tools to implement a full IT cloud solution for your school. It enables you to easily set up, control, and manage school resources such as apps, devices, and settings. Microsoft Store for Education acts as a **unique cloud platform** by bringing together school data sync, OneNote class notebook, Microsoft Teams, learning tools, whiteboard, and many more tools for a simple setup, use of affordable devices, collaboration, and inspiring learning.

Setting up Microsoft Store for Education

To set up Microsoft Store for Education, complete the following steps:

1. Set up an **Office 365 for Education** tenant

2. Import school, student, teacher, and class data with **School Data Sync**

3. Configure **Microsoft Store for Education** for browsing, buying, and distributing apps

4. Manage **Windows 10** devices, settings, and apps by configuring **Intune for Education** as your **Mobile Device Management** (MDM) solution

5. Quickly set up **Windows 10** devices with **Intune for Education** and the **Set up School PCs** utility

6. Log in and use your devices

Chapter lab – configuring Microsoft Store

In this chapter lab, you will learn how to do the following:

- Configure Microsoft Store

Configuring Microsoft Store

To **configure** Microsoft Store in your Windows 10 prior to signing-in with your Microsoft account, complete the following steps:

1. Click on the **Microsoft Store** icon in the taskbar to open it.
2. In the upper-right corner, click on the sign-in icon as shown in *Figure 9.18*:

Figure 9.18 Sign in Microsoft Store

3. Select **Sign in**, enter your Microsoft account, and then press *Enter*.
4. Enter a password, and then press *Enter*.
5. On the page **Use this account everywhere on your device** page, click **Next**, as shown in *Figure 9.19*:

Figure 9.19 Setting up Microsoft account to be used everywhere on your device

6. Shortly after, your **signed on profile** will show up in the Microsoft Store as shown in *Figure 9.20*:

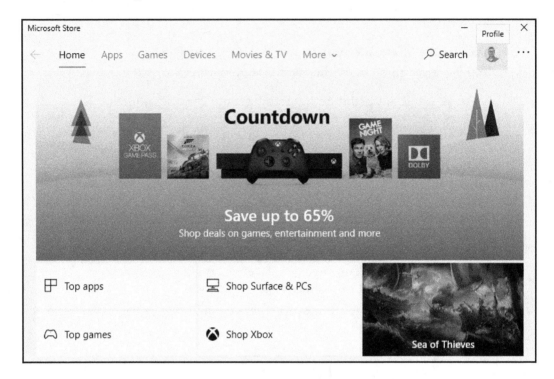

Figure 9.20 Microsoft Store displays the signed on profile

 A Microsoft account or just MSA is a free single sign-on Microsoft user account that enables you to easily access all Microsoft digital services. From Outlook to MSN, including Windows, you will be signed in to all these services to get things done, have more fun, stay in touch, keep things easy and personalized, earn rewards, and much more with enhanced security.

Summary

We can summarize the chapter with the following points:

- A general-purpose computer refers to a device with adequate applications that is capable of performing most computer work
- Desktop apps are larger and more complex, and are multipurpose programs designed for desktop, laptop, and tablet computers
- Usually when installing an application manually, you will end up executing a file with the `.exe` or `.msi` extension either downloaded from the internet or located on disk or supplied via DVD
- In addition to MDT, another way of implementing apps automatically is by using GPOs
- To uninstall a desktop app, open **Control Panel** and then click **Programs And Features**
- To change a desktop app, open **Control Panel** and then click **Programs And Features**
- Fast startup enables Windows to start faster than before
- Fast startup is also known as a **hybrid shutdown** because it is a state between hibernate and shutdown
- Another way to control the running apps at system startup is by using a system registry
- Microsoft Store serves as a digital platform for distributing Windows apps
- Microsoft Store apps are focused on performing a certain task, though there are also apps that can perform a small subset of tasks
- Another way of uninstalling Microsoft Store apps is through Windows Settings, **Apps & features**
- If you do not want the update of apps in the Microsoft Store to be done automatically, then in Microsoft Store settings you can turn off **Update Apps Automatically**
- In the Windows Server domain-based corporate network, it is recommended to use GPM to create and link GPO to the domain
- Microsoft Store for Business enables IT decision makers and system administrators to find, acquire, manage, and distribute free and paid apps
- Microsoft Store for Education offers cloud services and tools to implement a full IT cloud solution for your school
- A Microsoft account or just MSA is a free single sign-on Microsoft user account that enables you to easily access all Microsoft digital services

Questions

1. In addition to the **Microsoft Deployment Toolkit** (**MDT**), another way of implementing apps automatically is by using Microsoft Store for Business.
    1. True
    2. False

2. _____ enables IT decision makers and system administrators to find, acquire, manage, and distribute free and paid apps.

3. Which of the following are types of apps in Windows? (Choose two)
    1. Desktop apps
    2. Microsoft Store apps
    3. Mac apps
    4. Linux apps

4. Desktop apps are larger and more complex, and are multipurpose programs designed for desktop, laptop, and tablet computers.
    1. True
    2. False

5. _____ refers to a device with adequate applications that is capable of perform most computer work.

6. Which of the following Microsoft Store cloud solutions are valid? (Choose two).
    1. Microsoft Store for Business
    2. Microsoft Store for Education
    3. Office 365 for Education
    4. Intune for Education

7. If you do not want the updating of apps in the Microsoft Store to be done automatically, then in Microsoft Store Settings you can turn off **Update Apps Automatically**.
    1. True
    2. False

8. _____ enables Windows to start faster than before.

9. Which of the following enables you to automatically implement apps in Windows? (Choose two).
    1. Microsoft Deployment Toolkit (MDT)
    2. Group Policy Objects (GPOs)
    3. System registry
    4. Task Manager

10. A Microsoft account or just MSA is a free single sign-on Microsoft user account that enables you to easily access all Microsoft digital services.
    1. True
    2. False

Further reading

- **Windows 10 application management**: `https://docs.microsoft.com/en-us/windows/application-management/`
- **Setting up Windows Store for Business**: `https://stealthpuppy.com/setting-up-windows-store-for-business/#.XC0PPXdFyUk`
- **Configuring Microsoft Store for Education**: `https://docs.microsoft.com/en-us/education/get-started/configure-microsoft-store-for-education`

10
Configuring Remote Management

Now that you have learned how to install Windows 10 and run all the necessary configurations locally, it is time to try out remote management of the tools that Windows 10 supports. First, this chapter explains remote management tools. Specifically, this chapter will cover Remote Desktop, Remote Assistance, the **Microsoft Management Console** (**MMC**), and Windows PowerShell Remoting in Windows 10 so that you will become familiar with the ways you could manage remote computers. Other than that, you will get to know the types of Remote Desktop, such as Remote Desktop Connection and Microsoft Remote Desktop, as well as the EasyConnect feature in Remote Assistance so that you can manage remote computers without obstacles in your organization's IT infrastructure. Each topic is accompanied with step-by-step instructions driven by targeted, easy-to-understand graphics. The chapter concludes with chapter labs on configuring Remote Desktop Connection, installing EasyConnect from Microsoft Store, and configuring Windows PowerShell Remoting.

In this chapter, we will cover the following topics:

- Choosing the appropriate remote management tools
- Configuring remote management settings
- Modifying settings remotely by using the MMC or Windows PowerShell Remoting
- Configuring Remote Assistance including Easy Connect
- Chapter labs—Configuring Remote Desktop Connection, installing EasyConnect from the Microsoft Store, and configuring Windows PowerShell Remoting

Technical requirements

In order to complete the labs for this chapter, you will need the following equipment:

- A PC with Windows 10 Enterprise, at least 8 GB of RAM, 500 GB of HDD, and access to the internet

Choosing the appropriate remote management tools

Whether you access a remote computer to make some configurations or provide remote assistance to a remote user, the tool you choose for **remote management** depends largely on the task you are going to accomplish. Windows 10 is equipped with several tools for managing computers remotely. However, it is very important to know which tool you can use in which situation. That will enable you to address the user needs more quickly and efficiently. In the following sections lists the tools that can be used for remote management in Windows 10.

Remote Desktop

First things first, since Windows 10 supports desktop apps and Microsoft Store apps, then **Remote Desktop** comes in two formats: **Remote Desktop Connection** and **Microsoft Remote Desktop**. While the first one is a built-in tool that can be used to access a computer remotely over the **Remote Desktop Protocol** (**RDP**), the latter is the Microsoft Store app that lets you connect to a remote PC or virtual apps and desktops made available by you. Remote Desktop uses the 3389 port, thus in order to establish a successful remote connection it is required to enable the 3389 port in the Windows Firewall of the remote computer. Because Remote Desktop enables you access to the remote computer desktop in the same way as if you were sitting in front of that computer, then you are required to sign in before you can access the remote computer.

Remote Desktop Connection built-in app

To **access** the Remote Desktop Connection built-in app in your Windows 10 computer, complete the following steps:

1. Press the Windows key + R to start the **Run** dialog box.
2. In the **Run** dialog box, enter mstsc and press *Enter*.
3. Shortly after, the **Remote Desktop Connection** gets opened, as shown in *Figure 10.1*:

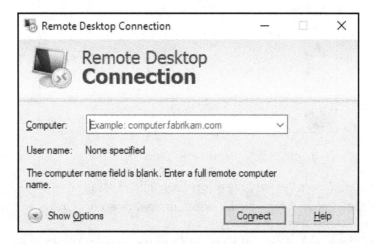

Figure 10.1 Remote Desktop Connection built-in app in Windows 10

Microsoft Remote Desktop app

To **install and access** the Microsoft Remote Desktop app in your Windows 10 computer, complete the following steps:

1. Press the Windows key + R to start the **Run** dialog box.
2. In the **Run** dialog box, enter ms-windows-store: and press *Enter*.
3. In the Microsoft Store window, click on the search icon and enter remote desktop.

4. From the list of search results, select **Microsoft Remote Desktop** as shown in *Figure 10.2*:

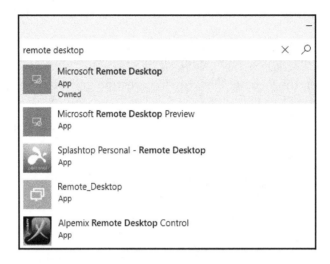

Figure 10.2 Installing Microsoft Remote Desktop app from Microsoft Store

5. On the Microsoft **Remote Desktop** page, click **Install**.
6. Once the Microsoft Remote Desktop app gets installed, you can then launch it from the start menu.
7. Shortly after, the Microsoft **Remote Desktop** app gets opened as shown in *Figure 10.3*:

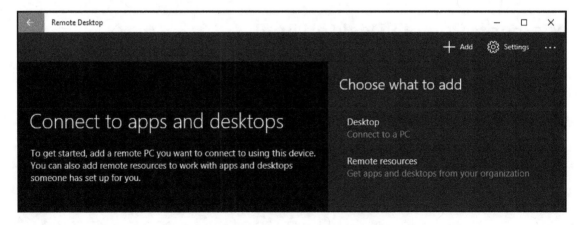

Figure 10.3 Microsoft Remote Desktop app in Windows 10

Remote Assistance

As the name suggests, Remote Assistance enables you to provide help to a friend's remote computer or invite a remote friend to offer you assistance on your computer. There are dozens of apps (free or paid) on the internet that you can use for remote assistance purposes; however, Microsoft has equipped Windows 10 with a built-in Remote Assistance app so that you can use it as often as you need it.

Remote Assistance app

To **access** the Remote Assistance built-in app in your Windows 10 computer, complete the following steps:

1. Press the Windows key + *R* to start the **Run** dialog box.
2. In the **Run** dialog box, enter `msra` and press *Enter*.
3. In the **Windows Remote Assistance** wizard (see *Figure 10.4*), you can **ask for help or offer help**:

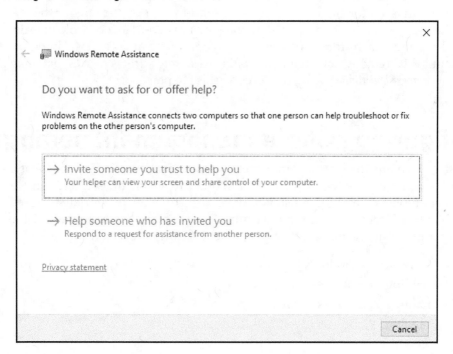

Figure 10.4 Remote Assistance built-in app in Windows 10

Windows PowerShell Remoting

If you like working with commands, then your favorite remote management tool will be **Windows PowerShell Remoting**. The reason for such a choice is that Windows PowerShell Remoting enables system administrators to execute commands on remote computers. If Remote Desktop has security concerns, the Windows PowerShell Remoting is a powerful remote management tool from a security perspective. In addition, Windows PowerShell Remoting provides a scripting environment too. Another advantage is that Windows PowerShell Remoting enables you to manage a single remote computer or multiple remote computers at once. For more about Windows PowerShell Remoting, see the *Modifying settings remotely by using the MMC or Windows PowerShell Remoting* section later in this chapter.

Microsoft Management Console

The **Microsoft Management Console** (**MMC**) is another way of managing applications on both local and remote computers. As you may know, to perform management using the MMC, a snap-in is loaded on the console. That snap-in is a specific tool for the management task. In this way, you may load the disk management snap-in in a console in order to manage disks and attach storage on the remote computer from the MMC interface. For more about MMC remote management, see the *Modifying settings remotely by using the MMC or Windows PowerShell Remoting* section later in this chapter.

Configuring remote management settings

Obviously, based on which remote management tool you have decided to use, it is necessary to configure the remote computer in order to enable the selected remote management tool. First and foremost, you have to ensure the appropriate feature is enabled on the **Windows Firewall** of the remote computer so it permits management. Thus, some of the configuration options for remote management settings are as follows:

- Configuring Windows Firewall
- Enabling Remote Desktop
- Enabling Remote Assistance
- Enabling Windows PowerShell Remoting

Configuring Windows Firewall

To **configure** Windows Firewall in your Windows 10 computer, complete the following steps:

1. Press the Windows key + R to start the **Run** dialog box.
2. In the **Run** dialog box, enter `control panel` and press *Enter*.
3. In the **Control Panel** window, select **System and Security** and then click **Windows Defender Firewall**.
4. In the **Windows Defender Firewall** window, select **Allow an app or feature through Windows Defender Firewall**.
5. In the **Allowed apps** window, click the **Change settings** button.
6. In the **Allowed apps and features** list, scroll down and select the appropriate management features as shown in *Figure 10.5*:

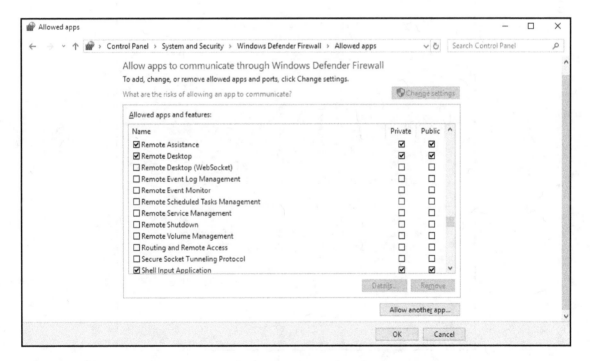

Figure 10.5 Allowing apps and features through Windows Defender Firewall

7. Ensure that the appropriate network location profile such as **Domain**, **Private**, or **Public** has been selected.
8. Click **OK**, and then close the **Windows Defender Firewall** window.

Enabling Remote Desktop

To **enable** Remote Desktop in your Windows 10 computer, complete the following steps:

1. Press the Windows key + *R* to start the **Run** dialog box.
2. In the **Run** dialog box, enter `sysdm.cpl` and press *Enter*.
3. In the **System Properties** dialog box, click the **Remote** tab.
4. In the **Remote Desktop** section, select the **Allow remote connections to this computer** option as shown in *Figure 10.6*:

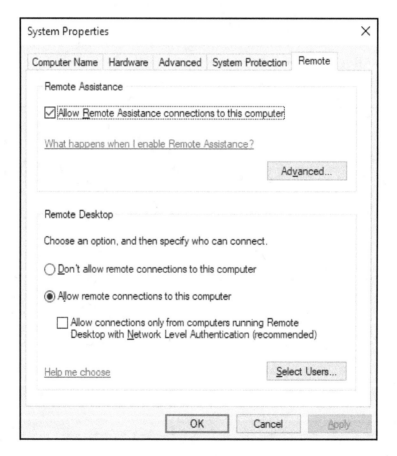

Figure 10.6 Enabling Remote Desktop in Windows 10

5. To add Remote Desktop users, click the **Select Users...** button.
6. In the **Remote Desktop Users** dialog box, click the **Add...** button to add Remote Desktop users (see *Figure 10.7*):

Figure 10.7 Adding Remote Desktop Users

7. When done with adding **Remote Desktop Users**, click **OK** twice.

Enabling Remote Assistance

To **enable** Remote Assistance in your Windows 10 computer, complete the following steps:

1. Repeat step 1 to step 3 from the previous section.
2. In the **Remote Assistance** section, check **Allow Remote Assistance connections to this computer** .
3. Click the **Advanced...** button.

4. In the **Remote Assistance Settings** dialog box, in the **Remote control** section, check **Allow this computer to be controlled remotely,** as shown in *Figure 10.8*:

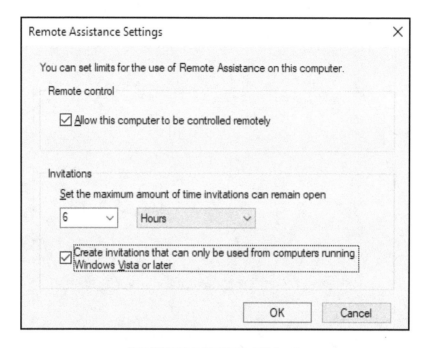

Figure 10.8 Remote Assistance Settings in Windows 10

5. In the **Invitations** section, you can **Set the maximum amount of time invitations can remain open** and **Create invitations that can only be used from computers running Windows Vista or later** (see the preceding screenshot).
6. When done with **Remote Assistance Settings**, click **OK** twice.

Enabling Windows PowerShell Remoting

To **enable** Windows PowerShell Remoting in your Windows 10 computer, complete the following steps:

1. Press the Windows key + R to start the **Run** dialog box.
2. In the **Run** dialog box, enter `powershell` and press *Enter*.

3. In the **Windows PowerShell** window, enter the `Enable-PSRemoting -Force` command and press *Enter* (see *Figure 10.9*):

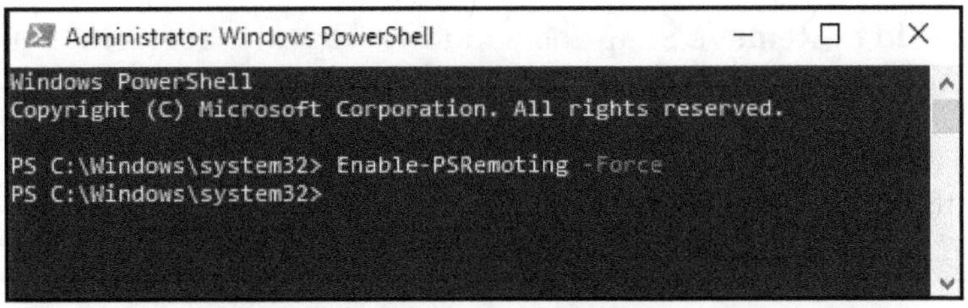

Figure 10.9 Enabling PowerShell Remoting in Windows 10

Modifying settings remotely by using the MMC or Windows PowerShell Remoting

In order to be able to remotely manage settings on a remote computer using the MMC, it is required to make the appropriate Windows Firewall settings (see the *Configuring Windows Firewall* section earlier in this chapter) on the remote computer. In contrast, in the case of **Windows PowerShell Remoting,** you must first enable the Windows Remote Management service by running the `winrm quickconfig` command (see the *Configuring Windows PowerShell Remoting* chapter lab later in this chapter) and then enable Windows PowerShell Remoting (see the previous *Enabling Windows PowerShell Remoting* section). The following sections will show how to modify settings remotely by using the MMC or Windows PowerShell Remoting.

MMC remote management

To **set up** MMC remote management in your Windows 10 computer, complete the following steps:

1. Press the Windows key + *R* to start the **Run** dialog box.
2. In the **Run** dialog box, enter mmc and press *Enter*.

3. Click the **Yes** button when asked **Do you want to allow this app to make changes to your device?**

4. In the **Console1** window, click **File** and select **Add/Remove Snap-in....**

5. In the **Add or Remove Snap-ins** window, select the **Services** snap-in and then click **Add**.

6. In the **Services** window, select **Another computer** and browse the **remote computer** (see *Figure 10.10*):

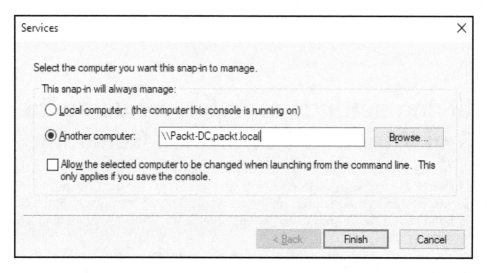

Figure 10.10 Browsing the remote computer in order to manage Services snap-in

7. Click **Finish**, and then click **OK**.

8. In the **Console1** window, click the **Services** snap-in you have just loaded.

9. Shortly after, the **Services** of the remote computer will be displayed in the middle pane, as shown in *Figure 10.11*:

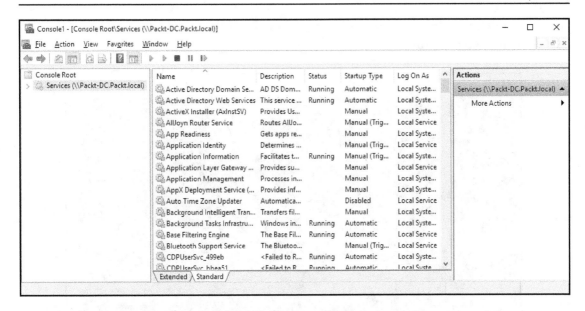

Figure 10.11 The Services of the remote computer accessed via MMC

Windows PowerShell Remoting remote management

To execute commands over Windows PowerShell Remoting to remote computers, complete the following steps:

1. Once the Windows PowerShell Remoting session to a remote computer is established (see the *Configuring Windows PowerShell Remoting* chapter lab later in this chapter), you may want to execute commands on the remote computer.
2. Enter the `ipconfig` command and press *Enter* to learn the IP address of the remote computer (see *Figure 10.12*)

3. Enter the `hostname` command and press *Enter* to learn the hostname of the remote computer (see *Figure 10.12*):

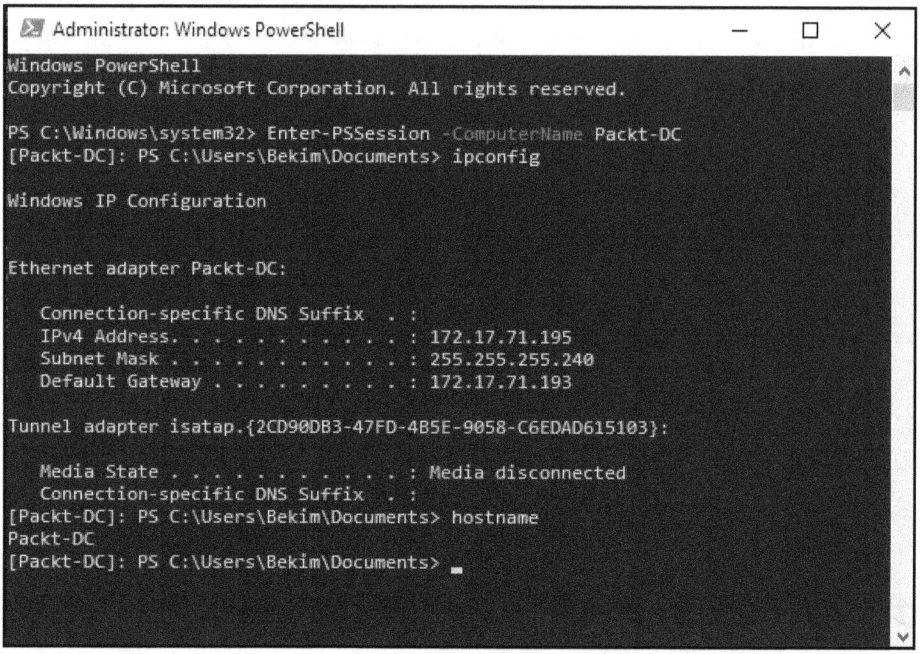

Figure 10.12 Executing commands on a remote computer

Configuring Remote Assistance including Easy Connect

Remote Assistance in Windows 10 features **Easy Connect**, which enables connection and control over the password between the invitee and trusted helper. Easy Connect simplifies the entire process through the use of a password. Once the trusting relationship is established between invitee and trusted helper, the password can be removed if the contact files are exchanged.

Using Easy Connect with Remote Assistance

To **configure** Remote Assistance including the Easy Connect app in your Windows 10 computer, complete the following steps:

1. Press the Windows key + *R* to start the **Run** dialog box.
2. In the **Run** dialog box, enter `msra` and press *Enter*.
3. In the **Windows Remote Assistance** wizard, select **Invite someone you trust to help you**.
4. On the **How do you want to invite trusted helper?** page, select **Use Easy Connect** as shown in *Figure 10.13*:

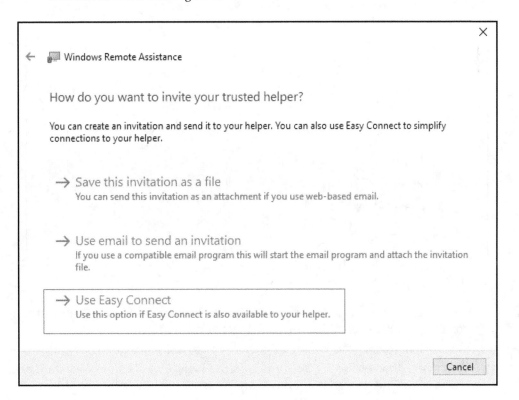

Figure 10.13 Using Easy Connect with Remote Assistance

5. Then, the Easy Connect password should be shared with the trusted helper.

6. On the other side, the trusted helper starts the **Windows Remote Assistance** and in the **Choose a way to connect to the other person's computer** window, selects **Use Easy Connect** as shown in *Figure 10.14*:

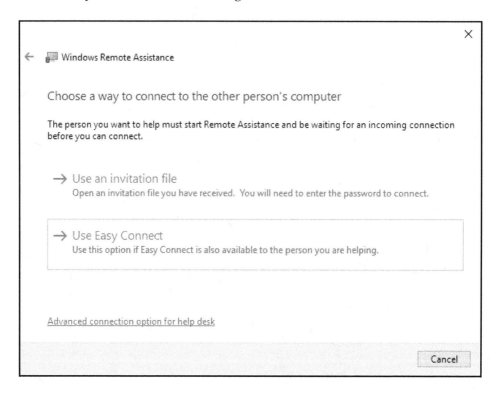

Figure 10.14 The trusted helper uses Easy Connect too

7. Then, the invitee clicks the **Yes** button in the **Windows Remote Assistance** dialog box to allow the trusted helper to connect of the invitee's computer.

8. In addition, the trusted helper **requests control** to the invitee's computer.

9. The invitee then clicks the **Yes** button in the **Windows Remote Assistance** dialog box to allow the trusted helper to share control of the invitee's desktop.

10. From now on, the trusted helper has **access and control** to provide the requested help to the invitee.

Chapter labs – Configuring Remote Desktop Connection, Installing EasyConnect from Microsoft Store, and Windows PowerShell Remoting

In these chapter labs, you will learn how to do the following:

- Configuring Remote Desktop Connection
- Installing EasyConnect from Microsoft Store
- Configuring Windows PowerShell Remoting

Configuring Remote Desktop Connection

To **configure** Remote Desktop Connection in your Windows 10 computer, complete the following steps:

1. Click the search box in the taskbar and enter `remote`.
2. Select **Open** on the right of the **Best match** list (see *Figure 10.15*):

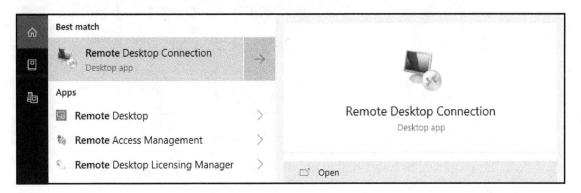

Figure 10.15 Opening Remote Desktop Connection in Windows 10

3. In the **Remote Desktop Connection** dialog box, in the **General** tab, enter the **name of the remote computer** and the **username**.
4. In the **Display** tab, within the **Display configuration** section, **change the size of your Remote Desktop** by dragging the slider.

5. In the **Local Resources** tab, in the **Local devices and resources** section, select **Printers** and **Clipboard**.

6. Return to the **General** tab, and click **Connect** as shown in *Figure 10.16*:

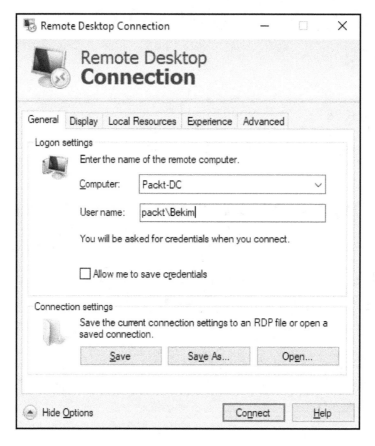

Figure 10.16 Configuring Remote Desktop Connection

7. The **Windows Security** dialog box asks you to enter a password, as shown in *Figure 10.17*, and then click **OK**:

Figure 10.17 Entering password to connect to a remote computer

8. In the **Remote Desktop Connection** dialog box, you may want to check **Don't ask me again for connections to this computer** if the identity of the remote computer cannot be verified (see *Figure 10.18*). Then, click the **Yes** button:

Figure 10.18 The certificate is not from a trusted certifying authority warning

9. Shortly after, you will get **connected** to the remote computer.

When you connect to the remote computer, if you are using a user who is part of the domain, then you must use the `domain\username` format in the username field of the **Remote Desktop Connection** dialog box.

Installing EasyConnect from Microsoft Store

To **install** the EasyConnect app in your Windows 10 computer from Microsoft Store, complete the following steps:

1. Press the Windows key + *R* to start the **Run** dialog box.
2. In the **Run** dialog box, enter `ms-windows-store:` and press *Enter*.
3. In the **Microsoft Store** window, click the **search icon** and enter `easyconnect`.
4. From the list of the search results, select **EasyConnect** as shown in *Figure 10.19*:

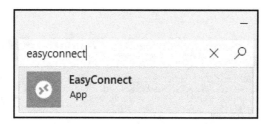

Figure 10.19 Installing EasyConnect app from Microsoft Store

5. On the **EasyConnect** page, click the **Get** button.
6. In the **EasyConnect** dialog box, ensure that the **System Drive** is selected and then click **Install** (see *Figure 10.20*):

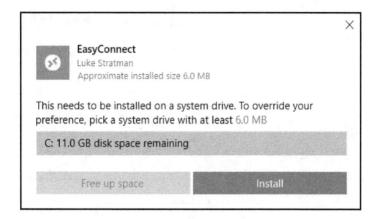

Figure 10.20 Easy Connect requires a system drive to be installed

7. Once the EasyConnect app gets installed, you can then launch it from the Start menu.

8. In the **Use RSA?** dialog box, click **Yes** if you want to use an RSA key container to encrypt your passwords, as shown in *Figure 10.21*:

Figure 10.21 Using RSA to encrypt passwords with EasyConnect

9. Shortly after, the EasyConnect app gets opened, as shown in *Figure 10.22*:

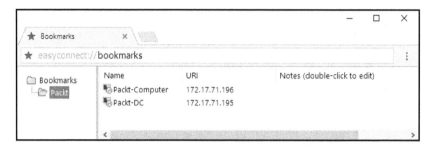

Figure 10.22 EasyConnect app in action

Configuring Windows PowerShell Remoting

To **configure** Windows PowerShell Remoting in your Windows 10 computer, complete the following steps:

1. In a remote computer, click the search box on the taskbar and enter `powershell`.

2. Right-click **Windows PowerShell** from the **Best match** list and click **Run as administrator** from the context menu (see *Figure 10.23*):

Figure 10.23 Opening Windows PowerShell with elevated privileges

3. In the **Windows PowerShell** window, enter the `winrm quickconfig` command and press *Enter* to set up the Windows Remote Management service as shown in *Figure 10.24*:

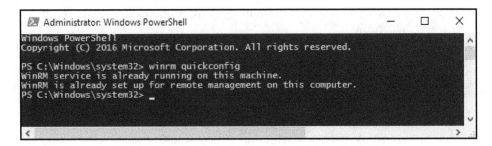

Figure 10.24 Setting up the Windows Remote Management service in a remote computer

4. In a local computer, right-click the Start button to open the system administrator menu.
5. Click **Windows PowerShell (Admin)**, and click the **Yes** button when asked **Do you want to allow this app to make changes to your device?**
6. In the **Windows PowerShell** window, enter the `Enter-PSSession -ComputerName <hostname>` command and press *Enter* to establish the Windows PowerShell Remoting session to the remote computer as shown *Figure 10.25*:

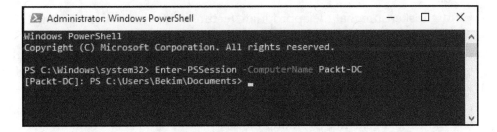

Figure 10.25 Establishing a remote PowerShell session

 If in the local computer the current connection type is set to public, then you might want to enter the `Enable-PSRemoting -Force -SkipNetworkProfileCheck` command and press *Enter* to enable the Windows Remote Management service. Once you enable WinRM, then enter the `Enter-PSSession -Computername "host" -Credential "host\administrator"` command and press *Enter* to establish a Windows PowerShell Remoting session with a remote computer.

Summary

We can summarize the chapter with the following points:

- The tool you choose for remote management depends largely on the task you are going to accomplish.
- The Remote Desktop Connection is a built-in tool that can be used to access a computer remotely over the RDP.
- The Microsoft Remote Desktop app is the Microsoft Store app that lets you connect to a remote PC or to the virtual apps and desktops made available by you.
- The 3389 port needs to be enabled in the remote computer's Windows Firewall for the Remote Desktop Connection to work properly
- Remote Assistance allows you to provide help on a friend's remote computer or invite a remote friend to offer you assistance on your computer.
- Windows PowerShell Remoting enables system administrators to execute commands on remote computers.
- Windows PowerShell Remoting also provides a scripting environment.
- The MMC is another way of managing applications in both local and remote computers by loading snap-ins into a console.
- Based on which remote management tool you have decided to use, it is necessary to configure the remote computer to enable the selected remote management tool.
- You must ensure that the appropriate feature is enabled in the Windows Firewall of the remote computer to allow the management of the remote computer.
- In order to be able to remotely manage settings on a remote computer via the MMC, you must make the appropriate Windows Firewall settings on the remote computer.
- In the case of Windows PowerShell Remoting, you must first enable Windows Remote Management by running the `winrm quickconfig` command, and then enable Windows PowerShell Remoting.
- Remote Assistance in Windows 10 features EasyConnect, which enables connection and control over the password between the invitee and trusted helper.

Questions

1. Remote Desktop Connection is a built-in tool that can be used to access a computer remotely over the **Remote Desktop Protocol** (**RDP**).
    1. True
    2. False

2. The 3389 port needs to be enabled in the remote computer's Windows Firewall for the _____ to work properly.

3. Which of the following are Remote Desktop types in Windows 10? (Choose two).
    1. Remote Desktop Connection
    2. Microsoft Remote Desktop
    3. EasyConnect
    4. Windows PowerShell Remoting

4. Remote Assistance in Windows 10 features Windows PowerShell Remoting, which enables connection and control over the password between the invitee and trusted helper.
    1. True
    2. False

5. It is mandatory to ensure that the appropriate feature is enabled on _____ of a remote computer to allow the management of a remote computer.

6. Other than Remote Desktop and Remote Assistance, which two further options are supported by Windows 10 for remote management? (Choose two).
    1. Remote Desktop Connection built-in
    2. Microsoft Remote Desktop app
    3. Windows PowerShell Remoting
    4. Microsoft Management Console (MMC)

7. The MMC is another way of managing applications in both local and remote computers by loading snap-ins into the console.
    1. True
    2. False

8. _____ enables system administrators to execute commands on remote computers.

9. Which of the following needs to be enabled so Windows PowerShell Remoting becomes functional?
    1. Remote Assistance
    2. Remote Desktop
    3. EasyConnect
    4. Windows Remote Management

Further reading

- **Remote Desktop clients**: `https://docs.microsoft.com/en-us/windows-server/remote/remote-desktop-services/clients/remote-desktop-clients`
- **Running Remote Commands**: `https://docs.microsoft.com/en-us/powershell/scripting/learn/remoting/running-remote-commands?view=powershell-6`
- **Manage your Windows computer with the Microsoft Management Console**: `https://www.geeksinphoenix.com/blog/post/2016/04/21/manage-your-windows-computer-with-the-microsoft-management-console.aspx`

11
Configuring Updates

Checking for updates is considered to be one of the most important Windows 10 post-installation tasks. In order to be aware of such important task, this chapter aims to focus your attention on Windows updates in Windows 10. With that in mind, this chapter explains updating in Windows 10 in general, and the **Windows Update** feature in particular. Specifically, this chapter will explain methods for updating and upgrading Windows 10 via **Windows Update**; **Windows Update** features, such as **Change active hours**, **View update history**, and **Advanced options**; going back to the previous version of Windows 10; and how to join the **Windows Insider Program**. Other than that, you will get to know the types of Windows 10 servicing channels, such as **Semi-Annual Channel (Targeted)**, **Semi-Annual Channel**, and **Long-Term Servicing Channel (LTSC)** so that you learn how to manage updates and upgrades in Windows 10 via **Windows Update**. Each topic is accompanied by step-by-step instructions driven by targeted, easy-to-understand graphics. This chapter concludes with a chapter lab on updating Windows Store apps.

In this chapter, we will cover the following topics:

- Configuring **Windows Update** options
- Managing the update history
- Rolling back updates
- Implementing Insider Preview
- **Current Branch (CB)**, **Current Branch for Business (CBB)**, and **Long-Term Servicing Branch (LTSB)** scenarios
- Chapter lab—updating Windows Store apps

Technical requirements

In order to complete the labs for this chapter, you will need the following equipment:

- PC with Windows 10 Enterprise, at least 8 GB of RAM, 500 GB of HDD, and access to the internet

Configuring Windows Update options

Ever since Windows 2000 Professional, after almost every installation of the Windows OS, I have immediately checked for **Windows Update**. I am sure you did the same too. And trust me, that approach is considered a best practice because that way, your computer is able to receive roll-up updates and feature upgrades. Above all, it receives security updates, too, which will keep your computer safe and protected from external threats, such as malware and hackers. Therefore, it is not good at all to neglect or, for whatever reason, disable the **Windows Update** process. So, when talking about **Windows Update** in general and *Windows 10* in particular, things have changed compared to previous Windows OSes. In Windows 10, you can no longer turn off **security updates**. That is because Windows 10 is categorized as a **Windows as a service**. Regularly updating your computer and keeping it up to date, both from the point of view of features as well as security, is known as **servicing**.

Updating and upgrading Windows 10

As you may know, Microsoft releases security updates every second **Tuesday** of every month, and that is unofficially known as **Patch Tuesday**. So, with Windows 10, in addition to monthly updates, Microsoft has set the practice of issuing feature upgrades twice a year. They are known as spring and fall feature upgrades, and because of that, these days we encounter Windows 10 builds with names such as **Windows 10 April 2018 Update**, and **Windows 10 October 2018 Update**. As such, these milestone builds are released by Microsoft as an entire package that includes all built-in updates and upgrades. The same serves as an upgrade of your existing Windows OS, or as a new installation.

New Windows updates

Since Windows 8, Microsoft has introduced a new **Windows Update** almost entirely different from what it was before. This is also evident in Windows 10, both from the interface perspective and from the way updates are downloaded and installed. As you know, in previous versions of Windows, users had the option to turn off Windows updates (see *Figure 11.1*), something that is not available with Windows 10. Also, in earlier versions of Windows, you could not receive the new version of Windows through Windows updates, while in Windows 10, your device is receiving the **new builds** of Windows 10 over Windows Updates. This is demonstrated in the following screenshot:

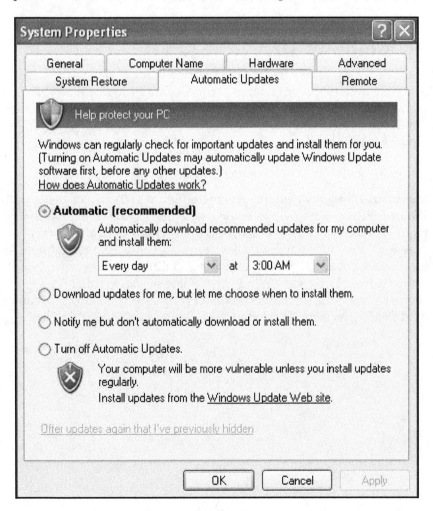

Figure 11.1: An option whereby Windows updates are turned off in Windows XP

In Windows 10, Windows updates have undergone a slight change in terms of its interface, too. The following options are available within the **Windows Update** page (see *Figure 11.2*):

- **Change active hours**: This option enables you to set active hours in order to avoid restarting your Windows 10 while you are working on your device.
- **View update history**: This option displays the list of updates that your device has received and their statuses. Also, it enables you to uninstall updates and provides you access to recovery options.
- **Advanced options**: This option enables you to set up update options and update notifications, pause updates, and to choose when updates are installed.

Updating Windows 10

Once updates are released by Microsoft as mentioned in the *Updating and Upgrading Windows 10* section, because of the fact that your Windows 10 system periodically checks for the latest updates and security features, then it may display a message similar to **You need some updates** in the **system tray**. Clicking on that message will redirect you to **Windows Update** from where you will then manage the available updates.

There are two ways to update Windows 10:

- **Microsoft Windows Update server** (see Figure 11.2) is a way of updating Windows 10 usually used by home users (that is, non-domain users). All that is required is access to the internet, and then Windows 10 will take care of downloading and installing the latest updates and security features. As you may have noticed, this method generates lots of traffic between your Windows 10 computer and Microsoft's Windows Update server. For that reason, in a corporate network, the WSUS method for updating Windows 10 computers is used instead, as demonstrated in the following screenshot:

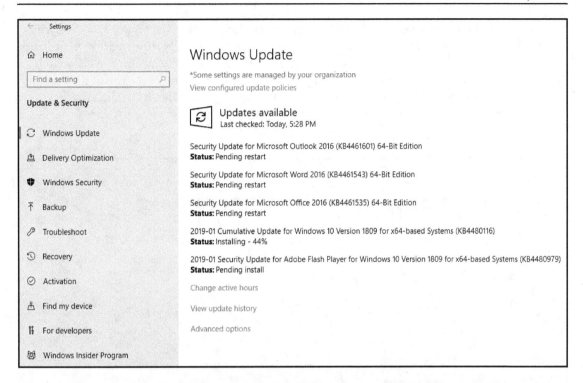

Figure 11.2: Updating Windows 10 from Microsoft's Windows Update server through Windows Update

Nowadays, according to Microsoft, Windows 10 updates released through the so-called Patch Tuesday are known to be **B** releases and these usually include security fixes, bug patches, and other non-security fixes. However, because of the continued intensity of Windows 10 development, Microsoft also releases updates in the third and fourth week of each month, which are known as **C** and **D** releases, respectively. Interestingly, these updates are not automatic but appear in your Windows 10 device after you click the **Check for updates** button in **Windows Update**.

- The **Windows Server Update Services** (**WSUS**) server (see *Figure 11.3*) is a way of updating Windows 10 in a corporate network. Usually, this method is utilized by organizations in order to avoid generating any external traffic because such traffic is reserved for business-priority services. By deploying WSUS, the end-user devices in the corporate network will receive updates from the WSUS server, while the WSUS server downloads the updates directly from the Microsoft Windows Update server:

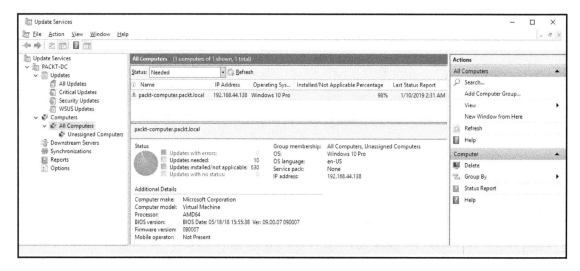

Figure 11.3: WSUS reports that updates are required by a client computer

Upgrading Windows 10

As mentioned earlier, because Windows 10 is categorized by Microsoft as **Windows as a service**, your existing Windows 10 system will receive the new Windows 10 builds as an upgrade option twice a year. All that is done through **Windows Update**, as shown in Figure 11.4:

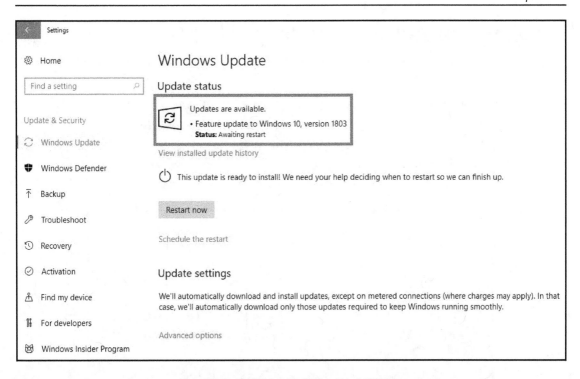

Figure 11.4: Upgrading Windows 10 to Windows 10 April 2018 Update

In Windows 10, if you don't want to receive new builds, then you can benefit from an option known as **Defer feature updates**. To learn more about the **Defer feature updates** feature, navigate to the following URL: `https://www.onmsft.com/news/mean-defer-feature-updates-windows-10`.

Managing update history

Checking the status of updates received by your Windows 10 device after every installation update is considered to be a best practice. The **Update history** page of **Windows Update** enables you to view the updates that have been installed and those that have failed to install. You will notice that every update received by your Windows 10 device contains a unique name, the status with a date, and, if you click on each update, you will be redirected to the **Microsoft Support website**, where detailed information on an update is presented.

Viewing your update history

To **view** your update history in your Windows 10 computer using **Windows Update**, complete the following steps:

1. Press the Windows key + *I* to open **Windows Settings**.
2. In the **Windows Settings** window, click **Updates & Security**.
3. In the **Updates & Security** page, by default, **Windows Update** in the navigation menu is highlighted.
4. Select **View update history**, as in *Figure 11.5*:

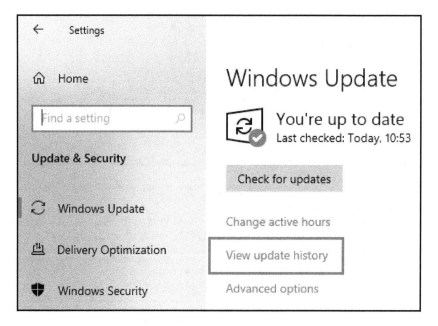

Figure 11.5: Viewing your update history through Windows Updates

Uninstalling an update

To **uninstall** an update in your Windows 10 computer using the **Update history** page, complete the following steps:

1. **Repeat steps 1 to 4** from the previous section.
2. In the **View update history** page, select **Uninstall updates**, as shown in Figure 11.6:

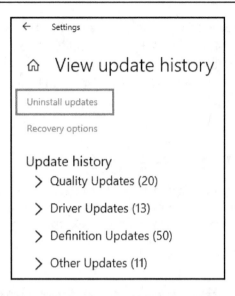

Figure 11.6: An option of uninstalling updates in the View update history page

3. In the **Installed Updates** window, select an **update** and then click **Uninstall** (see Figure 11.7):

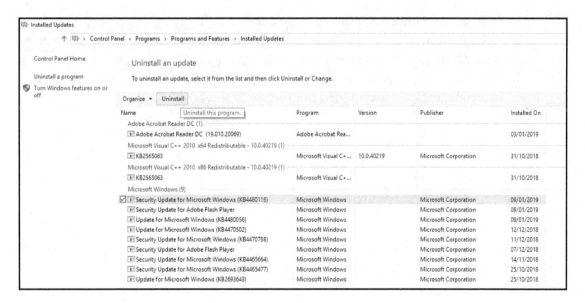

Figure 11.7: Uninstalling an update in Windows 10

4. In the **Uninstall an update** dialog box, click the **Yes** button.
5. Shortly after, the **Microsoft Windows** window displays the **bar** that indicates the uninstalling of an update.
6. Once the update has been **uninstalled**, you will be asked to **Restart Now** your Windows 10 computer.

Rolling back updates

You may have already completed the installation of the latest version of Windows 10, and it happened that you have encountered problems and issues with it. Then, you have nothing else left to do with the new version of Windows 10 except roll back to the previous version of Windows 10.

Rolling back to the previous version of Windows 10

To **roll back** to the previous version of Windows 10, complete the following steps:

1. Press the Windows key + *I* to open **Windows Settings**.
2. In the **Windows Settings** window, click **Updates & Security**.
3. In the **Updates & Security** page, select **Recovery** from the navigation menu.
4. In the **Recovery** page, within the **Go back to the previous version of Windows 10** section, click the **Get started** button (see *Figure 11.11*):

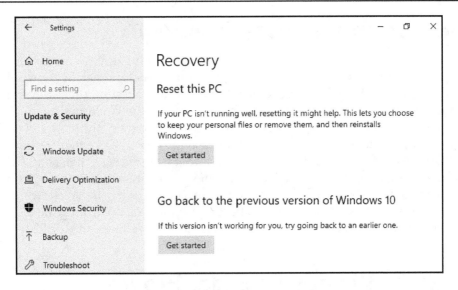

Figure 11.11: Rolling back to the previous version of Windows 10

5. In the **Go back to earlier build** dialog box, provide the reason **Why are you going back?** and then click **Next**.

6. Before you go back, try installing the latest updates by clicking the **Check for updates** button.

7. If **Check for updates** fails to solve your problem, repeat steps 1 to 6 and, instead of clicking on **Check for updates**, click **No thanks**.

8. In the **What you need to know** page, click **Next**.

9. In the **Don't get locked out** page, note down the **username and password** and then click **Next**.

10. In the **Thanks for trying out this build** page, click the **Go back to earlier build** button, as in Figure 11.12:

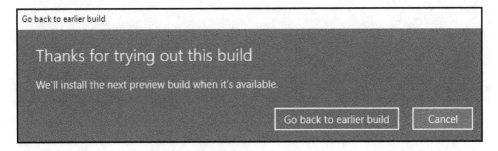

Figure 11.12: Going back to the previous build of Windows 10

Implementing Insider Preview

I recall years ago how Microsoft, through so-called **beta testing**, invited interested individuals to test products during the development phase before they became public release. Nowadays, with the introduction of Windows 10, the testing process has assumed another form by being structured into something known as the **Windows Insider Program**. In the same way as before, through the Windows Insider Program, the so-called **enthusiast crowd** has the option to test the **Windows 10 release previews** before they become public releases. Participation in the program is optional and it features Fast, Slow, and Release Preview rings. Unlike before, when aspects of Windows 10 are being tested, Microsoft requires feedback from Windows Insiders. While this book covers the Windows 10 October 2018 Update, as a Windows Insider, it may be the case that you are testing the latest developments of an incremental build that is expected to be released in April 2019.

Joining the Windows Insider Program

To **join** the Windows Insider Program in testing the new features of Windows 10, complete the following steps:

1. Press the Windows key + *I* to open **Windows Settings**.
2. In the **Windows Settings** window, click **Updates & Security**.
3. In the **Updates & Security** page, select **Windows Insider Program** from the navigation menu.
4. In the **Windows Insider Program** page, within the **Get Insider Preview builds** section, click **Get started** (see *Figure 11.13*):

Figure 11.13: Joining the Windows Insider program

5. In the **Pick an account to get started** window, click **Link an account**.

6. In the **Sign in** dialog box, select **Microsoft account** and then click **Continue**, as in Figure 11.14:

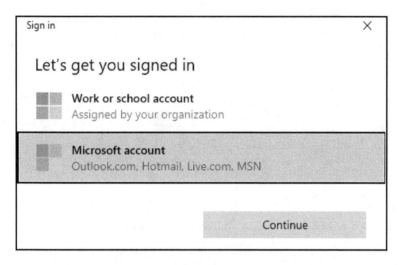

Figure 11.14: Joining the Windows Insider Program with a Microsoft account

7. Enter your Microsoft account and click **Next**.
8. Enter your password and click **Sign in**.
9. In the **What kind of content would you like to receive?**, select **Active development of Windows** and then click **Confirm**.
10. In the **A better Windows for everyone** window, take your time to read both the **Microsoft Insider Privacy Statement** and **Microsoft Insider Program Agreement**, and then click **Confirm**.
11. In the **One more step to go...**, click **Restart Now** (see Figure 11.15):

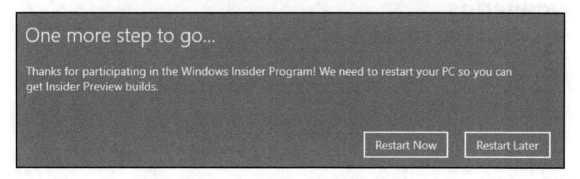

Figure 11.15: Restarting your Windows 10 device after signing in to the Windows Insider Program

12. Once *restarting* completes, sign in to your Windows 10 device and go ahead and **Check for updates** so you can receive all of the latest Windows content, including regular new builds of Windows 10, as in Figure 11.16:

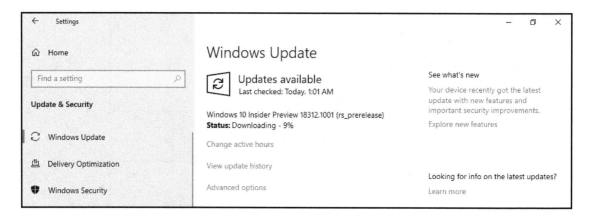

Figure 11.16: Downloading Windows 10 Insider Preview

 Alpha testing is usually a phase of a software development life cycle in which a group of internal users test the software with the aim of finding bugs and ensuring the quality of the software.

Current Branch, Current Branch for Business, and Long-Term Servicing Branch scenarios

From what has been discussed so far, Windows 10 has incorporated new stuff in almost every aspect. From Windows Update to the Windows Insider Program, these are just a few of the new things introduced with Windows 10. Similarly, the three servicing channel options, such as **CB**, **CBB**, and **LTSB**, represent a new approach in terms of how updates are managed in Windows 10.

Current Branch servicing branch

CB is now known as **Semi-Annual Channel (Targeted)** and presents the latest version of Windows 10. **Semi-Annual Channel (Targeted)** means the updates are ready for download for most home users. This servicing channel enables your Windows 10 device to receive all of the updates and the latest upgrade from the Microsoft Windows Update server within a few days of their release.

Verifying the Semi-Annual Channel (Targeted) servicing channel

To verify the **Semi-Annual Channel (Targeted)** servicing channel in your Windows 10 computer, complete the following steps:

1. Press the Windows key + *I* to open **Windows Settings**.
2. In the **Windows Settings** window, click **Updates & Security**.
3. In the **Updates & Security** page, by default, the **Windows Update** in the navigation menu is highlighted.
4. Select **Advanced options**.
5. In the **Advanced options** page, within the **Choose when updates are installed** section, you will find the chosen servicing branch on your computer (see Figure 11.17):

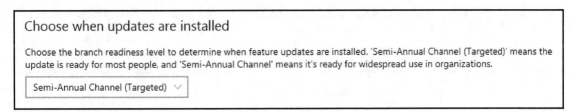

Figure 11.17: Verifying the Semi-Annual Channel (Targeted) servicing branch

Current Branch for Business

CBB is now known as **Semi-Annual Channel** and presents the latest version of Windows 10 with four months' deferred updates from the official release of the latest version of Windows 10. **Semi-Annual Channel** means the updates are ready for widespread use in organizations by providing sufficient time for the organizations to use the **Semi-Annual Channel (Targeted)** computers for pilot deployments to ensure compatibility with existing apps and infrastructure. Once **Semi-Annual Channel (Targeted)** is declared as **Semi-Annual Channel** by Microsoft, it will then be serviced with quality updates for a minimum of 18 months after it is released.

Enabling the Semi-Annual Channel servicing channel

To enable the **Semi-Annual Channel** servicing channel in your Windows 10 computer, complete the following steps:

1. **Repeat steps 1 to 4** from the *Verifying the Semi-Annual Channel (Targeted) servicing channel* section.
2. In the **Advanced options** page, within the **Choose when updates are installed** section, select the **Semi-Annual Channel** servicing branch, as shown in *Figure 11.18*:

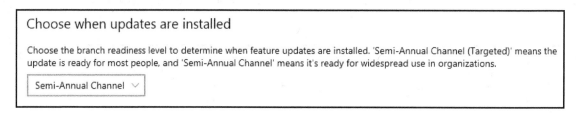

Figure 11.18: Enabling the Semi-Annual Channel servicing branch

Long-Term Servicing Branch

LTSB is now known as **Long-Term Servicing Channel** (**LTSC**) and reminds us of earlier versions of Windows on which we have been receiving new updates, but not new features (that is, upgrades). LTSC lacks a considerable number of programs. In addition, this servicing branch has a minimum servicing lifetime of 10 years. In the same way as **Semi-Annual Channel**, the LTSC servicing channel is also aimed at businesses, the only difference being that its functionality and features don't change over time.

Verifying the Long-Term Servicing Channel servicing branch

To verify the LTSC servicing branch in your Windows 10 computer, complete the following steps:

1. Right-click the **Start** button and select **Windows PowerShell (Admin)**.
2. Enter the `gwmi win32_operatingsystem | select OperatingSystemSKU` command and press *Enter*.
3. A value of 48 means you are using the **Semi-Annual Channel (Targeted)** servicing branch, whereas a value of 125 means you are using the LTSC servicing branch

 Changes to the names of the three service branches in Windows 10 have been introduced since Windows 10 version 1709.

Chapter lab – updating Windows Store apps

In this chapter lab, you will learn how to do the following:

- Update Windows Store apps

Updating Windows Store apps

To update apps in your Windows 10 computer using **Microsoft Store**, complete the following steps:

1. Click the Microsoft Store icon on the taskbar to open it.
2. In the **Microsoft Store** window, click **see more...** on the far right-hand side, next to your profile picture.

3. From the menu displayed, select **Downloads and updates**, as shown in Figure 11.19:

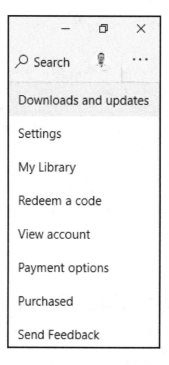

Figure 11.19: Downloading and updating apps in the Microsoft Store

4. In the **Downloads and updates** page, click the **Get updates** button, or, alternatively, select which apps to update manually.

 If you don't want the updating of apps in the Microsoft Store to be effected automatically, then, in the Microsoft Store settings, you can turn off **Update Apps Automatically**. In doing so, you may want to update the apps manually.

Summary

We can summarize this chapter with the following points:

- In Windows 10, you can no longer turn off security updates.
- Windows 10 is categorized as a Windows as a Service.
- Microsoft releases security updates every second Tuesday of every month, and that is unofficially known as *Patch Tuesday*.
- In addition to monthly updates, Microsoft has established a practice of issuing feature upgrades twice a year.
- With Windows 10, Microsoft has introduced a new Windows Update that is almost entirely different from what it was before.
- In Windows 10, your device is receiving the new builds of Windows 10 over Windows Updates.
- **Change active hours** enables you to set active hours in order to avoid restarting Windows 10 while you are working on your device.
- **View update history** displays the list of updates that your device has received and their statuses. Also, it enables you to uninstall updates and provides you with access to recovery options.
- **Advanced options** enable you to set up update options, update notifications, pause updates, and to choose when updates are installed.
- Microsoft Windows Update server is a way of updating Windows 10 usually used by home users.
- The **Windows Server Update Services** (**WSUS**) server is a way of updating Windows 10 in a corporate network.
- The **Rolling back updates** option enables you to go back to the previous version of Windows 10.
- Windows Insider Program enables interested users to test the Windows 10 Release Previews before they become public releases.
- **Semi-Annual Channel (Targeted)** means the updates are ready for download for most home users.
- **Semi-Annual Channel** means the updates are ready for widespread use in organizations.
- The **Long-Term Servicing Channel** (**LTSC**) servicing channel is recommended for businesses where functionality and features don't change over time.

Questions

1. Microsoft releases security updates every second Tuesday of every month, and that is unofficially known as Patch Tuesday.
   1. True
   2. False

2. _____ servicing branch is recommended for businesses where functionality and features don't change over time.

3. Which of the following options are available on the **Windows Update** page? (Choose two)
   1. Uninstall updates
   2. Change active hours
   3. Advanced options
   4. Recovery options

4. **Advanced options** enable you to set up update options, update notifications, pause updates, and to choose when updates are installed.
   1. True
   2. False

5. _____ enables you to set active hours in order to avoid restarting Windows 10 while you are working on your device.

6. Which of the following servicing channels are introduced with Windows 10?
   1. Semi-Annual Channel (Targeted)
   2. Semi-Annual Channel
   3. Long-Term Servicing Channel (LTSC)
   4. All of the above

7. In Windows 10, you can no longer turn off security updates.
   1. True
   2. False

8. _____ server is a way of updating Windows 10 in a corporate network.

9. Which of the following constitute methods for updating Windows 10 devices? (Choose two)
   1. Microsoft Windows Updates server
   2. Windows 10 Installation Media
   3. Windows Server Update Services (WSUS) server
   4. Going back to the previous version of Windows 10

10. In addition to monthly updates, Microsoft has established a practice of issuing feature upgrades twice a year.
    1. True
    2. False

11. _____ option enables you to go back to the previous version of Windows 10.

Further reading

For more information on what was covered in this chapter, check out the following links:

- **Overview of Windows as a service**: `https://docs.microsoft.com/en-us/windows/deployment/update/waas-overview`
- **Update Windows 10 in enterprise deployments**: `https://docs.microsoft.com/en-us/windows/deployment/update/`
- **Windows Update and Security settings in Windows 10**: `https://www.thewindowsclub.com/windows-update-security-settings-windows-10`
- **Windows 10 Update and Servicing Branches Explained**: `https://www.makeuseof.com/tag/windows-10-update-servicing-branches/`
- **Troubleshoot problems updating Windows 10**: `https://support.microsoft.com/en-us/help/4089834/windows-10-troubleshoot-problems-updating`

12
Monitoring Windows 10

This chapter is designed to teach you the tools to monitor your Windows 10 device system resources. By understanding the importance of key system components and how their performance affects the overall performance of your Windows 10 device, it will help you to maintain the optimal performance of your device both in normal and heavy use. With that in mind, this chapter covers Event Viewer, Task Manager, Resource Monitor, Performance Monitor, and Reliability Monitor. Anyone of these tools, or all together, will enable you to run both real-time monitoring of the system resources, and create a baseline. Other than that, you will get to know the Windows Security Center that includes Windows Defender that ensures that your Windows 10 device is kept safe and protected from threats. Each topic is accompanied with step-by-step instructions driven by targeted, easy-to-understand graphics. The chapter concludes with *Chapter labs* section on Configuring indexing options, configuring Windows Defender Advanced Threat Detection, and troubleshooting performance issues.

In this chapter, we will cover the following topics:

- Configuring and analyzing Event Viewer logs
- Configuring event subscriptions
- Monitoring performance using Task Manager
- Monitoring performance using Resource Monitor
- Monitoring performance using Performance Monitor and Data Collector Sets
- Monitoring system resources
- Monitoring and managing printers
- Managing client security using Windows Defender
- Managing security using the Windows Defender Security Center
- Evaluating system stability using Reliability Monitor
- Chapter labs - configuring indexing options, configuring Windows Defender Advanced Threat Detection, and troubleshooting performance issues

Technical requirements

In order to complete the labs for this chapter, you will need the following equipment:

- A PC with Windows 10 Pro, at least 4 GB of RAM, 500 GB of HDD space, and access to the internet

Configuring and analyzing Event Viewer logs

The **Event Viewer**, as the name suggests, is a **Microsoft Management Console** (**MMC**) snap-in that enables IT professionals to view events in Windows 10. In addition, it servers as handy troubleshooting tool because it provides detailed information about what is going on in your Windows 10 computer. It should be acknowledged that the Event Viewer is not a new feature in Windows 10, but a legacy utility inherited from earlier versions of Windows. As such, due to its importance in maintaining your computer system, it is recommended that each user knows about the Event Viewer. The **Windows Event log** service which is responsible for the Event Viewer, starts automatically when Windows 10 starts.

There are five types of events that you can monitor with *Event Viewer*.

- **Application**: Displays applications or programs events.
- **Security**: Displays security related events.
- **Setup**: Displays applications setup events.
- **System**: Displays Windows system components events.
- **Forwarded Events**: Displays remote computers events.

Other than displaying the types of events, by clicking at a certain type of event, Event Viewer displays three main event notifications in both XML and plain text format:

- **Error**: Represents a problem on your Windows 10 device that you need immediately.
- **Warning**: Represents an alert that needs to be taken into consideration because it might become a problem.
- **Information**: Represents information triggered by activity on your computer system or remote.

Analyzing Event Viewer logs

To **run** Event Viewer in your Windows 10 computer and analyze the event logs, complete the following steps:

1. Press Windows key + *R* to open **Run**.
2. Enter `eventvwr.msc` and press *Enter*.
3. In the *Event Viewer* window, expand **Windows Logs**.
4. Click **Application** event type, and view the **application notifications** in the details pane as in *Figure 12.1*:

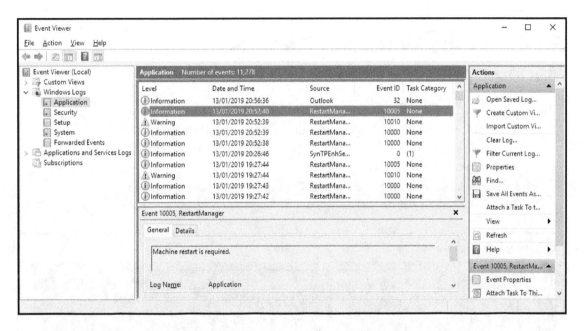

Figure 12.1. Event Viewer and the event notifications in Windows 10

5. Click a *specific event* in the details pane, and then click **General** and **Details** tabs to learn more about that specific event.

Configuring event subscriptions

In the section: *Configuring and analyzing Event Viewer logs,* you have learned that Forwarded Events displays event logs from remote computers. This is useful particularly for system administrators when analyzing event viewer logs on servers. Because manually connecting to servers on a regular basis can be inconvenient. Thus, event subscription enables automatic collection of event logs from servers. Prior to configuring event subscriptions, it is required to enable **Windows Remote Management** service on the source computer to allow remote administration. On the collector computer, you need to enable **Windows Event Collector** service so it can collect events from remote devices.

Enabling the Windows Remote Management service

To **enable** Windows Remote Management service on a server, complete the following steps:

1. Right-click the Start button and select **Command Prompt (Admin)**.
2. Click the **Yes** button, when asked **Do you want to allow this app to make changes to your device?**.
3. In the **Administrator: Command Prompt** window, enter `winrm quickconfig` command and press *Enter* as in *Figure 12.2:*

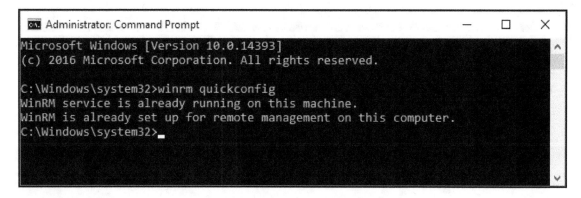

Figure 12.2. Enabling remote collection of events on the server

4. Enter `Y` and press *Enter.*

Enabling Windows Event Collector service

To **enable** Windows Event Collector service in a Windows 10 computer, complete the following steps:

1. Right-click the Start button and select **Windows PowerShell (Admin)**.
2. Click the **Yes** button, when asked **Do you want to allow this app to make changes to your device?**.
3. In the **Administrator: Windows PowerShell** window, enter `wecutil qc` command and press *Enter* as in *Figure 12.3*:

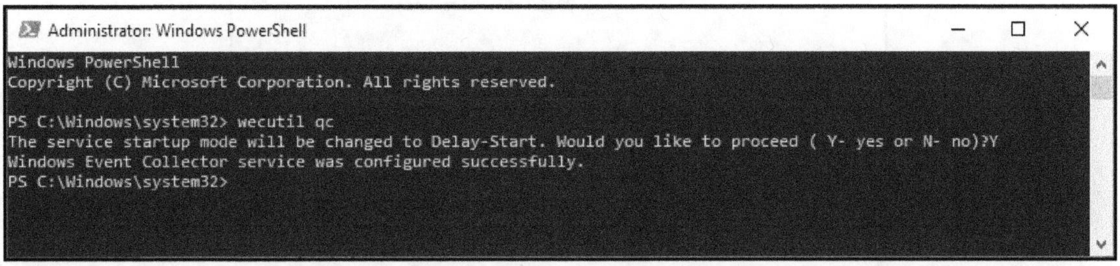

Figure 12.3. Enabling Windows 10 computer to view subscriptions

4. Enter `Y` and press *Enter*.

Creating Subscription...

To **create** event subscription in a Windows 10 computer, complete the following steps:

1. Press Windows key + *R* to open **Run**.
2. Enter `eventvwr.msc` and press *Enter*.

3. In the **Event Viewer** window, right-click **Subscriptions** and then select **Create Subscription...** from the context menu as shown in *Figure 12.4*:

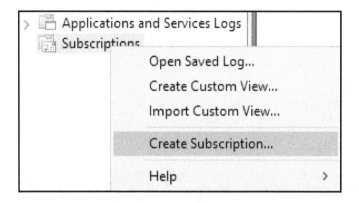

Figure 12.4. Creating an event subscription in Windows 10

4. In the **Subscriptions Properties** dialog box, enter a name and a description for the subscription, as in *Figure 12.5*:

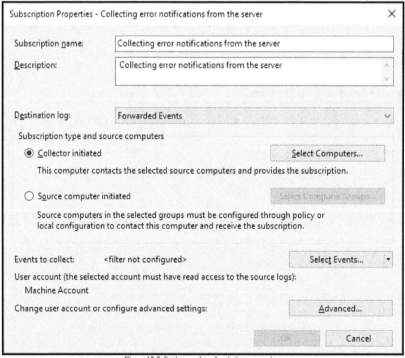

Figure 12.5. Setting up the subscription properties

5. Within **Subscription type and source computers** section, choose **Collector initiated** and then click **Select Computers...** button.
6. In the **Computers** dialog box, click **Add Domain Computers...** button.
7. In the **Select Computer** dialog box, enter the **name of the server** and click **OK**.
8. In the **Computers** dialog box, click **Test** button to test the connectivity with the server (see *Figure 12.6*) and then click **OK** twice:

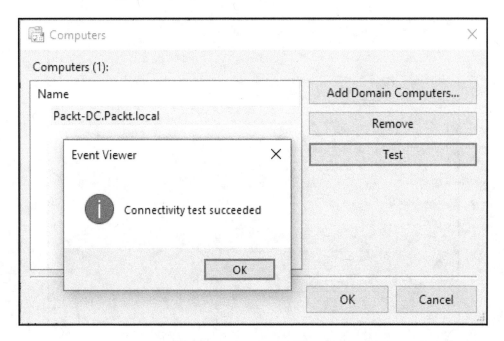

Figure 12.6. Testing connectivity with the server

9. Within the **Events to collect** section, click **Select Events...** button.

10. In the **Query Filter** dialog box, define **Logged**, **Event level**, and **Event logs** as in *Figure 12.7*, and then click **OK**:

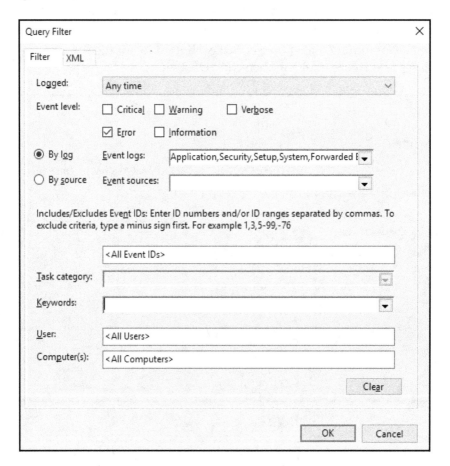

Figure 12.7. Defining the event criteria

11. Within **Events to collect** section, click **Select Events...** button.
12. Within **Change user account or configure advanced settings** section, click **Advanced...** button.

13. In the **Advanced Subscription Settings** dialog box, choose **Specific User** and click **User and Password...** button.

14. In the **Credentials for Subscription Source** dialog box, enter username and password of specific user and then click **OK**.

15. Click **OK** to close **Advanced Subscription Settings** dialog box (see *Figure 12.8*):

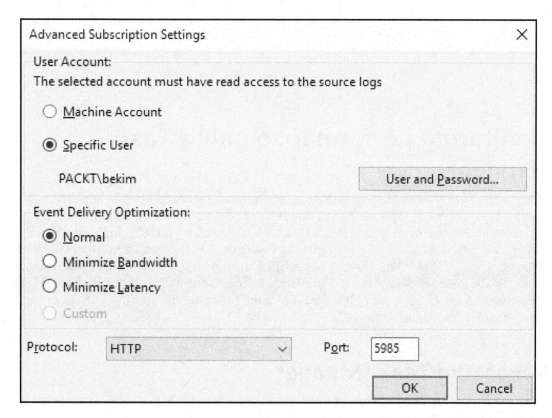

Figure 12.8. Setting up the user account

16. Click **OK** to save the subscription.

17. The newly created subscription is listed in the details pane of **Event Viewer** window as shown in *Figure 12.9*:

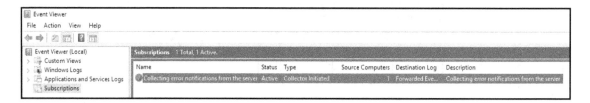

Figure 12.9. The newly created subscription becomes active once it is saved

Monitoring performance using Task Manager

Along with Event Viewer, also **Task Manager** is another legacy utility that enables monitoring the processes, performance, app history, startup, users, and services running on Windows 10 devices. In addition, Task Manager lets you start and stop applications and background processes. Task Manager offers a **Fewer details** view and a **More details** view of the system. By default, the Task Manager opens to showing the **running applications** in **Fewer details** view. While most users may only be interested in fewer details view of Task Manager window, IT professionals might prefer the **More details** view as it offers more detailed information in each tab.

Accessing Task Manager

To **access** Task Manager and view real-time information about key system components of the computer system, complete the following steps:

1. Press Windows key + *R* to open **Run**.
2. Enter `taskmgr.exe` and press *Enter*.
3. In the *Task Manager* window, in the lower-left corner select **More details**.
4. In the **More details** view of **Task Manager** window, click **Performance** tab (see *Figure 12.10*):

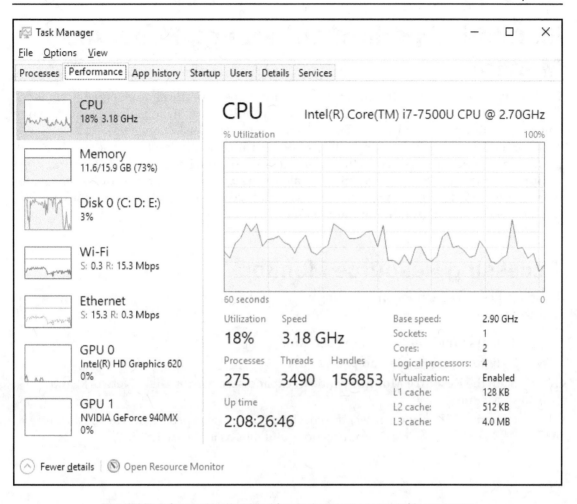

Figure 12.10. The Performance tab provides real-time information about key system components of the computer system

The key system components are considered to be the **CPU**, **memory**, **disk**, and **network** interface devices.

Monitoring performance using Resource Monitor

If recently, your Windows 10 computer is showing signs of performance degradation, then Microsoft has taken care to offer us the **Resource Monitor** tool that enables to monitor your computer's slow performance. Similar to Event Viewer and Task Manager, Resource Monitor too is a legacy monitoring utility that helps also identifying the cause of the performance problem. It provides the real-time usage of both hardware and software resources. Otherwise, Resource Monitor is said to be an advanced form of Task Manager as it enables to dive deep into the actual processes and see how they affect the performance of key system components of the computer system.

Accessing Resource Monitor

To **access** Resource Monitor and creating a real-time filter of processes, complete the following steps:

1. Press Windows key + *R* to open **Run**.
2. Enter `resmon.exe` and press *Enter*.
3. In the **Resource Monitor** window, expand sections for **Disk**, **Network**, and **Memory**.
4. In the **CPU** section, select the check box of a certain process to **create filter** for that process across all four sections and tabs as in *Figure 12.11*:

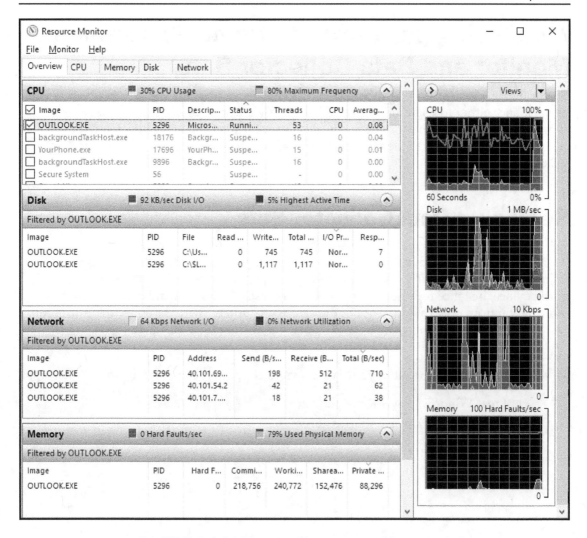

Figure 12.11. Filtering the Outlook process across all key system components of the computer system

You can open Resource Monitor by using the link on the **Performance** tab of **Task Manager**.

Monitoring performance using Performance Monitor and Data Collector Sets

Performance Monitor is an MMC snap-in that enables you to monitor Windows 10 device performance either in real time or from a log file. By creating **Data Collector Sets** to configure and schedule performance counters, event traces, and configuration data collection, you can analyze the performance results in formats such as a line graph, histogram bar, or as report.

Setting up Data Collector Sets

The Data Collector Set is the data collected from the computer system in order to evaluate its performance. To achieve that, the Data Collector Set uses **counters** and **instance**. Like that, counters represent the various hardware components that are used to measure their performance, instance represent a unique copy of a selected object and are used to collect information from only that instance of the selected counter. Then, the collected information is stored in a log file at the location that is specified during the creation of the Data Collector Set.

To set up a Data Collector Set in your Windows 10 computer, complete the following steps:

1. Press Windows key + *R* to open **Run**.
2. Enter perfmon.msc and press *Enter*.

3. In the **Performance Monitor** window, expand **Data Collector Sets**, right-click **User Defined**, select **New** from the context menu and then **Data Collector Set** as in *Figure 12.12*:

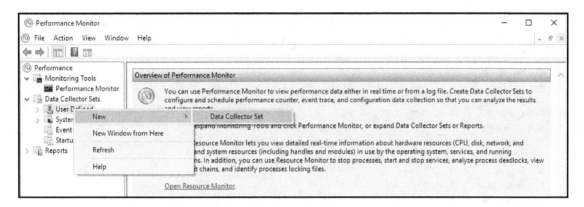

Figure 12.12. Creating Data Collector Set in Performance Monitor

4. In the **Create new Data Collector Set** wizard, enter the name for the New Data Collector Set, select **Create manually (Advanced)** and then click **Next**.

5. In the **What type of data do you want to include?** page, check **Performance counter** and then click **Next**.

6. In the **Which performance counters would you like to log?** page, click **Add...** button.

7. Select **counters** from the **Available counters** section, and then click the **Add** button to add them to the list in the **Added counters** section as in *Figure 12.13*:

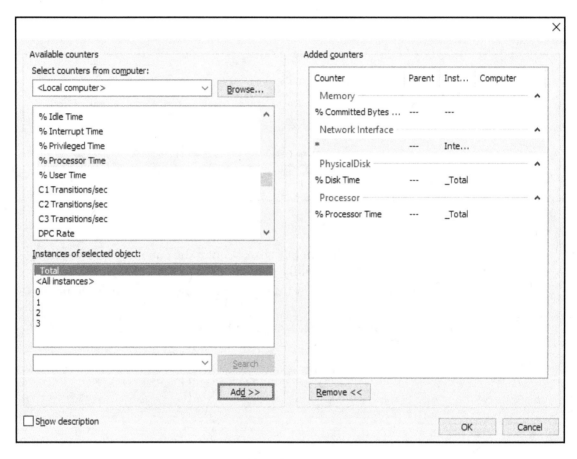

Figure 12.13. Adding Performance counters and instances

8. Click **OK** and then click **Next** as in the *Figure 12.14*:

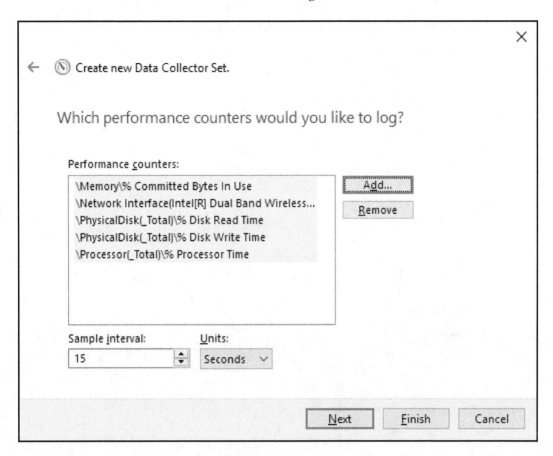

Figure 12.14. Confirming the added performance counters

9. In the **Where would you like the data to be saved?** page, click **Browse...** button to set the saving location and then click **Next**.

10. In the **Create the data collector set?** page, click **Change** and enter the **username** and the **password** in the **Performance Monitor** dialog box and click **OK**, then select **Save and close** and click **Finish** as in *Figure 12.15*:

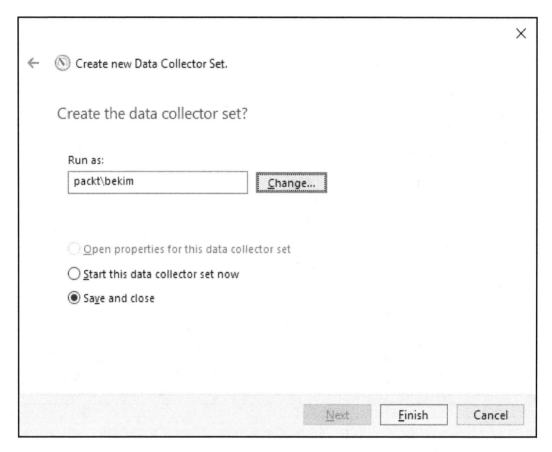

Figure 12.15. Setting the user for the data collector set

11. In the **Performance Monitor** window, select the **newly created data collector set** and then click Start the data collector set from the toolbar (see *Figure 12.16*)

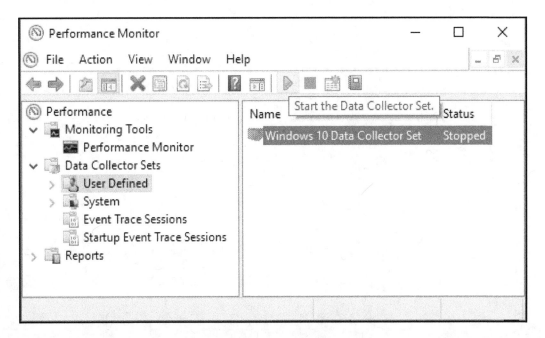

Figure 12.16. Starting the newly created data collector set

12. To view the logged data, select the newly created data collector set under **User Defined**, and then click Stop the data collector set from the toolbar.

13. Expand **Reports** I **User Defined** I **Newly created data collector set** and then click the generated report as shown in *Figure 12.17*:

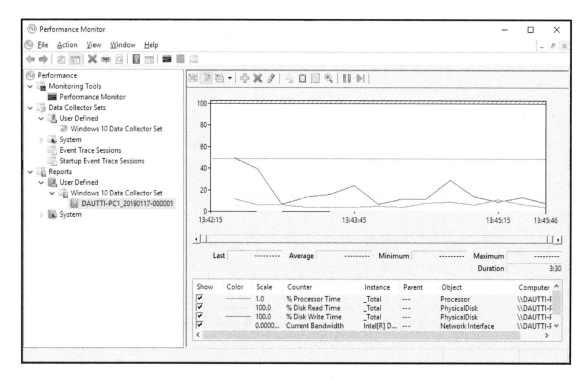

Figure 12.17. Viewing the logged data in the User Defined report

You can find more information regarding performance monitoring thresholds and other useful monitoring information for various technologies from `https://www.manageengine.com/network-monitoring/` `network-performance-monitoring.html`.

Monitoring system resources

If you have already completed CompTIA Server+ certification, then you are familiar with the **performance threshold** of key system components. If it happens to exceed the defined levels of utilization of key system components, then such a situation will compromise the overall computer's system performance. Therefore, it is recommended that when selecting hardware for the computer system attention is paid to the processor, RAM, hard disk, and network interface. Such a consideration presents the only guarantee that your Windows 10 device will perform optimally even in heavy use.

Computer's baseline

As discussed so far in this chapter, the Task Manager, Resource Monitor and Performance Monitor helps you monitor system resources in general, and key system components in particular. Anyone of these tools, or all together, will enable you to run real-time monitoring of the system resources that can be useful during instant diagnosis. In addition, the same tools enable you to run baseline on your Windows 10 device. Then, what is the computer's baseline? In short, a baseline represents a performance snapshot of your Windows 10 device under a normal workload. Like that, it enables to compile a detailed report in relation to how the key system components affect the overall performance of the Windows 10 device. That implies that **system resources monitoring tools** are not confined solely to just collecting information from the key system resources in real-time monitoring, instead to analyze the collected information over a certain period of time both during normal and heavy use.

Monitoring and managing printers

In addition to monitoring key system components, Windows 10 also provides tools that enable you to monitor and manage printers either connected directly to your Windows 10 device or on your LAN. Such an MMC console can be found within the **Administrative Tools** of Windows 10 Pro, Education, and Enterprise editions. **Print Management** (see *Figure 12.18*) MMC is a single console that enables you to add printers and drivers, share printers, and manage the printers' properties.

Managing printers with Print Management

To **manage** printers in your Windows 10 computer using Print Management, complete the following steps:

1. Press Windows key + *R* to open **Run**.
2. Enter `printmanagement.msc` and press *Enter* to open **Print Management** as shown in *Figure 12.18*:

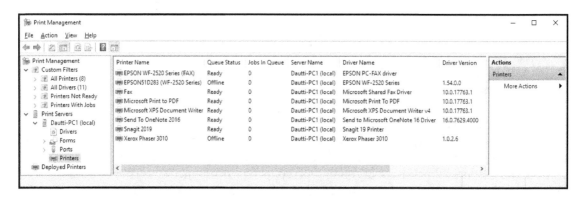

Figure 12.18. Print Management MMC console

Managing printers with Windows PowerShell

Enter the following command to **list** all the available Windows PowerShell cmdlets in your Windows 10 computer:

```
Get-Command -Module PrintManagement
```

Letting Windows 10 managing the default printer

To enable Windows 10 to manage the default printer, complete the following steps:

1. Press **Windows key + I** to open **Windows Settings**.
2. Click **Devices**, and then select **Printers & scanners** from the navigation menu.
3. Below the **Printers & scanners** list, check **Let Windows manage my default printer** as shown in *Figure 12.19*:

 Let Windows manage my default printer

When this is on, Windows will set your default printer to be the one you used most recently at your current location.

Figure 12.19. Letting Windows manage the default printer

Managing security using the Windows Security

Windows Security in Windows 10 acts as a platform that enables to view and manage the security and health of your Windows 10 device. It helps keep you protected while you are online, maintain your Windows 10 device's health, run periodic scans, manage your threat protection settings and more. From the moment you turn on your device for the first time and sign in to Windows 10, your device will be actively protected. It downloads the updates automatically, provides continuous real-time protection, and continually scans your device for viruses, malware, and security threats. All that is done through **Windows Defender** ensuring that your Windows 10 device is kept safe and protected from threats. Interesting, from the time it was introduced as a downloadable free anti-spyware program for Windows XP and up to now in Windows 10, Windows Defender has become more proactive and has improved significantly. However, not every individual and organizations are aware of the Windows Defender being part of Windows 10. As a results, they end up using third-party antivirus and antimalware solutions.

Accessing Windows Defender settings

To **access** Windows Defender settings in your Windows 10 computer using **Windows Settings**, complete the following steps:

1. Press Windows key + *I* to open **Windows Settings**.
2. In the **Windows Settings** window, click **Update & Security**.
3. In the **Update & Security** page, select **Windows Security** from the navigation menu (see *Figure 12.20*):

Figure 12.20. Windows Defender settings in Windows 10

Opening Windows Security

To **open** Windows Security in your Windows 10 computer using **Windows Settings**, complete the following steps:

1. **Repeat step 1 to step 3** from the previous section.
2. In the *Windows Security* page, click **Open Windows Security** button (see *Figure 12.20*).
3. The **Windows Security** dashboard is shown in *Figure 12.21*:

Figure 12.21. Windows Security dashboard in Windows 10

Updating Windows Defender Antivirus

To **update** Windows Defender Antivirus in your Windows 10 computer using Windows Security, complete the following steps:

1. Right-click the **Windows Security** icon on the system tray.
2. Select **View security dashboard** from the context menu.
3. In the **Security at a glance** page, click **Virus & threat protection**.
4. In the **Virus & threat protection** page, within **Virus & threat protection updates** section select **Check for updates**.

5. In the **Protection updates** page, within **Threat definitions** section click **Check for updates** button (see *Figure 12.22*):

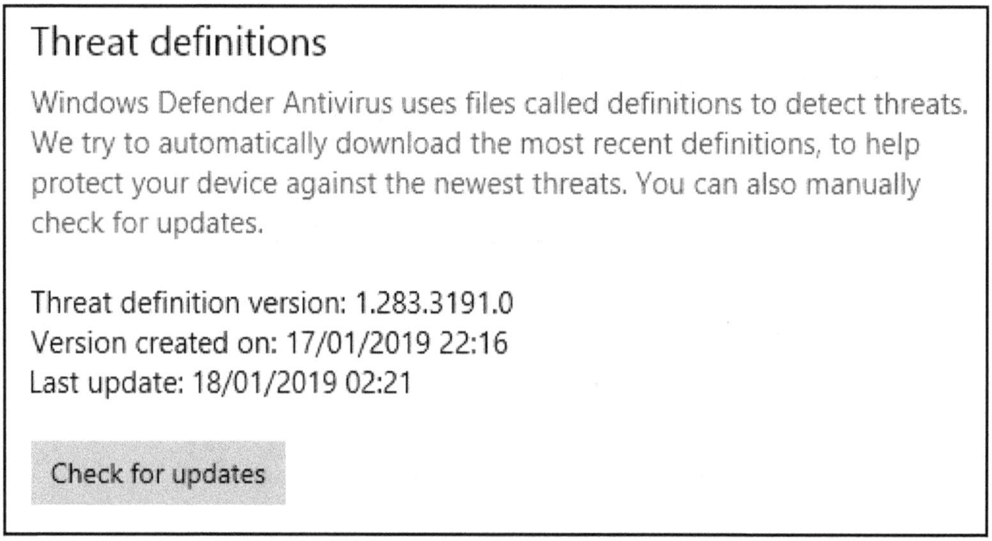

Threat definitions

Windows Defender Antivirus uses files called definitions to detect threats. We try to automatically download the most recent definitions, to help protect your device against the newest threats. You can also manually check for updates.

Threat definition version: 1.283.3191.0
Version created on: 17/01/2019 22:16
Last update: 18/01/2019 02:21

Check for updates

Figure 12.22. Updating Windows Defender Antivirus in Windows 10

Evaluating system stability using Reliability Monitor

If you have recently purchased a used computer and want to know if the Windows has been stable, then you can use the so-called **Reliability Monitor**. It enables you to view the stability history of Windows. Reliability Monitor is an MMC snap-in in Windows 10 and it utilizes the **RacTask** (an analysis task) in order to process system reliability data. Like that, it allows the user to identify previous warnings, as well as past critical and informational events. The interface of the Reliability Monitor is organized into two parts:

- The **top part** shows a line graph with a scale of 1 to 10 and date timeline along the bottom axis.
- The **bottom part** lists the **Reliability details** that relate to system configuration changes like software and driver installations.

By selecting a **specific period in time**, you may review the specific hardware and software problems that have impacted your Windows 10 device.

Accessing Reliability Monitor

To access Reliability Monitor and evaluate the system stability of your Windows 10 computer, complete the following steps:

1. Press Windows key + *R* to open **Run**.
2. Enter `perfmon /rel` and press *Enter*.
3. Make sure that **View by: Days** is selected, and then click any of the dates in the top part where failures have occurred as shown in *Figure 12.23*:

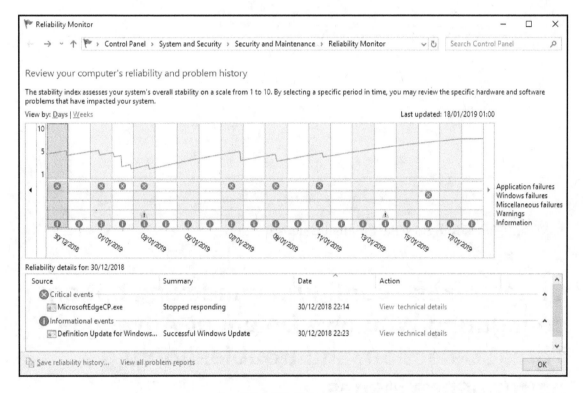

Figure 12.23. Reliability Monitor in Windows 10

4. In the bottom part, the **Reliability details** for that specific date lists information, warnings, and application, Windows and miscellaneous failures.

5. Click **View technical details** to display the **Description** of the failure as in *Figure 12.24:*

Figure 12.24. Description of failure in Reliability Monitor

6. Click **OK** to close the **Problem Details** window.

Chapter labs - configuring indexing options, configuring Windows Defender Advanced Threat Detection, and troubleshooting performance issues

In these chapter labs, you will learn how to do the following:

- Configuring indexing options
- Configuring Windows Defender Advanced Threat Detection
- Troubleshooting performance issues

Configuring Indexing Options

To **rebuild** the search index in your Windows 10 computer using Indexing Options, complete the following steps:

1. Press Windows key + *R* to open **Run**.
2. Enter `control.exe srchadmin.dll` and press *Enter*.
3. In the **Indexing Options** dialog box, click **Advanced** button (see *Figure 12.25*):

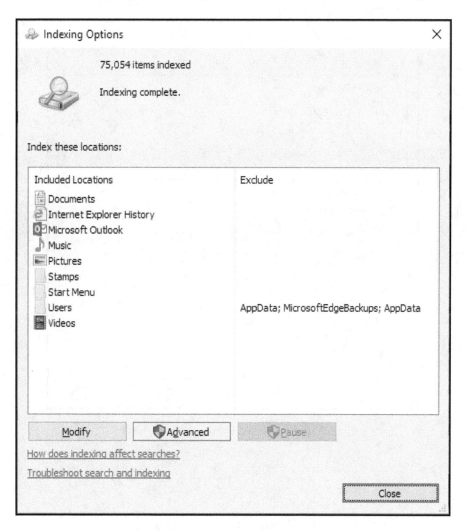

Figure 12.25. Accessing Advanced options of the search index in Windows 10

4. In the **Advanced Options** dialog box, within the troubleshooting section click **Rebuild** button as in *Figure 12.26*:

Figure 12.26. Rebuilding search index in Windows 10

Configuring Windows Defender Advanced Threat Detection

To configure Windows Defender Advanced Threat Detection, complete the following steps:

1. Press Windows key + *R* to open **Run**.
2. Enter `microsoft-edge:` and press *Enter*.
3. In the Microsoft Edge, click the address, and enter `https://www.microsoft.com/en-us/WindowsForBusiness/windows-atp?ocid=docs-wdatp-main-abovefoldlink`, and press *Enter*.
4. In the **Windows Defender Advanced Threat Protection** page, click **START FREE TRIAL** as shown in *Figure 12.27*:

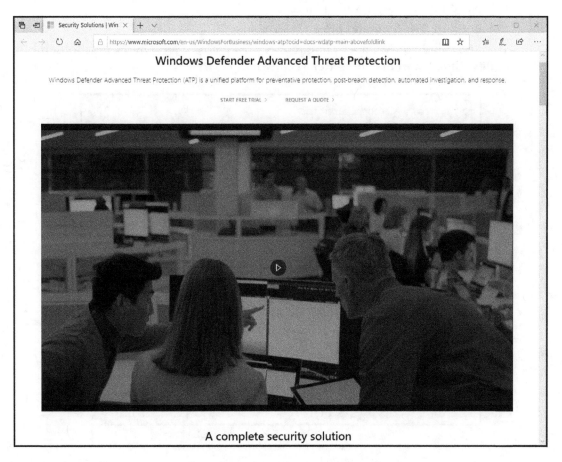

Figure 12.27. Signing up for free trial with Windows Defender ATP

5. In the **Please read the Trial Online Service Terms...** page, check **I accept these terms and conditions** and then click **Next** button.

6. In the **Please enter your details below:** page, fill up the form and then click **Submit** button.

7. On the **We're now reviewing your application...** page, you will be thanked for your application, and within 7 business days you will get contacted by email.

Troubleshooting performance issues

To run Windows Memory Diagnostics tool in your Windows 10 computer, complete the following steps:

1. Press Windows key + *R* to open **Run**.

2. Enter `mdsched.exe` and press *Enter*.

3. In the **Windows Memory Diagnostics** dialog box, select **Check for problems the next time I start my computer** as shown in *Figure 12.28*:

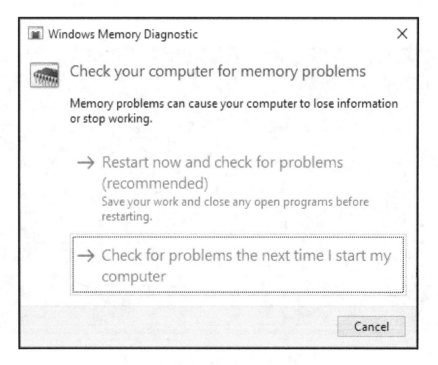

Figure 12.28. Running Windows Memory Diagnostics in Windows 10

Summary

We can summarize the chapter with the following points:

- The Event Viewer is an MMC snap-in that enables IT professionals to view events in Windows 10
- There are five types of events that you can monitor with Event Viewer: application, security, setup, system, and forwarded events
- Event Viewer displays three main event notifications in both XML and plain text format: error, warning, and information
- Task Manager is another legacy utility that enables monitoring the processes, performance, app history, startup, users, and services running on Windows 10 devices
- Resource Monitor too is a legacy monitoring utility that helps also identifying the cause of the performance problem
- Performance Monitor is a MMC snap-in that enables you to monitor Windows 10 device performance either in real time or from a log file
- Data Collector Sets enables you to analyze the performance results in formats such as a line graph, histogram bar, or as report
- Instance represents a unique copy of a particular type of object
- Counters provide performance information on how well an operating system, application, service, or driver is working
- A baseline represents a performance snapshot of your Windows 10 device under a normal workload
- System resource monitoring tools are not confined solely to just collecting information from key system resources in real-time monitoring, instead to analyze the collected information over a certain period of time both during normal and heavy use
- Print Management MMC is a single console that enables you to add printers and drivers, share printers, and manage the printers properties
- Windows Security in Windows 10 acts as a platform that enables to view and manage the security and health of your Windows 10 device
- Windows Defender ensures that your Windows 10 device is kept safe and protected from threats
- Reliability Monitor enables you to view the stability history of Windows

Questions

1. Task Manager is another legacy utility that enables monitoring the processes, performance, app history, startup, users, and services running on Windows 10 devices.
   1. True
   2. False

2. A _____ represents a performance snapshot of your Windows 10 device under a normal workload.

3. Which of the following events are part of Event Viewer? (Choose two)
   1. Application
   2. Software
   3. System
   4. Program

4. Print Management MMC is a single console that enables you to add printers and drivers, share printers, and manage the printers properties.
   1. True
   2. False

5. _____ ensures that your Windows 10 device is kept safe and protected from threats.

6. Which of the following tools can be used for monitoring system resources in Windows 10?
   1. Task Manager
   2. Resource Monitor
   3. Performance Monitor
   4. All of the above

7. Reliability Monitor enables you to view the stability history of Windows.
   1. True
   2. False

8. _____ acts as a platform that enables to view and manage the security and health of your Windows 10 device.

9. Which of the following event notifications are displayed by Event Viewer?
   1. Error
   2. Warning
   3. Information
   4. All of the above

10. Data Collector Sets enables you to analyze the performance results in formats such as a line graph, histogram bar, or as report.
    1. True
    2. False

11. _____ provide performance information on how well an operating system, application, service, or driver is working.

12. Which of the following are part of Data Collector Set? (Choose two)
    1. Counters
    2. Instance
    3. Baseline
    4. Reliability details

Further reading

- **How to start the Event Viewer in Windows (all versions)**: https://www.digitalcitizen.life/how-start-event-viewer-windows-all-versions
- **Guide to Windows 10 Task Manager – Part I**: https://www.online-tech-tips.com/windows-10/windows-10-task-manager-overview-part-i/
- **How to use Resource Monitor in Windows 10**: https://www.thewindowsclub.com/use-resource-monitor-windows-10
- **How to use Performance Monitor on Windows 10**: https://www.windowscentral.com/how-use-performance-monitor-windows-10
- **How to work with Windows 10's Reliability Monitor**: https://www.cio.com/article/2998906/windows/how-to-work-with-windows-10-reliability-monitor.html
- **Windows 10 Enterprise Security**: https://docs.microsoft.com/en-us/windows/security/
- **Windows Defender Advanced Threat Protection**: https://www.microsoft.com/en-us/WindowsForBusiness/windows-atp?ocid=docs-wdatp-main-abovefoldlink

13

Configuring Systems and Data Recovery

This chapter explains various methods and techniques to recover files and folders from a Windows 10 device. Also, this chapter will help you learn the ways you can recover a Windows 10 OS. With that in mind, tools such as Recovery Drive, System Restore, Device Manager, Previous Versions, and File History are explained both in terms of their concepts and their how-to instructions. In addition, Backup and Restore (Windows 7) and `WBAdmin.exe` are advanced tools for creating a system backup of your Windows 10 device. You will also learn how to reset your PC, roll back the device driver, access recovery options through advanced startup options, and recover deleted files from the `OneDrive.com` website. Each topic is accompanied by step-by-step instructions driven by targeted, easy-to-understand graphics. The chapter concludes with chapter labs on performing a refresh or recycle, driver rollback, backup and restore with `WBAdmin.exe`, recovery operations using Windows recovery, and recovering files from OneDrive.

In this chapter, we will cover the following topics:

- Configuring a recovery drive
- Configuring a system restore
- Configuring restore points
- Resolving hardware and device issues
- Interpreting data from Device Manager
- Restoring previous versions of files and folders
- Configuring File History
- Use Windows Backup and Restore
- Chapter labs – performing a refresh or recycle, driver rollback, backup and restore with WBAdmin, recovery operations using Windows Recovery, and recovering files from OneDrive

Technical requirements

To complete the labs for this chapter, you will need the following equipment:

- A PC with Windows 10 Enterprise, at least 8 GB of RAM, 500 GB of HDD, and access to the internet

Configuring a recovery drive

If, recently, you have had a situation when a Windows 10 device acted unstably, among the available solutions may be that you have chosen clean install as a solution if you have used a non-**OEM** (**Original Equipment Manufacturer**) device. As you may know, OEM devices do have a **recovery drive** that will help troubleshoot and fix problems in Windows 10 devices. But the question arises as to what solutions have custom build computers available? Obviously, there are many third-party apps out there on the internet, whether paid or free, that will enable you to create a recovery drive. But, to simplify and facilitate that at the same time, Microsoft in Windows 10 has included a recovery tool that will help create a recovery drive. With that tool and a USB flash drive of a minimum capacity of 8 GB, you can create your own recovery drive and use it every time to recover your Windows 10 computer.

Creating a recovery drive

To create a recovery drive in your Windows 10 computer using the recovery tool, complete the following steps:

1. Press the Windows key + *R* to open **Run**.
2. Enter `control panel` and press *Enter*.
3. In the **Control Panel** window, click **System and Security**.
4. In the **System and Security** window, click on **Security and Maintenance**.
5. In the **Security and Maintenance** window, within the **If you don't see your problem listed, try one of these:** section, select **Recovery**, as shown in *Figure 13.1*:

Figure 13.1: Selecting recovery to create a recovery drive

6. In the **Recovery** window, within the **Advanced recovery tools** section, select **Create a recovery drive**.

7. Click the **Yes** button when asked **Do you want to allow this app to make changes to your device?**.

8. In the **Recovery Drive** wizard, within the **Create a recovery drive** page, make sure that **Back up system files to the recovery drive** is checked, and then click **Next**.

9. In the **Select the USB flash drive** page, once the **Recovery image** has been prepared, insert the USB flash drive that is able to hold at least 8 GB, and then click on **Next** (see *Figure 13.2*):

Figure 13.2: Inserting a USB drive to store the recovery image

10. In the **Create the recovery drive** page, once you have read the warning message **Everything on the drive will be deleted...**, click **Create**.

11. The **Creating recovery drive** process begins; and be patient, as your computer will take considerable time to copy the **recovery image** to the USB flash drive.

12. In the **The recovery drive is ready** page, once the copying completes, click **Finish**, as in *Figure 13.3*:

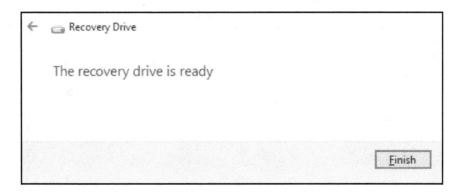

Figure 13.3: The recovery drive is ready

Configuring a system restore

System Restore is a feature that has been part of the Windows operating system from the version of Windows XP. As you might know, it is a feature that enables you to restore your computer to a state in which it worked well. System Restore uses **restore points** to create a snapshot of a computer's state at a given time and date. These restore points are created automatically and help restore personal files as well. In Windows 10, you must enable System Restore, as it is not enabled by default.

Enabling System Restore

To **enable** System Restore in your Windows 10 computer, complete the following steps:

1. **Repeat Step 1 to Step 3** from the *Creating a recovery drive* section.
2. In the **System and Security** window, click on **System**.
3. In the **System** window, from the navigation menu, select **System Protection**.

4. In the **System Properties** dialog box, with the **System Protection** tab selected, within the **Protection Settings** section, select the system drive (**C:**) and then click on the **Configure...** button, as in *Figure 13.4*:

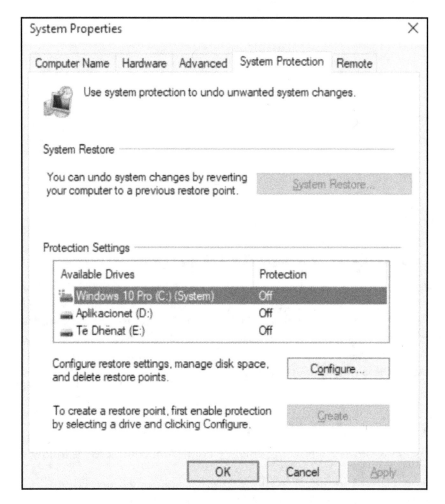

Figure 13.4: Enabling System Protection in Windows 10

5. In the System Protection for System Drive (C:) dialog box, within the **Restore Settings** section, select the **Turn on system protection** option and then click **OK**.

6. Click **OK** again to close the **System Properties** dialog box.

Configuring restore points

Now that you know about System Restore and have learned how to enable it, it is time to learn how to create a **restore point**. Part of the restore point configuration process is also the configuration of **disk space usage**. This will then be used by the restore point to save the computer's states on it.

Configuring the amount of disk space

To **configure** the amount of the disk space in your Windows 10 computer using *System Properties*, complete the following steps:

1. **Repeat step 1 to step 3** from the *Enabling System Restore* section.

2. In the System Protection for System Drive (C:) dialog box, within the **Disk Space Usage** section, adjust the **Max Usage** slider to the preferred percentage as shown in *Figure 13.5*, and then click **OK**:

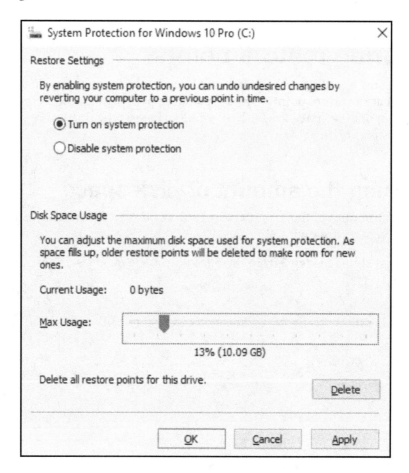

Figure 13.5: Configuring disk space usage for restore points

Creating a restore point

To **create** a restore point in your Windows 10 computer using **System Properties**, complete the following steps:

1. Continue from where you left off in the previous section.
2. In the **System Properties** dialog box, with the **System Protection** tab selected, within **Protection Settings**, select System Drive (C:) and then click the **Create...** button.
3. In the **System Protection** dialog box, **enter the description** to help you identify the restore point (see *Figure 13.6*) and then click **Create**:

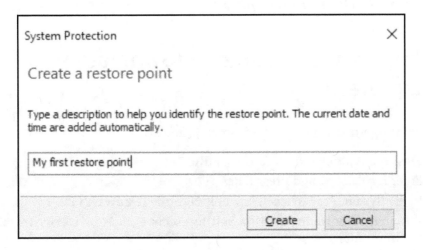

Figure 13.6: Creating a restore point in Windows 10

4. Create a restore point begins.
5. Once the restore point has been created successfully, click **Close**.
6. Click **OK** to close **System Properties** dialog box.

Resolving hardware and device issues

Have you ever installed a Windows 2000 driver in Windows XP, or a Windows Vista driver in Windows 7, or a Windows 7 one in Windows 8? As you know, such a thing is not recommended by Microsoft! However, it might have helped you overcome a problem, right? Well, in Windows 10, things have changed radically in regard to device drivers. Windows 10 is **not supporting** the installation of device drivers designed for earlier versions of Windows. Thus, even if an **unsigned driver** might seem to work, you should avoid doing that, especially in a production environment. That being said, you should always go for digitally signed device drivers. In addition, Windows 10 does not allow you to install a 32-bit device in a Windows 10 64-bit architecture. Just as you cannot use a 64-bit device driver in a Windows 10 32-bit architecture.

Disabling to automatically downloading manufacturers' apps

To **disable** the automatic download of manufacturers' apps in your Windows 10 computer using **System Properties**, complete the following steps:

1. Press the Windows key + *R* to open **Run**.
2. Enter `sysdm.cpl` and press *Enter*.
3. In the **System Properties** dialog box, click the **Hardware** tab.
4. Within the **Device Installation Settings** section, click the **Device Installation Settings** button.
5. In the **Device installation settings** dialog box, select the **No (your device might not work as expected)** option, as shown in *Figure 13.7*:

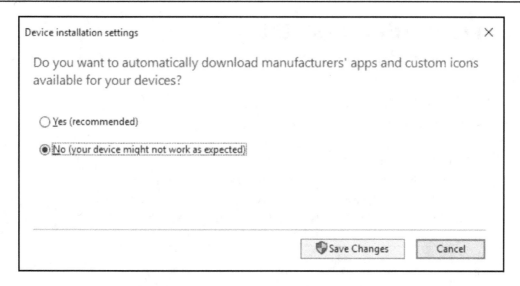

Figure 13.7: Disabling to automatically downloading manufacturers' apps in Windows 10

6. Click **Save Changes**, and then click **OK** to close the **System Properties** dialog box.

Interpreting data from Device Manager

When adding new hardware to a Windows 10 computer, it is **installed automatically**. That is because **Windows 10 DriverStore** is rich in device drivers, and that **Plug and Play** plays an important role in recognizing the new hardware too. Also, Windows 10 is equipped with a variety of connection methods, such as USB, Wi-Fi, and Bluetooth. Additionally, Windows 10 has built-in support for emerging technologies such as **Near-Field Communication** (**NFC**) and **Miracast**. Despite all that, it is worth mentioning Device Manager; although it is a legacy management tool, which is one of the favorite system administrators tools, Device Manager helps getting first-hand information about every hardware component, including device type, device status, manufacturer, device-specific properties, and device driver information.

Viewing the device's status

To **view** the device status in your Windows 10 computer using Device Manager, complete the following steps:

1. Press the Windows key + *R* to open **Run**.
2. Enter `devmgmt.msc` and press *Enter*.
3. In the **Device Manager** window, expand any of the hardware components from the tree structure.
4. Right-click a device, and select **Properties** from the context menu.
5. In the **Device's Properties** dialog box, within the **Device status** section, check whether it reads **This device is working properly**, as in *Figure 13.8*:

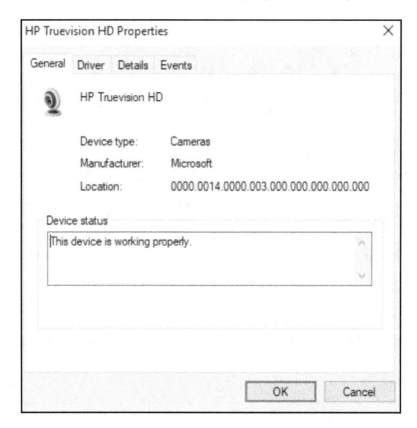

Figure 13.8: Checking the device's status in Device Manager

6. Click **OK** to close the device's properties dialog box.

If you want more information about Plug and Play, Device Manager, and how to operate with device drivers, you can find it in `Chapter 15`, *Configuring Advanced Management Tools*.

Restoring previous versions of files and folders

The **Volume Shadow Copy Service** (**VSS**), introduced for the first time in Windows Server 2003, is a feature that enables you to restore **previous versions** of files and folders quickly. With VSS, there is no need to take the applications offline to back them up. So, just like that, the VSS reduces the administrative effort. However, all that should not be taken to the point where the VSS is better than backup! Instead, VSS is a technology that facilitates the communication between the backup application, the applications that are being backed up, and the storage, to allow them all to work better together. From the point of view of work, the VSS generates **local shadow copies**, which serves as a platform for the Previous Versions feature, so that the latter then can enable users to view, revert, or recover files and folders that have been modified or deleted. Prior to using the Previous Versions feature, the **File History** feature or the restore points need to be configured.

Introduced in Windows 8.1., **File History** is a feature that enables you to back up your data periodically to an external disk or a network share. To be able to use File History, it needs to be enabled. Once enabled, File History backs up your data every hour in a format of a schedule. It will continue backing up changes until the disk, respectively the network share is filled. However, that can be modified in Advanced Settings. To turn on File History, see the section *Troubleshooting data recovery*, in `Chapter 8`, *Configuring Data Access and Usage*. While, to create a restore point, see the section: *Creating a restore point*, earlier in this chapter.

Adding a backup drive

To **add** an external drive to be used by File History in your Windows 10 computer, complete the following steps:

1. Press the Windows key + *I* to open **Windows Settings**.
2. In the **Windows Settings** window, click the **Update & Security**.
3. In the **Update & Security** window, select **Backup** from the navigation menu.

4. In the **Backup** page, within the **Back up using File History** section, click the **Add a drive** button, as shown in *Figure 13.9*:

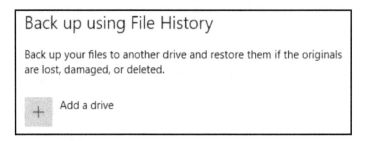

Figure 13.9: Adding an external drive to your computer

5. Once you add the drive, if the File History is turned on, then it will start saving data on your backup drive.

6. In the **Backup** page, within the **Back up using File History** section, select **More options**.

7. In the **Backup options** page, within the **Back up these folders** section, click the **Add a folder** button to add a folder that you want to back up it and its content (see *Figure 13.10*):

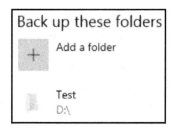

Figure 13.10: Adding a folder to backup with File History

Restoring previous versions of a file

To **restore** previous versions of a file in your Windows 10 computer, complete the following steps:

1. Make sure that File History is turned on (see *Figure 13.11*):

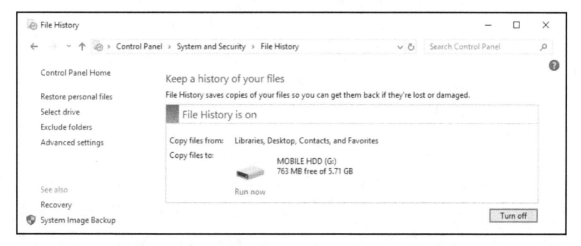

Figure 13.11: Checking whether File History is turned on in Windows 10

2. Locate the **folder** that you have created in the **Adding a backup drive** section, and within the same folder, create a text file and enter a sample text.
3. Save the added text and close the file.
4. In **File History**, click **Run now**.
5. Open the text file and **modify** the sample text, and then **save** and **close** the file.
6. In the **File History**, click **Run now**.
7. Right-click the text file and select **Properties** from the context menu.

8. In the file's properties dialog box, click the **Previous Versions** tab, as in *Figure 13.12*:

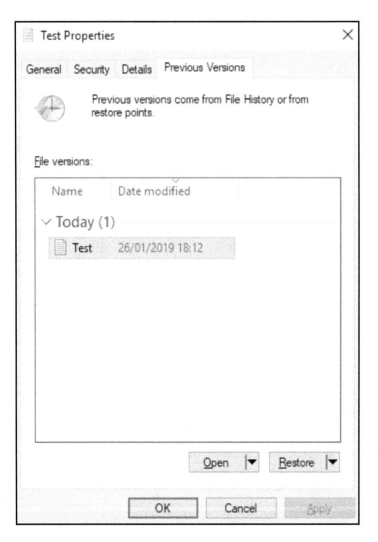

Figure 13.12: Previous Versions in Windows 10

9. Within the **File version** section, you will notice that one previous version of the file is listed.

10. Click the **Restore** button, and then in the **Replace or Skip Files** dialog box, select **Replace the file in the destination**, as shown in *Figure 13.13*:

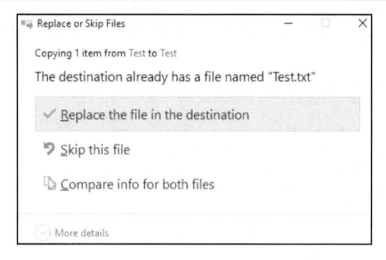

Figure 13.13: Restoring the file in the original location

11. Click **OK** to close the file's properties dialog box.

Using Windows Backup and Restore (Windows 7)

From my experience as a **Microsoft-Certified Trainer** (**MCT**), I have encountered many users who do not back up their personal data. Perhaps that is because today, most rely on cloud services such as OneDrive, Google Drive, Dropbox, and so on. However, you have to be prepared for any unexpected situation, because computer devices are simply unpredictable. Hence, to be prepared for situations when your computer does not work and you cannot access your data, it is recommended that you make a regular backup of your data. Simply put, a **backup** is the method of creating another set (that is, copy) of your data. That way, if loss of a data occurs, then a backup can be used to recover the data. To do that, **restore** is a method that enables data recovery from the backup. Windows 10 is equipped with backup tools in both **Windows Settings** and the **Control Panel**. Interestingly, in Windows 10, Microsoft has returned again the old **Backup and Restore (Windows 7)** tool. With regard to storing the backup, the media you have chosen is very important. Usually, it depends on the importance and the quantity of the data. CD-RW, DVD-RW, and external HDDs are a few of the technologies that can be used for backup on PCs.

Accessing and running Backup and Restore (Windows 7)

To access the Backup and Restore (Windows 7) tool in your Windows 10 computer, complete the following steps:

1. Press the Windows key + *R* to open **Run**.
2. Enter `control panel` and press *Enter*.
3. In the **Control Panel** window, select **System and Security**.
4. In the **System and Security** window, select **Backup and Restore (Windows 7)**, as shown in *Figure 13.14*:

Figure 13.14: Backup and Restore (Windows 7) tool in Windows 10

5. In the **Backup and Restore (Windows 7)** window, within the **Back up or restore your files** section, select **Set up backup**.
6. Shortly after, the **Set up backup** wizard opens, as in *Figure 13.15*:

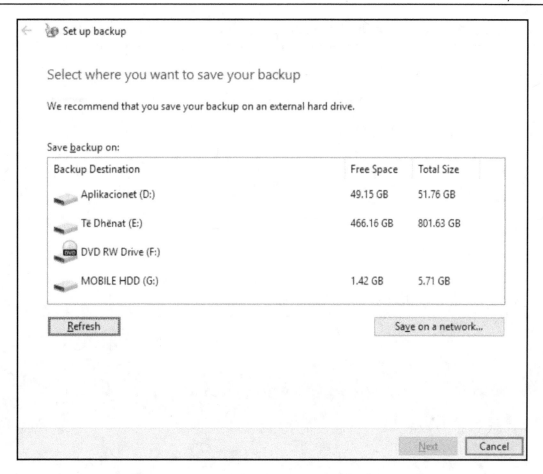

Figure 13.15: Setting up the backup in Windows 10

7. Plug an external hard drive in your computer, and then click the **Refresh** button.
8. Within the **Save backup on** section, select the external hard drive and click **Next**.
9. In the **What do you want to back up?** page, select the **Let me choose** option and then click **Next**.
10. In the next page of the **Set up backup** wizard, select the **checkboxes of the items** that you want to include in the backup and then click **Next**.

11. In the **Review your backup settings** page, review the items within **Backup Summary** section and then click **Save settings and run backup** (see *Figure 13.16*):

← 🖳 Set up backup

Review your backup settings

Backup Location: MOBILE HDD (G:)

Backup Summary:

Items	Included in backup
E:\Dokumentet\Packt Publishing Book Writing\	All local data files

Schedule: Every Sunday at 19:00 Change schedule

[Save settings and run backup] [Cancel]

Figure 13.16: Running the backup in Windows 10

12. Shortly after, the **Backup and Restore (Windows 7)** window opens and the **Back up or restore your files** page displays the backup progress, as in *Figure 13.17*:

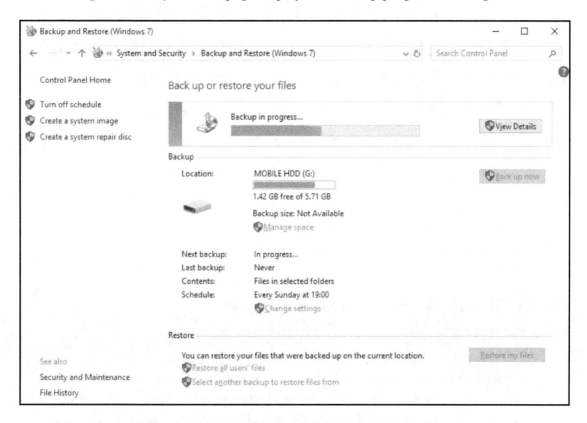

Figure 13.17: Backup progress in Backup and Restore (Windows 7)

13. Once the backup progress disappears from the view, the backup of the data has been completed.

Chapter labs – performing a refresh or recycle, driver rollback, backup and restore with WBAdmin, recovery operations using Windows Recovery, and recovering files from OneDrive

In these chapter labs, you will learn how to do the following:

- Performing a refresh or recycle
- Performing a driver rollback
- Performing a backup and restore with WBAdmin
- Performing recovery operations using Windows Recovery
- Recovering files from OneDrive

Performing a refresh or recycle

To reset your Windows 10 computer, complete the following steps:

1. Press the Windows key + *I* to open **Windows Settings**.
2. In the **Windows Settings** window, click **Update & Security**.
3. In the **Update & Security** window, select **Recovery** from the navigation menu.
4. In the **Recovery** page, within the **Reset this PC** section, click the **Get started** button, as shown in *Figure 13.18*:

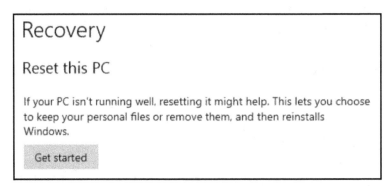

Figure 13.18: Resetting your Windows 10 computer

5. In the **Reset this PC** dialog box, select **Keep my files**.
6. In the **Ready to reset this PC** page, click on the **Reset** button (see *Figure 13.19*):

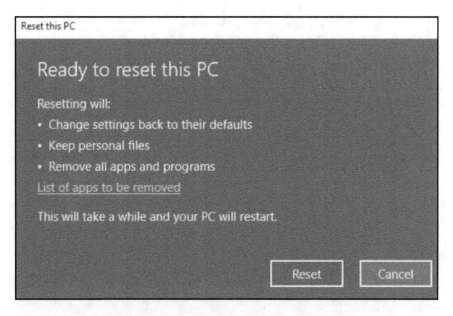

Figure 13.19: Ready to reset your Windows 10 computer

7. Once your Windows 10 computer completes resetting, you are presented with the **logon screen**.

Performing a driver rollback

To **perform** a driver rollback in your Windows 10 computer, complete the following steps:

1. Press the Windows key + R to open **Run**.
2. Enter devmgmt.msc and press *Enter*.
3. In the **Device Manager** window, **expand** any of the devices from the tree structure.
4. Right-click a device and select **Properties** from the context menu.

5. In the device's properties dialog box, click the **Driver** tab and then click the **Roll Back Driver** button, as shown in *Figure 13.20*:

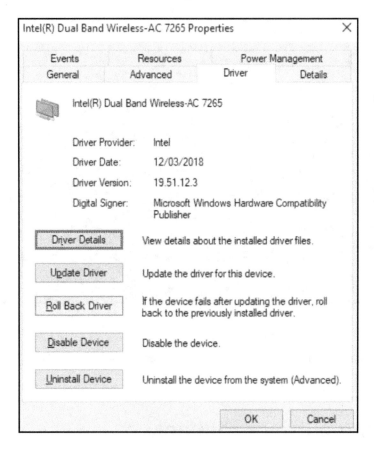

Figure 13.20: Rolling back the driver in Windows 10

6. In the **Driver Package rollback** dialog box, within the **Why are you rolling back?** section, select an **option or enter a reason**, and then click **Yes**.

7. Click **Close** to close the device's properties dialog box.

You may want to roll back the driver if you have installed more than one driver for your device and the last one installed is not performing to the expected level, or, perhaps recently, the driver has been updated via Windows Updates and the newest driver is not performing as expected.

Performing a backup and restore with WBAdmin

To **perform** a backup and restore in your Windows 10 computer using WBAdmin, complete the following steps:

1. Click the search box in the taskbar and enter `cmd`.
2. With **Command Prompt** highlighted in the **Best match** list, select **Run as administrator**.
3. In the **User Account Control** dialog box, click the **Yes** button when asked **Do you want to allow this app to make changes to your device?**.
4. In the **Administrator: Command Prompt** window, enter the `WBAdmin start backup -BackupTarget:D: -allcritical -Include:C:\Test\Test.txt` command to back up a text file.
5. When asked **Do you want to start the backup operation?**, enter **Y** and press **Enter**, as shown in *Figure 13.21*:

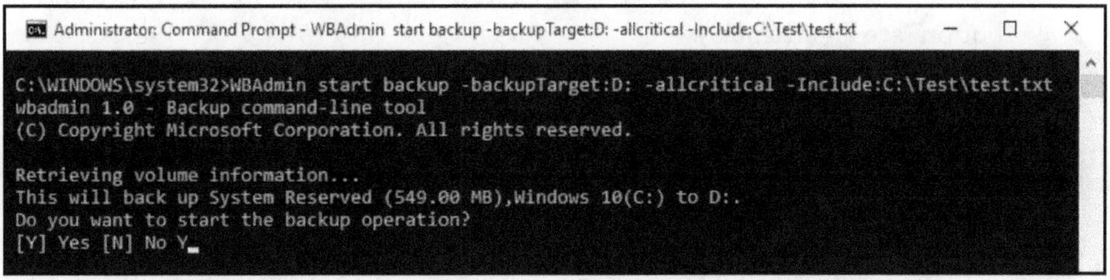

```
Administrator: Command Prompt - WBAdmin start backup -backupTarget:D: -allcritical -Include:C:\Test\test.txt    —    □    ×

C:\WINDOWS\system32>WBAdmin start backup -backupTarget:D: -allcritical -Include:C:\Test\test.txt
wbadmin 1.0 - Backup command-line tool
(C) Copyright Microsoft Corporation. All rights reserved.

Retrieving volume information...
This will back up System Reserved (549.00 MB),Windows 10(C:) to D:.
Do you want to start the backup operation?
[Y] Yes [N] No Y_
```

Figure 13.21: Backing up a file with the WBAdmin tool in Windows 10

6. Once the backup completes, enter the `WBAdmin get versions -BackupTarget:D:` command to list the **backup images**, as shown in *Figure 13.22*:

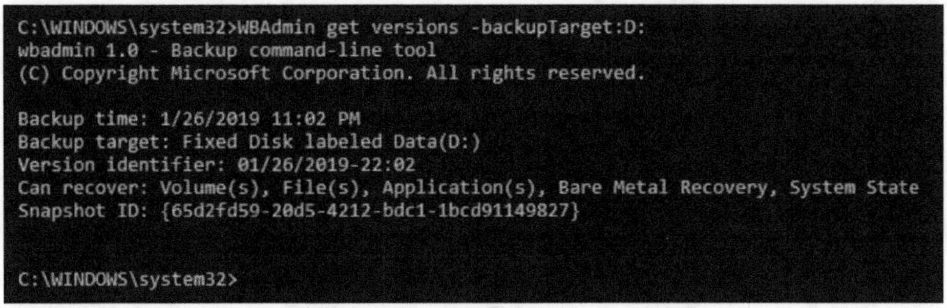

```
C:\WINDOWS\system32>WBAdmin get versions -backupTarget:D:
wbadmin 1.0 - Backup command-line tool
(C) Copyright Microsoft Corporation. All rights reserved.

Backup time: 1/26/2019 11:02 PM
Backup target: Fixed Disk labeled Data(D:)
Version identifier: 01/26/2019-22:02
Can recover: Volume(s), File(s), Application(s), Bare Metal Recovery, System State
Snapshot ID: {65d2fd59-20d5-4212-bdc1-1bcd91149827}

C:\WINDOWS\system32>
```

Figure 13.22: Listing the backup images with WBAdmin tool

7. To restore the backup image, enter the `WBAdmin start recovery -version:01/26/2019-22:02 -itemType:Volume -items:\\?\Volume{65d2fd59-20d5-4212-bdc1-1bcd91149827}\ -BackupTarget:D: -RecoveryTarget:C:` command.

Performing recovery operations using Windows Recovery

To access the advanced startup option in your Windows 10 computer, complete the following steps:

1. Press the Windows key + *I* to open **Windows Settings**.
2. In the **Windows Settings** window, click **Update & Security**.
3. In the **Update & Security** window, select **Recovery** from the navigation menu.
4. In the **Recovery** page, within the **Advanced startup** section, click the **Restart now** button (see *Figure 13.23*):

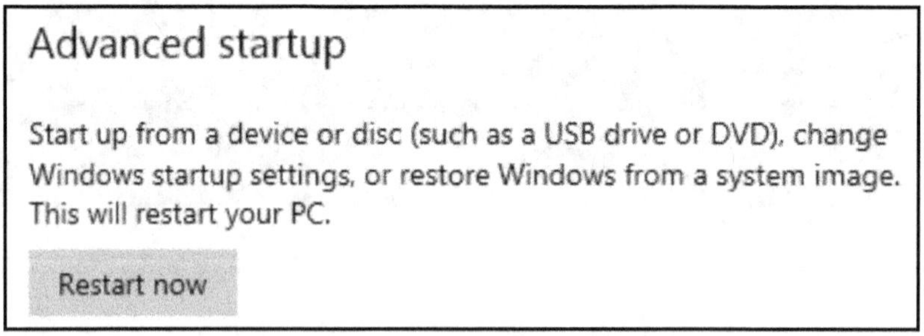

Advanced startup

Start up from a device or disc (such as a USB drive or DVD), change Windows startup settings, or restore Windows from a system image. This will restart your PC.

Restart now

Figure 13.23: Recovering on a Windows 10 computer through the Advanced Startup option

5. In the **Choose an option** page, click **Troubleshoot**.
6. In the **Troubleshoot** page, click **Advanced options**.
7. In the **Advanced options** page, select any of the recovery tools listed, as in *Figure 13.24*:

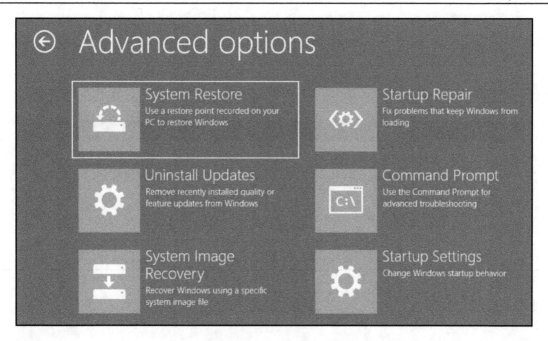

Figure 13.24: Advanced startup option in Windows 10

 In Windows 10, there is no *F8* key as there was in Previous Versions of Windows. However, you can use the advanced startup options to recover your Windows 10 computer.

Recovering files from OneDrive.com

To **recover** deleted files from OneDrive.com website, complete the following steps:

1. Press the Windows key + *R* to open **Run**.
2. Enter microsoft-edge: and press *Enter*.
3. In the **Microsoft Edge** window, click the **address bar**, enter onedrive.com and press *Enter*.
4. Sign in to the OneDrive website with your **Microsoft account**.

5. In the OneDrive website, select **Recycle bin** from the navigation menu, then select the file that you want to recover, and then click **Restore**, as shown in *Figure 13.25*:

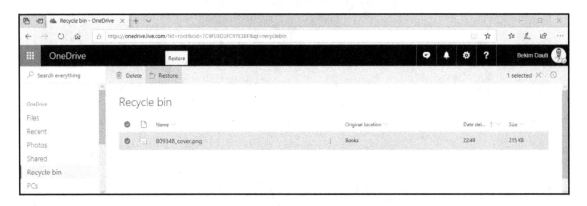

Figure 13.25: Recovering the deleted files from the OneDrive website

Summary

We can summarize the chapter with the following points:

- The recovery tool enables the creation of a recovery drive
- System Restore is a feature that enables you to restore your computer to a state in which it worked well
- System Restore uses restore points to create a snapshot of a computer's state at a given time and date
- Windows 10 doesn't support the installation of device drivers designed for earlier versions of Windows
- Adding new hardware in a Windows 10 computer is installed automatically
- The VSS, is a feature that enables you to restore previous versions of files and folders quickly
- The VSS generates local shadow copies that serve as a platform for the Previous Versions feature, so that the latter then can enable users to view, revert, or recover files and folders that have been modified or deleted
- File History is a feature that enables you to back up your data periodically to an external disk or network share
- Backup is the method of creating another set (that is, copy) of your data
- Restore is a method that enables data recovery from the backup

Questions

1. System Restore uses restore points to create a snapshot of a computer's state at a given time and date.
    1. True
    2. False

2. _____ tool enables you to create a recovery drive.

3. Which of the following is used by File History to store backups? (Choose two)
    1. Internal disk
    2. External disk
    3. Network share
    4. Folder in internal disk

4. Backup is the method of creating another set (that is, copy) of your data.
    1. True
    2. False

5. _____ is a method that enables data recovery from a backup.

6. Which of the following advanced options enables you to restore Windows, using a restore point?
    1. System Image Recovery
    2. Backup and Restore (Windows 7)
    3. System Restore
    4. Startup Repair

7. System Restore is a feature that enables you to restore your computer to a state where it worked well.
    1. True
    2. False

8. The _____ is a feature that enables you to restore previous versions of files and folders quickly.

9. Which of the following Command Prompt tools creates System Backup?
    1. Reset this PC
    2. Advanced Startup options
    3. Backup and Restore (Windows 7)
    4. WBAdmin.exe

Further reading

- **How to Fix Device Manager Errors in Windows 10**: `https://hetmanrecovery.com/recovery_news/how-to-fix-device-manager-error-in-windows-10.htm`
- **Recovery options in Windows 10**: `https://support.microsoft.com/en-us/help/12415/windows-10-recovery-options`
- **How to Configure a File History Backup for Windows 10**: `https://redmondmag.com/articles/2018/03/23/file-history-backup-windows-10.aspx`
- **Using the Windows 7 Back up and Restore Tool in Windows 10**: `https://www.thewindowsclub.com/use-windows-7-back-up-and-restore-tool-windows-10`
- **WBAdmin**: `https://docs.microsoft.com/en-us/windows-server/administration/windows-commands/wbadmin`

14
Configuring Authorization and Authentication

If you like the security of Windows 10, and especially the authentication technologies, then this chapter is for you. This chapter explains various authentication methods and technologies supported by Windows 10. Other than that, this chapter explains protection technologies such as Windows Defender Device Guard and Windows Defender Credential Guard. With that in mind, you will get acquainted with features and technologies such as Microsoft Passport, picture password, Credential Manager, device registration, Windows Hello for Business, Device Guard, and Credential Guard, which are presented both as concepts and also as configurations. In addition, **Device Health Attestation** (**DHA**) and Dynamic Lock are two other new features of Windows 10 that determine the health status of your Windows 10 device, and automatically lock down your Windows 10 device when you step away from your desk. Each topic is accompanied with step-by-step instructions driven by targeted, easy-to-understand graphics. The chapter concludes with chapter labs on configuring workgroups, domain settings, Azure Active Directory Domain Join, and Microsoft accounts.

In this chapter, we will cover the following topics:

- Configuring Microsoft Passport
- Configuring picture passwords and biometrics
- Configuring Credential Manager
- Configuring Device Registration
- Configuring Windows Hello for Business
- Configuring Device Guard
- Configuring Credential Guard
- Configuring DHA

- Configuring Dynamic Lock
- Chapter labs – configuring workgroups, domain settings, Azure AD Domain Join, and Microsoft accounts

Technical requirements

In order to complete the labs for this chapter, you will need the following equipment:

- A PC with Windows 10 Enterprise, at least 8 GB of RAM, 500 GB of HDD, and access to the internet

Configuring Microsoft Passport

Traditionally, users are usually authenticated by **username** and **password**. However, in today's technological trends in which a user needs to log in to different environments to access applications, websites, and other services, the traditional format of authentication is neither viable nor secure. The same goes for Microsoft's operating systems and services. Therefore, Microsoft has introduced **Microsoft Passport**, which enables users to authenticate without a password. Microsoft Passport is based on the **Fast IDentity Online Alliance** (**FIDO**) standards, and consists of two components: a **single sign-in** service and a **wallet service**. From that, we can deduce that Microsoft Passport is a two-factor authentication mechanism with which users will be able to prove who they are by providing something that they uniquely posses. In Windows 10, Microsoft Passport has been introduced along with **Windows Hello**, which is a built-in biometrics authentication technology. Thus, to avoid confusion, try to understand the fact that Windows Hello is a feature that uses the Microsoft Passport platform.

Configuring picture passwords and biometrics

With the introduction of Windows 10, Microsoft has provided a variety of authentication technologies alongside traditional formats of authentication. Thus, in addition to using username and password, technologies such **personal identification number** (**PIN**), **biometric gestures**, and a **picture passwords** can all be used to authenticate you in a Windows 10 devices. However, in the case of biometric gestures and a picture passwords your Windows 10 device should be equipped with the appropriate hardware.

Setting up a picture password

To **set up** a picture password on your Windows 10 computer, complete the following steps:

1. Press Windows key + *I* to open **Windows Settings**.
2. In the **Windows Settings** window, click **Accounts**.
3. On the **Accounts** page, select **Sign-in options** from the navigation menu.
4. On the **Sign-in options** page, within the **Picture password** section click the **Add** button as shown in *Figure 14.1*:

Figure 14.1. Setting up a picture password in Windows 10

5. In the **Windows Security** dialog box, verify your account by entering the **password** and press *Enter*.
6. In the **Picture password** window, click the **Choose picture** button.
7. Locate your favorite picture and click **Open**.
8. On the **How's this look?** page, click **Use this picture** button.
9. On the **Set up your gestures** page, **draw** three gestures on your picture.
10. On the **Confirm your gestures** page, **repeat** your three gestures.
11. On the **Congratulations** page, click the **Finish** button.

Configuring Credential Manager

Usually, when we access websites, online services, network applications, and computers and servers on a network, we will be asked to provide a username and a password so we can

access those sites and services. To ease access to such sites and services the next time, Windows 10 stores the user credentials in Credential Manager. Usernames, passwords, and IP addresses usually represent the information that is stored in Credential Manager. **Vaults** are the folders where the Credential Manager stores user credentials, whereas the **Windows vault** is the default storage of Credential Manager information. In addition, Credential Manager is organized into two lists. User credentials that are used to access web services are stored in the **Web Credentials** list, while user credentials for accessing network services are stored in the **Windows Credentials** list.

Accessing Credential Manager

To access Credential Manager in your Windows 10 computer using Control Panel, complete the following steps:

1. Press Windows key + *R* to open **Run**.
2. Enter `control panel` and press *Enter*.
3. In the **Control Panel** window, select **User Accounts**.
4. In the **User Accounts** window, select **Credential Manager** as in *Figure 14.2*:

Figure 14.2. Accessing Credential Manager in Windows 10

5. In the **Credential Manager** window, **Web Credentials** and **Windows Credentials** are shown.

Configuring device registration

If you want to access restricted resources on your organization's network without having to join your Windows 10 devices to your organization's domain, then you can do that by using the new feature known as **Access work or school**. It enables you to register your Windows 10 device on your organization's network, and facilitates a **single sign-on** (**SSO**) experience so you are able to get access to resources such as email, apps, and other network services. Registering your device to your organization's network means that your work might control some things on your device. Thus, it is recommended that you ask your organization's IT department about what is being controlled on your device.

Registering your device

To **register** your Windows 10 computer to your organization's network, complete the following steps:

1. Press Windows key + *I* to open **Windows Settings**.
2. In the **Windows Settings** window, click **Accounts**.
3. On the **Accounts** page, select **Access work or school** from the navigation menu.
4. On the **Access work or school** page, on the far right of your screen in the **Related settings** section, select **Enroll only in device management**, as shown in *Figure 14.3*:

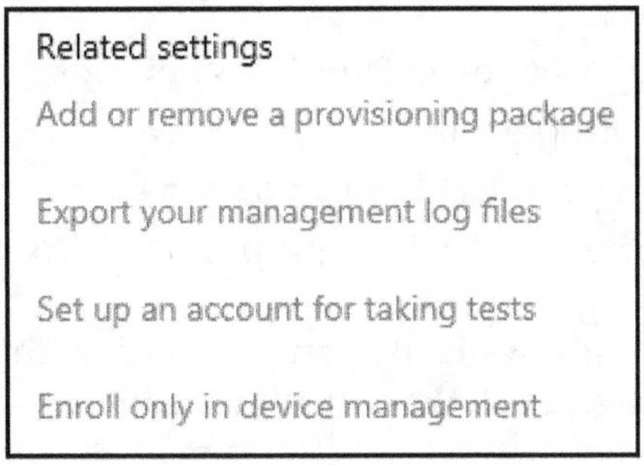

Figure 14.3. Enabling registration of Windows 10 device to organization's network

5. In the Microsoft **ACCOUNT** dialog box, within the **Set up a work or school account** page, enter your email address for your work or school account and then click **Next**.

6. On the **Connecting to a service** page, enter the **password** for your work or school account and then click **Sign in**.

7. Once your device gets registered by the enterprise registration host, the connected information will be listed below the **Connected** button in the **Access work or school** page.

Configuring Windows Hello for Business

As mentioned in the *Configuring Microsoft Passport* section, Microsoft Passport enables users to sign in to Windows 10 devices with Windows Hello or a PIN. Usually, a **PIN** is a numeric or an alphanumeric password, whereas Windows Hello is a biometrics-based authentication technology. With Windows Hello, you can sign in to your Windows 10 device using fingerprints or facial recognition. Since Windows Hello is part of the Microsoft Passport framework, then, just like Microsoft Passport, Windows Hello is a two-factor biometric authentication mechanism built into Windows 10. From that, Windows Hello authentication is based on the concept that users prove who they are by providing something they uniquely possess. As a method of enforcing security in organizations, Windows Hello for Business is being used to authenticate users and enable them to access network resources in a corporate network.

Setting up Windows Hello

To **set up** Windows Hello on your Windows 10 computer, complete the following steps:

1. Press Windows key + *I* to open **Windows Settings**.
2. In the **Windows Settings** window, click **Accounts**.
3. On the **Accounts** page, select **Sign-in options** from the navigation menu.
4. On the **Sign-in options** page, in the **Window Hello** section, click the **Set up** button under **Face**.
   1. In the **Windows Hello setup** wizard, within the **Welcome to Windows Hello** page, click the **Get started** button.
5. In the **Windows Security** dialog box, enter your PIN or password to verify your identity.
6. In the **Windows Hello setup** wizard, keep looking directly at your camera to allow Windows Hello to capture your facial features.

7. In the **Windows Hello setup** wizard, on the **All set** page, click the **Close** button (see *Figure 14.4*):

Figure 14.4. Setting up Windows Hello in Windows 10

Configuring Device Guard

Windows Defender Device Guard is another layer of security in the so-called *defense in depth* strategy. It is a combination of the enterprise hardware and software security features so that it can mitigate threats coming from **malicious software** (**malware**). With that being said, Device Guard only allows the execution of **trusted applications**, and trusted applications are considered to be applications that are **signed digitally**. Thus, to verify an application's digital signature, Device Guard uses virtualization-based security. In that way, if an attacker manages to get control of your Windows 10 device, Device Guard will lock down your device. Once locked, your device will only run trusted applications that you have previously defined in your code integrity policies. No untrusted apps are permitted to run.

Adding Guarded Host

To **add** the Guarded Host feature to your Windows 10 computer using **Turn Windows features on or off**, complete the following steps:

1. Click the search box in the taskbar and enter `turn windows`.
2. With **Turn Windows features on or off** highlighted in the **Best match** list, to their right, select **Open**.
3. In the **Windows Features** window, check the **Guarded Host** option as in *Figure 14.5* and then click **OK**:

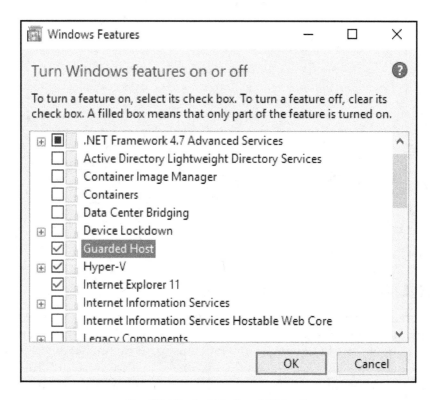

Figure 14.5. Adding Guarded Host feature in Windows 10

4. Once the feature has been added, select the **Restart now** button to restart your computer.

Enabling Device Guard

To **enable** Device Guard on your Windows 10 computer using **Local Group Policy Editor**, complete the following steps:

1. Press the Windows key + *R* to open **Run**.
2. Enter `gpedit.msc` and press *Enter*.
3. In the **Local Group Policy Editor** window, expand **Computer Configuration | Administrative Templates | System | Device Guard** and then, on the details pane, double-click **Turn On Virtualization based Security** (see *Figure 14.6*):

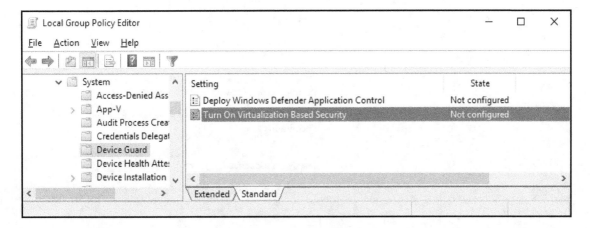

Figure 14.6. Enabling Device Guard in Windows 10

4. In the **Turn On Virtualization based Security** window, check the **Enabled** option.
5. In the **Options** section, select the **Secure Boot** option for **Select Platform Security Level**.
6. For **Virtualization Based Protection of Code Integrity**, select the **Enabled with UEFI lock** option.
7. For **Credential Guard Configuration**, select the **Enabled with UEFI lock** option.

8. For **Secure Launch Configuration**, select the **Enabled** option, as shown in *Figure 14.7*, and then click **OK**:

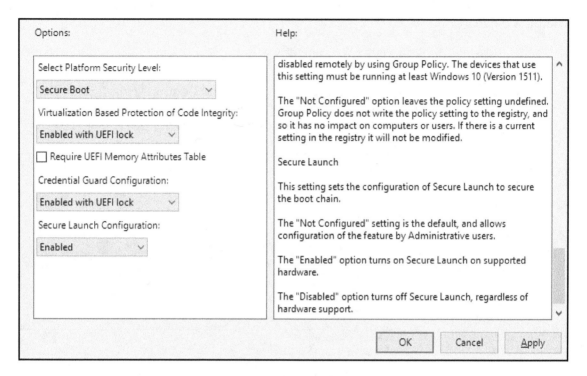

Figure 14.7. Configuring Device Guard Options

9. Close the **Local Group Policy Editor** window.

Verifying whether Device Guard is enabled using System Information

To **verify** whether Device Guard is enabled on your Windows 10 computer using System Information, complete the following steps:

1. Press the Windows key + *R* to open **Run**.
2. Enter `msinfo32` and press *Enter*.
3. In the **System Information** window, scroll through the information on the details pane to the end, as in *Figure 14.8*:

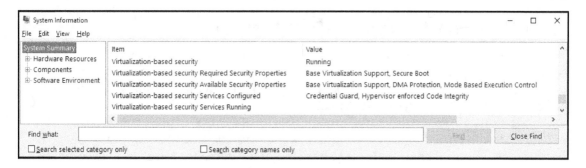

Figure 14.8. Verifying whether Device Guard is enabled using System Information

Verifying whether Device Guard is enabled using Windows PowerShell

To **verify** whether Device Guard is enabled on your Windows 10 computer using Windows PowerShell, complete the following steps:

1. Right-click the Start button and select **Windows PowerShell (Admin)**.
2. In the **Administrator: Windows PowerShell** window, enter `Get-CimInstance –ClassName Win32_DeviceGuard –Namespace root\Microsoft\Windows\DeviceGuard` and press *Enter*.
3. The detailed description of Device Guard properties is listed as shown in *Figure 14.9*:

```
Administrator: Windows PowerShell                                              —  □  ×

Windows PowerShell
Copyright (C) Microsoft Corporation. All rights reserved.

PS C:\Windows\system32> Get-CimInstance -ClassName Win32_DeviceGuard -Namespace root\Microsoft\Windows\DeviceGuard


AvailableSecurityProperties                  : {1, 3, 7}
CodeIntegrityPolicyEnforcementStatus         : 0
InstanceIdentifier                           : 4ff40742-2649-41b8-bdd1-e80fad1cce80
RequiredSecurityProperties                   : {1, 2}
SecurityServicesConfigured                   : {1, 2}
SecurityServicesRunning                      : {0}
UsermodeCodeIntegrityPolicyEnforcementStatus : 0
Version                                      : 1.0
VirtualizationBasedSecurityStatus            : 2
PSComputerName                               :



PS C:\Windows\system32>
```

Figure 14.9. Verifying whether Device Guard is enabled using Windows PowerShell

Configuring Credential Guard

Windows Defender Credential Guard, as the name suggests, is a new Windows 10 security feature whose task is to protect credentials from theft. It does so by separating the user credentials from the rest of the operating system in order to block access to credentials stored in the **Local Security Authority** (**LSA**). But what is *LSA*? It has to do with the user authentication by **Active Directory Domain Services** (**AD DS**) in an organization's network. Usually, in a domain environment, a user provides the username and the password to a domain controller. In the backend of the domain controller, it is **Kerberos** that takes care of the user's successful authentication once the requirements are met. As a result, Kerberos grants an authentication ticket to the user's computer, which then uses that ticket to access the network services by establishing sessions with servers in the same domain. With that said, it is the LSA that stores the Kerberos tickets and related security tokens.

 Refer to examples in the *Enabling Device Guard* and *Verifying whether Device Guard is enabled using Windows PowerShell* sections in order to see how to enable Windows Defender Credential Guard, and to verify whether Credential Guard is enabled on your Windows 10 computer.

Configuring DHA

From what we have discussed so far in this chapter, here are some of the best practices for the maintenance and security of your Windows 10 device:

- Being up to date with important Windows updates
- Having the latest Windows Defender signatures installed
- Having the Windows Defender Device Guard
- Windows Defender Credential Guard enabled and configured

In some way, these features also determine the health status of your Windows 10 device in your organization's network to make sure that only healthy devices can access the network resources. Thus, in the context of the discussions in this chapter on Windows 10 security features, DHA presents another security stack in Windows 10 layered security. That being said, DHA is included in Windows 10 Enterprise version and enables you to determine the health of your Windows 10 devices connected to your corporate network. Once the Windows 10 device is booted, DHA determines whether the security features are enabled. Thus, in the platform consisting of the **Trusted Platform Module (TPM)** chip, the **Mobile Device Management (MDM)** framework, and **Microsoft Intune**, enables the data collected by DHA in the boot process of Windows 10 devices to be sent to a remote attestation service called **Windows Health Attestation Service**. Then the collected data is being checked by the DHA service to determine whether any changes have been made on the device.

 To set up DHA on your corporate network, you need to have a server running Windows Server 2016, clients running Windows 10 Enterprise with a TPM chip, and DHA SSL, signing, and encryption certificates. More information regarding setting up the DHA you can find from `https://docs.microsoft.com/en-us/windows-server/security/device-health-attestation`.

Configuring Dynamic Lock

Dynamic Lock is another Windows 10 security feature. It enables users who, in addition to computers, also use mobile devices such as smartphones and tablets so to automatically lock their device whenever they step away from their PC. Prior to enabling Dynamic Lock on your Windows 10 computer, you should pair your computer and your mobile device via Bluetooth.

Enabling Dynamic Lock

To **enable** Dynamic Lock in your Windows 10 computer, complete the following steps:

1. Press the Windows key + *I* to open **Windows Settings**.
2. In the **Windows Settings** window, click **Accounts**.
3. On the **Accounts** page, select **Sing-in options** from the navigation menu.

4. On the **Sign-in options** page, in the **Dynamic Lock** section, check the **Allow Windows to automatically lock your device when you're away** option as in *Figure 14.10*:

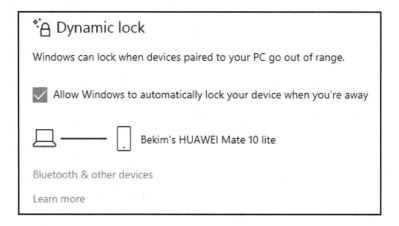

Figure 14.10. Enabling Dynamic Lock in Windows 10

 Dynamic Lock has been introduced with Windows 10 Creators Update version, and it will automatically lock your computer once your computer detects via Bluetooth that your paired smartphone has moved away from your computer for 30 seconds.

Chapter labs – configuring workgroups, domain settings, Azure AD Domain Join, and Microsoft accounts

In these chapter labs, you will learn how to do the following:

- Configure workgroups
- Configure domain settings
- Configure Azure AD Domain join
- Configure Homegroup settings
- Configure Microsoft accounts

Configuring workgroups

To **set up** a workgroup in your Windows 10 computer, complete the following steps:

1. Press the Windows key + *R* to open **Run**.
2. Enter `sysdm.cpl` and press *Enter*.
3. In the **System Properties** dialog box, click the **Change** button (see *Figure 14.11*):

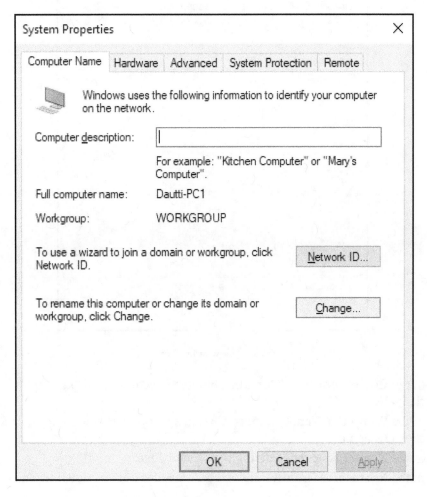

Figure 14.11. System Properties dialog box in Windows 10

4. In the **Computer Name/Domain Changes** dialog box, click the **Workgroup** text box and enter the name of your workgroup as shown in *Figure 14.12* and then click **OK**:

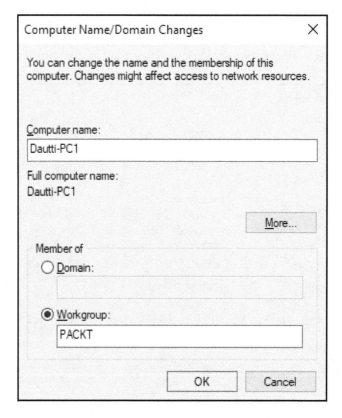

14.12. Setting up workgroup in Windows 10

5. In the **Computer Name/Domain Changes** welcome to workgroup dialog box, click **OK**.
6. In the **Computer Name/Domain Changes** restarting your computer dialog box, click **OK** again.
7. In the **System Properties** dialog box, click **Close**.
8. In the **Microsoft Windows** dialog box, click the **Restart now** button.

Configuring domain settings

To **set up** domain in your Windows 10 computer, complete the following steps:

1. **Repeat step 1 to step 3** from the previous section.
2. In the **Computer Name/Domain Changes** dialog box, click the **Domain** text box and enter the name of your domain and then click **OK**.
3. In the **Windows Security** dialog box, enter the system administrator's username and password as in *Figure 14.13* and then click the **OK** button:

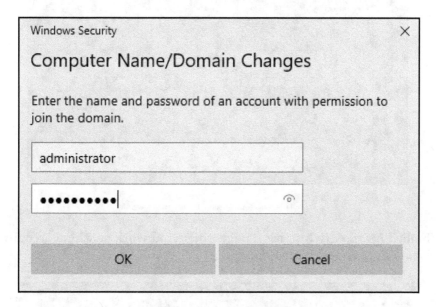

Figure 14.13. Joining the domain in Windows 10

4. In the **Computer Name/Domain Changes** welcome to domain dialog box, click **OK**.
5. In the **Computer Name/Domain Changes** restarting your computer dialog box, click **OK** again.
6. In the **System Properties** dialog box, click **Close**.
7. In the **Microsoft Windows** dialog box, click **Restart Now** button.

Configuring Azure AD Domain Join

To **join** your Windows 10 computer to Azure AD during **Windows Out-of-Box Experience** (**OOBE**), complete the following steps:

1. When you reach the **How would you like to setup?** page, select **Set up for an organization** (see *Figure 14.14*) and then click **Next**:

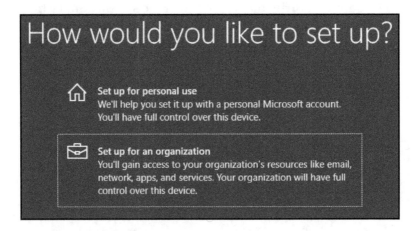

Figure 14.14. Joining your Windows 10 computer to Azure AD

2. In the **Sign in with Microsoft** page, enter your **work or school account** as in *Figure 14.15* and then press *Enter*:

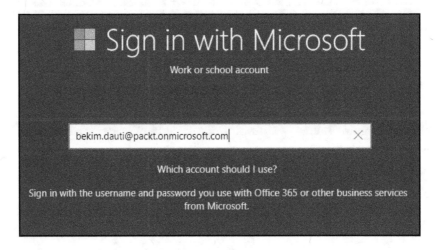

Figure 14.15. Entering work or school account when joining Azure AD

3. In the **Enter your password** page, enter the **password** for the work or school account as shown in *Figure 14.16* and then press *Enter*:

Figure 14.16. Entering the password for the work or school account when joining Azure AD

4. On the **Your organization requires Windows Hello** page, click the **Set up PIN** button.
5. Once you have logged in using your newly created PIN, you can **verify** that your Windows 10 computer is connected to the Azure AD by opening **Windows Settings | Access work or school**.

Configuring Microsoft accounts

To **connect** your Microsoft account to your Windows 10 computer, complete the following steps:

1. Press the Windows key + *I* to open **Windows Settings**.
2. In the **Windows Settings** window, click **Accounts**.
3. In the **Your info** page, select **Sign in with a Microsoft account instead** as shown in *Figure 14.17*:

> Windows is better when your settings and files automatically sync. Use a Microsoft account to easily get all your stuff on all your devices.
>
> Sign in with a Microsoft account instead

Figure 14.17. Connecting your Microsoft account in Windows 10

4. In the **Microsoft Account** dialog box, on the **Sign in** page, enter your email and press *Enter*.
5. In the **Microsoft Account** dialog box, enter your **password** and press *Enter*.
6. In the **Microsoft Account** dialog box, within the **Sign into this computer using your Microsoft account** page, enter your computer's **current password** and press *Enter*.
7. In the **Microsoft Account** dialog box, within the **Create a PIN** page, click the **Next** button.
8. In the **Windows Security** dialog box, enter a new PIN, confirm your PIN, and then click **OK** as in *Figure 14.18*:

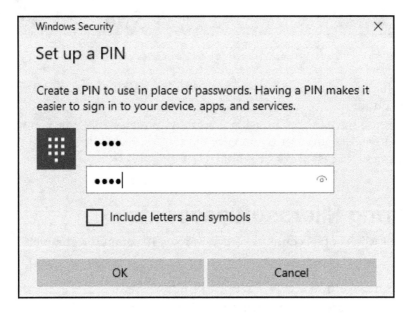

Figure 14.18. Setting up a PIN in Windows 10

Shortly after, your Microsoft account connects to your Windows 10 computer.

 It is recommended that you go ahead and verify your identity once you connect your Microsoft account to Windows 10, so you can sync your password across your devices.

Summary

We can summarize the chapter with the following points:

- Traditionally, users are usually authenticated by username and password.
- Microsoft Passport is a two-factor authentication mechanism that users will be able to prove who they are by providing something that they uniquely possess.
- In addition to using username and password, technologies such as PIN, biometric gestures, and a picture password can all be used to authenticate you in a Windows 10 devices.
- Usernames, passwords, and IP addresses usually represent the information that is stored in Credential Manager.
- Vaults are the folders where Credential Manager stores user credentials, whereas the Windows vault is the default storage of Credential Manager information.
- Access work or school enables you to register your Windows 10 device on your organization's network, and facilitates an **SSO** experience so you are able to get access to resources such as email, apps, and other network services.
- Registering your device to your organization's network means that your workplace might control some things on your device.
- Usually, a PIN is a numeric or an alphanumeric password, whereas Windows Hello is a biometrics-based authentication technology.
- Windows Hello for Business is used to authenticate users and enable them to access network resources in a corporate network.
- The Windows Defender Device Guard feature is a combination of enterprise hardware and software security features, so it can mitigate threats coming from malicious software (malware).
- Windows Defender Credential Guard, as the name suggests, is a new Windows 10 security feature whose task is to protect credentials from theft.
- DHA is included in Windows 10 Enterprise and enables you to determine the health of the Windows 10 devices connected to your corporate network.
- Dynamic Lock enables users who, in addition to computers, also use mobile devices such as smartphones and tablets so to automatically lock their device whenever they step away from their PC.

Questions

1. In addition to using username and password, technologies such **Personal Identification Number** (**PIN**), biometric gestures, and picture passwords can all be used to authenticate you in Windows 10 devices.
    1. True
    2. False

2. _____ is used to authenticate users and enable them to access network resources in a corporate network.

3. Which of the following Windows 10 authentication technologies requires appropriate hardware? (Choose two)
    1. Username and password
    2. PIN
    3. Picture password
    4. Windows Hello

4. **Device Health Attestation** (**DHA**) is included in Windows 10 Enterprise version and enables you to determine the health of the Windows 10 devices connected to your corporate network.
    1. True
    2. False

5. _____ enables users who, in addition to computers, also use mobile devices such as smartphones and tablets to automatically lock their device whenever they step away from their PC.

6. Where in the Windows Defender Credential Guard are Kerberos tickets stored?
    1. **Virtualization-Based Protection** (**VBP**)
    2. **Local Security Authority** (**LSA**)
    3. **Device Health Attestation** (**DHA**)
    4. **Personal Identification Number** (**PIN**)

7. Microsoft Passport is a two-factor authentication mechanism that users will be able to prove who they are by providing something that they uniquely posses.
    1. True
    2. False

8. Usually, _____ is a numeric or an alphanumeric password, whereas _____ is a biometrics-based authentication technology.

9. The Dynamic Lock feature relies on which of the following technologies?
    1. Kerberos
    2. PIN
    3. Windows Hello
    4. Bluetooth

10. To verify an application's digital signature, Device Guard uses virtualization-based security.
    1. True
    2. False

11. User credentials that are used to access web services are stored in the _____ list, while user credentials for accessing network services are stored in the _____ list.

12. Which of the following protection technologies are introduced with Windows 10? (Choose two)
    1. Username and password
    2. Windows Defender Device Guard
    3. Active Directory Domain Services
    4. Windows Defender Credential Guard

Further reading

- **Set up your Microsoft account on your devices**: https://account.microsoft.com/account/connect-devices
- **Device Guard and Credential Guard**: https://docs.microsoft.com/en-us/windows-hardware/drivers/bringup/device-guard-and-credential-guard
- **Windows Hello biometrics in the enterprise**: https://docs.microsoft.com/en-us/windows/security/identity-protection/hello-for-business/hello-biometrics-in-enterprise
- **Control the health of Windows 10-based devices**: https://docs.microsoft.com/en-us/windows/security/threat-protection/protect-high-value-assets-by-controlling-the-health-of-windows-10-based-devices
- **Offline Domain Join (Djoin.exe) Step-by-Step Guide**: https://docs.microsoft.com/en-us/previous-versions/windows/it-pro/windows-server-2008-R2-and-2008/dd392267(v=ws.10)

15
Configuring Advanced Management Tools

This chapter explains advanced management tools, such as Windows Services, Windows Registry, the **Microsoft Management Console** (**MMC**), and Task Scheduler. The chapter is organized into two parts. The first part explains the importance of services and registry of Windows 10. Topics such as understanding Windows Services and Windows Registry, and how to manage both the Services and Registry in Windows 10, are discussed. As far as the second part is concerned, it covers the MMC and Task Scheduler. Examples of how to access and add a snap-in, respectively creating a basic task, are presented. Each topic is accompanied by step-by-step instructions driven by targeted, easy-to-understand graphics. The chapter concludes with chapter labs on configuring the automation of management tasks using Windows PowerShell and converting Group Policy Objects to MDM policies using the MDM Migration Analysis tool.

In this chapter, we will cover the following topics:

- Configuring device system resources
- Configuring Windows Services
- Configuring Windows Registry
- Configuring and using the MMC
- Configuring Task Scheduler
- Chapter labs – configuring automation of management tasks using Windows PowerShell, and converting Group Policy Objects to MDM policies using the MDM Migration Analysis tool

Technical requirements

In order to complete the labs for this chapter, you will need a PC with Windows 10 Pro, at least 4 GB of RAM, 500 GB of HDD, and access to the internet.

Configuring device system resources

In a computer system, devices use system resources to work with one another. As such, a **system resource** is any computer component, physical or virtual, and internal or external. The **operating system** is responsible for managing the system resources, whereas users use system resources to open programs and utilities. System resources are considered to be **limited**, and as such, computer systems are usually running low on resources. Such situations reduce the overall performance of your device, which results in an error similar to *your computer is low on memory*. So, in the following sections, you will get acquainted with computer system resources.

Plug and Play (PnP)

If you have heard the expression that *Windows is all about Plug & Play*, then it can be said that it really is! In that line of discussion, do you remember when you last installed Windows 10 drivers? No? That's because **Plug and Play** has tremendously simplified the work involved with devices and drivers. As the name implies, once a device is plugged in to a Windows 10 computer, the device is immediately recognized by the operating system. Windows 10 uses its driver store to install the device's drivers. As you know now, the path to driver store in Windows 10 can be found at `C:\Windows\System32\DriverStore`.

Interrupt Request and Direct Memory Access

The beauty of technological names is that they are self-explanatory, right? The same applies to both **Interrupt Request** (**IRQ**) and **Direct Memory Access** (**DMA**). While the first is the signal sent to the CPU whenever any computer component needs processing, the latter is a way of bay-passing CPU and accessing the computer's memory by any computer component. Thus, while IRQ momentarily interrupts the processor, DMA bypasses the processor. In both cases, numeric values help the CPU to identify hardware components that interrupt and bypass the processor. Thus, IRQ uses the segment of numbers from 0 to 31, whereas DMA uses a smaller segment of numbers from 0 to 8.

Viewing IRQ and DMA system resources

To view IRQ and DMA system resource settings in your Windows 10 computer, complete the following steps:

1. Press Windows key + *R* to open **Run**.
2. Enter devmgmt.msc and press *Enter.*
3. In the **Device Manager** window, right-click any of the *devices* and select **Properties** from the context menu.
4. Click the **Resources** tab, and view the information within the **Resource settings** section, as shown in *Figure 15.1*:

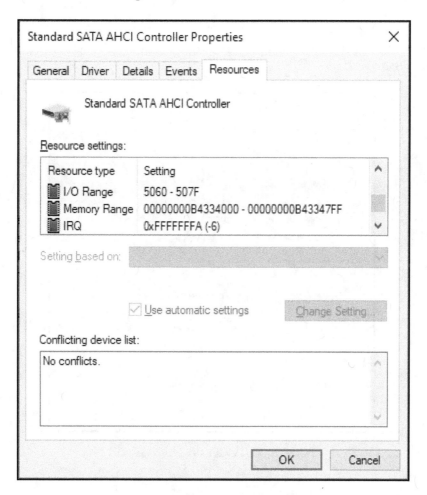

Figure 15.1: Viewing a device's system resources in Windows 10

Driver signing

Driver signing represents the device's driver **digital signature** and identifies the **publisher** of the driver package. Technically speaking, a device's driver's digital signature ensures you that Microsoft has tested and approved a device driver package and that its installation will not cause any reliability or security issues in your Windows 10 device.

Viewing a driver's digital signing information

To verify a device's driver digital singing information in your Windows 10 computer, complete the following steps:

1. **Repeat step 1 to step 3** from the previous section.
2. Click the **Driver** tab, and verify the **Digital Signer** information, as shown in *Figure 15.2*:

Figure 15.2: Verifying a device's driver Digital Signer information

Configuring Windows Services

In a computer system, **Windows Services** are the long-running background processes that keep the Windows programs and utilities alive. These **Windows 10 core components** are started along with the operating system without user intervention and will continue to run even after the user has signed out. Whether you are running a program, utility, or network service, it is Windows Services that operates behind the scenes to support their execution. That being said, Windows Services can be stopped, paused, started, delayed, or resumed through Windows Services Control Manager.

Services startup types

Once you access Windows Services Control Manager in your Windows 10 device, other than managing the status of services, you will notice that each service contains a description that helps you to understand its purpose. In addition, it lets you maintain the following start-up mechanisms:

- **Automatic**: Starts automatically along with the operating system
- **Automatic (delayed start)**: Starts approximately 2 minutes after automatic services have started
- **Manual**: Must be started either by a user or dependent services
- **Disable**: Cannot be started by the OS, or dependent services

Accessing Windows Services Control Manager

To the Windows Services Control Manager in your Windows 10 computer, complete the following steps:

1. Press Windows key + *R* to open **Run**.
2. Enter `services.msc` and press *Enter*.

3. Shortly after, Windows Services Control Manager opens up, as shown in *Figure 15.3*:

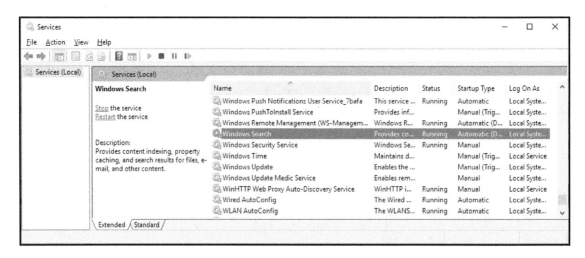

Figure 15.3: Windows Services Control Manager console in Windows 10

Setting up service recovery options

To set up service recovery options in your Windows 10 computer, in the event that a service fails, complete the following steps:

1. **Repeat step 1 to step 3** from the previous section.
2. In the Windows Services Control Manager window, right-click a certain service and then from the context menu, select **Properties**.
3. From the **Services** window's **Properties** dialog box, click the **Recovery** tab.
4. Within the **Select the computer's response if the service fails** section, set up **First failure**, **Second failure**, and **Subsequent failures** (see *Figure 15.4*):

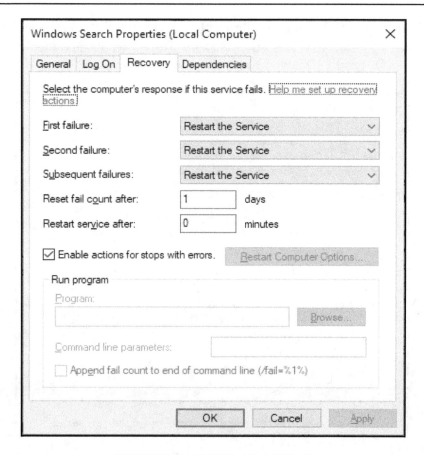

Figure 15.4: Setting up service recovery options in Windows 10

5. Click **OK** to close the **Services** windows' **Properties** dialog box.

Setting up the service delayed startup

To delay the startup of a service in your Windows 10 computer, complete the following steps:

1. **Repeat step 1 to step 3** from the *Accessing Windows Services Control Manager* section.

2. In the Windows Services Control Manager window, right-click a **certain service** and then from the context menu select **Properties**.

3. From the **Services** window's **Properties** dialog box, click the **General** tab.
4. Within the **Startup type** section, click the drop-down list and then select **Automatic (Delayed start)**, as shown in *Figure 15.5*:

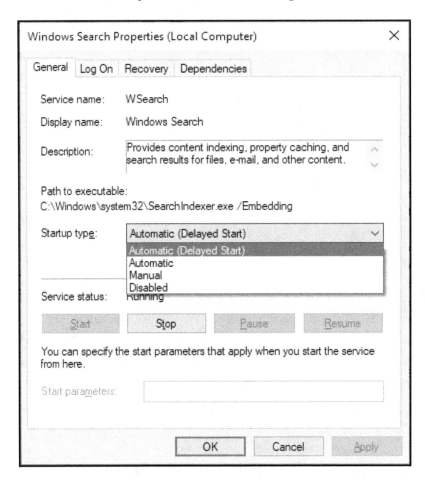

Figure 15.5: Setting up the service delayed startup in Windows 10

5. Click **OK** to close the **Services** window's **Properties** dialog box.

Setting up the Log On as settings for a service

To set up the log on as settings for a service in your Windows 10 computer, complete the following steps:

1. **Repeat step 1 to step 3** from the *Accessing Windows Services Control Manager* section.
2. In the Windows Services Control Manager window, right-click a **certain service** and then, from the context menu, select **Properties**.
3. From the **Services** window's **Properties** dialog box, click the **Log On** tab.
4. Within the **Log on as** section, select **This account** option then enter a user account, password, and confirm the password, as shown in *Figure 15.6*:

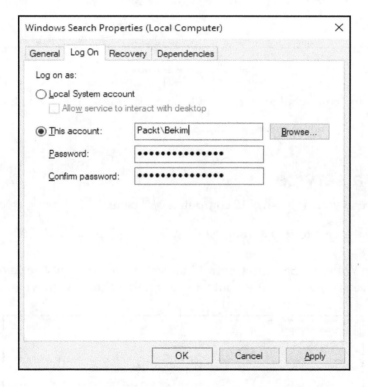

Figure 15.6: Setting up Log on as settings for a service in Windows 10

5. Click **OK** to close the **Services** window's **Properties** dialog box.

Starting a service

To start a service in your Windows 10 computer, complete the following steps:

1. **Repeat step 1 to step 3** from the *Accessing Windows Services Control Manager* section.
2. In the Windows Services Control Manager window, right-click a **certain service** and then from the context menu, select **Start**, as shown in *Figure 15.7*:

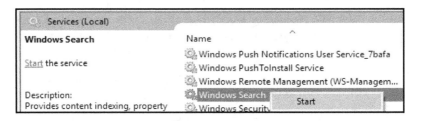

Figure 15.7: Starting a service in Windows 10

Enter the following command to start a service with Windows PowerShell:

```
Start-service - name <name of the service>
```

Stopping a service

To stop a service in your Windows 10 computer, complete the following steps:

1. **Repeat step 1 to step 3** from the *Accessing Windows Services Control Manager* section.
2. In the Windows Services Control Manager window, right-click a **certain service** and then from the context menu, select **Stop**, as shown in *Figure 15.8*:

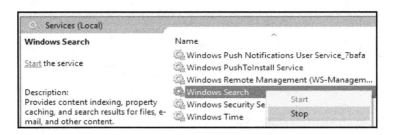

Figure 15.8: Stopping a service in Windows 10

Enter the following command to stop a service with Windows PowerShell:

```
Stop-service - name <name of the service>
```

Restarting a service

To restart a service in your Windows 10 computer, complete the following steps:

1. Repeat step 1 to step 3 from the *Accessing Windows Services Control Manager* section.
2. In the Windows Services Control Manager window, right-click a **certain service** and then from the context menu, select **Restart**, as shown in *Figure 15.9*:

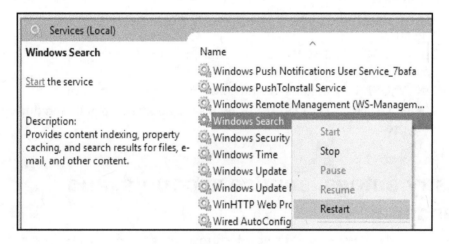

Figure 15.9: Restarting a service in Windows 10

Enter the following command to restart a service with Windows PowerShell:

```
Restart-service - name <name of the service>
```

Configuring Windows Registry

In contrast to Windows Services, Windows Registry is considered to be **the heart** of the Windows operating system. When you install an application or a device driver in your Windows 10 computer, it is stored in Windows Registry. That way, Windows Registry acts as a hierarchical database that stores the hardware and software configurations and system security information. Once you access Windows Registry, you will notice that its root keys pane has five registry keys, known as **hives** (that is, HKEYs). Note that the syntax of the registry keys and sub-keys follows the standard of the Windows file paths separated by a backslash. The following are the five HKEYs in Windows 10:

- **HKEY_CLASSES_ROOT**: Stores the information of installed applications and their extensions
- **HKEY_CURRENT_USER**: Stores the information about the user that is currently logged in
- **HKEY_LOCAL_MACHINE**: Stores the information specific to the local computer
- **HKEY_USERS**: Contains the information of logged-in user profiles
- **HKEY_CURRENT_CONFIG**: Contains the information gathered during the boot process

Registry entries, service accounts, and dependencies

Often, when you fix an issue or add a new feature in your Windows 10 device, you might end up adding a **new registry key** or a **registry value** in Windows Registry. Regardless of your actions, you should always be careful when working with Windows Registry. In contrast to registry entries, the **service accounts** are the Windows 10 native accounts or accounts created by an administrator to manage the *Log On as services*. From a security standpoint, the service accounts enable the services to access both local and network resources. From the account perspectives that the services accounts are running, the following are available in Windows 10:

- **Local System**: This is a built-in account with the most privileges. In a Windows 10 system, it is known as a superuser, and it is more powerful than your administrator account.

- **NT Authority\LocalService**: This is a built-in account with the same privileges as members of the users group.
- **NT Authority\NetworkService**: This is a built-in account that has more privileges than members of the users group.

As far as **service dependencies** are concerned, there are applications that use more than one service. So, sometimes while you are stopping a service, you will end up being asked to stop a few others dependent services too. Conversely, while you start a service, a few other dependent services will require to be started too. Thus, that is a typical example of the dependencies between the services.

Accessing the Windows Registry Editor

To access the Windows Registry Editor in your Windows 10 computer, complete the following steps:

1. Press Windows key + *R* to open **Run**.
2. Enter `regedit.exe` and press *Enter*.
3. Click the **Yes** button when asked **Do you want to allow this app to make changes to your device?**
4. Shortly after, the Windows **Registry Editor** opens up, as shown in *Figure 15.10*:

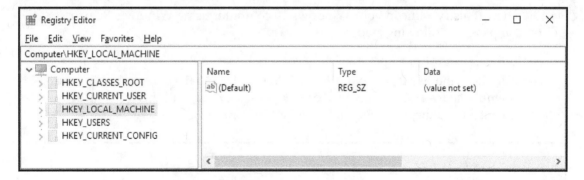

Figure 15.10: Windows Registry Editor in Windows 10

Adding a new registry key

To add a new registry key in your Windows 10 computer using Windows Registry Editor, complete the following steps:

1. **Repeat step 1 to step 3** from the previous section.
2. In the Windows **Registry Editor** window, in the root keys pane, right-click any of the five registry keys and select **New** from the context menu, and then select **Key** from its context sub-menu, as shown in *Figure 15.11*:

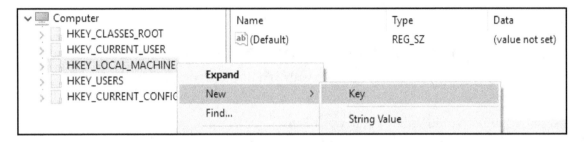

Figure 15.11: Adding a new registry key in Windows 10

Adding a new registry value

To add a new registry value in your Windows 10 computer using Windows Registry Editor, complete the following steps:

1. **Repeat step 1 to step 3** from the *Accessing Windows Registry Editor* section.
2. In the Windows **Registry Editor** window, in the details pane right-click the **empty space** and select **New** from the context menu, and then select **Key** from its context sub-menu, as shown in *Figure 15.12*:

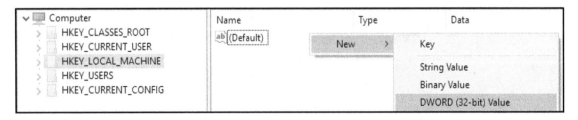

Figure 15.12: Adding a new registry value in Windows 10

Modifying a registry value

To modify a registry value in your Windows 10 computer using Windows Registry Editor, complete the following steps:

1. **Repeat step 1 to step 3** from the *Accessing Windows Registry Editor* section.
2. In the Windows **Registry Editor** window, in the root keys pane, locate the registry key and its subkey(s).
3. In the details pane, right-click the **registry value** that you want to change the value of and select **Modify** (see *Figure 15.13*):

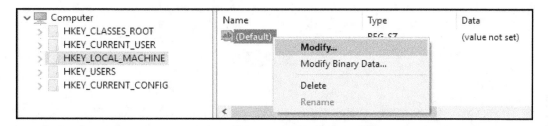

Figure 15.13: Modifying a registry value in Windows 10

Renaming a registry value

To rename a registry value in your Windows 10 computer using Windows Registry Editor, complete the following steps:

1. **Repeat step 1 to step 3** from the *Accessing Windows Registry Editor* section.
2. In the Windows **Registry Editor** window, in the root keys pane, locate the registry key and its subkey(s).
3. In the Details pane, right-click the **registry value** that you want to change the name of and select **Rename** (see *Figure 15.14*):

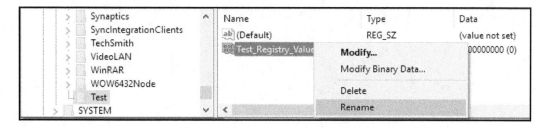

Figure 15.14: Renaming a registry value in Windows 10

Deleting a registry value

To delete a registry value in your Windows 10 computer using Windows Registry Editor, complete the following steps:

1. **Repeat step 1 to step 3** from the *Accessing Windows Registry Editor* section.
2. In the Windows **Registry Editor** window, in the root keys pane, locate the registry key and its subkey(s).
3. In the details pane, right-click the **registry value** that you want to delete and select **Delete** (see *Figure 15.15*):

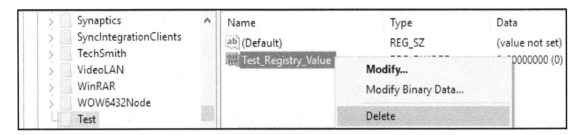

Figure 15.15: Deleting a registry value in Windows 10

Configuring and using the MMC

As you may have noticed, the MMC has been mentioned several times in this book since the first chapter. That is because MMC has accompanied the Windows operating system since its introduction with Windows 2000, and as such, it serves as a platform for the majority of administrative and management tools. MMC is the most preferred tool for system administrators and advanced users, because it provides an interface to configure and monitor Windows. MMC enables you to manage Windows 10 devices, both locally and over a network.

Accessing MMC

To **access** the MMC in your Windows 10 computer, complete the following steps:

1. Press Windows key + *R* to open **Run**.
2. Enter `mmc.exe` and press *Enter*.
3. Click the **Yes** button when asked **Do you want to allow this app to make changes to your device?**
4. Shortly after, the MMC opens up, as shown in *Figure 15.16*:

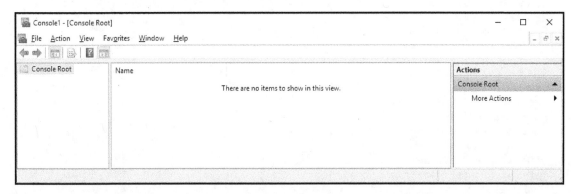

Figure 15.16: MMC in Windows 10

Adding a snap-in in MMC

To add the snap-in in MMC in your Windows 10 computer, complete the following steps:

1. **Repeat step 1 to step 3** from the previous section.
2. Click the **File** menu and select **Add/Remove Snap-in...**.
3. In the **Add or Remove Snap-ins** dialog box, from within **Available snap-ins** section, choose one or more snap-ins to add to your console.

4. Once you select the needed snap-in, click the **Add** button and then **OK**. as shown in *Figure 15.17*:

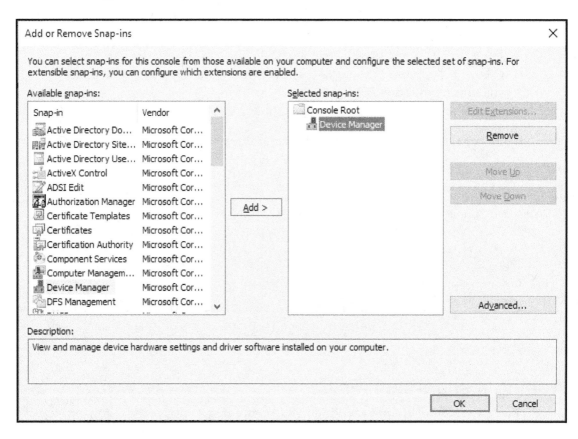

Figure 15.17: Adding a snap-in MMC in Windows 10

Configuring Task Scheduler

Like MMC, **Task Scheduler** is also a tool that accompanies the **Windows operating system** from **Window 2000** onwards. Task Scheduler allows system administrators and advanced users to perform automated tasks on a chosen computer. This service enables you to schedule a task that will run at a convenient time. Task Scheduler is based on time monitoring, and once the condition is met, then it executes the task. Similar to MMC, Task Scheduler can also help you schedule simple or complex tasks both on a **local computer** or on a **remote computer**.

Chapter 15

Accessing Task Scheduler

To access Task Scheduler in your Windows 10 computer, complete the following steps:

1. Press *Windows key + R* to open **Run**.
2. Enter `taskschd.msc` and press *Enter*.
3. Shortly after, **Task Scheduler** opens up, as shown in *Figure 15.18*:

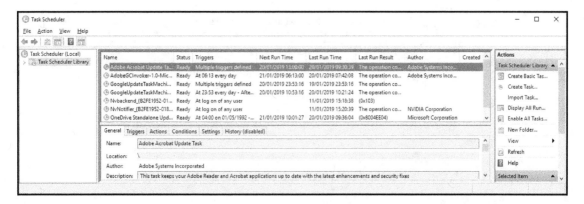

Figure 15.18: Task Scheduler in Windows 10

Scheduling a task with Task Scheduler

To **schedule a task** in your Windows 10 computer using Task Scheduler, complete the following steps:

1. Repeat step 1 and step 2 from the previous section.
2. In the **Task Scheduler** window, within the **Actions** pane, select **Create Basic Task...**.

3. In the **Create Basic Task Wizard**, within the **Create a Basic Task** page, enter the name and description of the task, as shown in *Figure 15.19*, and then click **Next**:

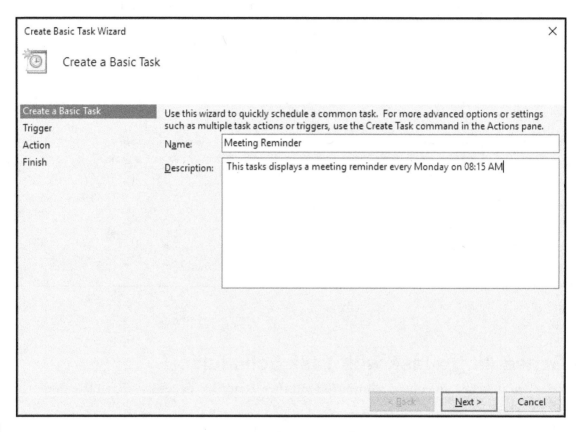

Figure 15.19: Creating a basic task using Task Scheduler in Windows 10

4. In the **Task Trigger** page, within the **When do you want the task to start?**, section select the preferred option and then click **Next**.
5. In the **Weekly** page, set the starting date and time, recurrence, and the day, and then click **Next**.
6. In the **Action** page, within the **What action do you want the task to perform?** section, select the preferred option and then click **Next**.
7. In the **Summary** page, review the entries you have made so far and then click **Finish** (see *Figure 15.20*):

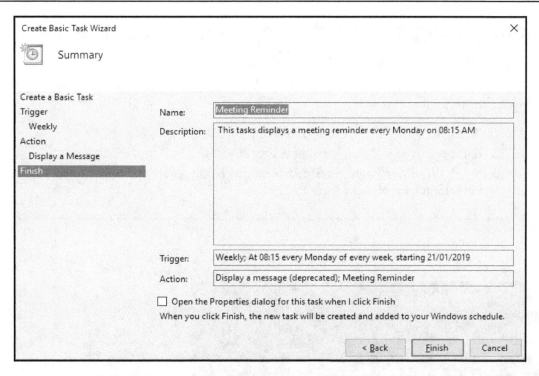

Figure 15.20: Completing the Create a Basic Task Wizard

Chapter labs – configuring automation of management tasks using Windows PowerShell, and converting Group Policy Objects to MDM policies using the MDM Migration Analysis tool

In these chapter labs, you will learn how to do the following:

- Configuring the automation of management tasks using Windows PowerShell
- Converting Group Policy Objects to MDM policies using the MDM Migration Analysis tool

Configuring automation of management tasks using Windows PowerShell

To **create and run** scripts in your Windows 10 computer using Windows PowerShell (ISE), complete the following steps:

1. Press Windows key + *R* to open **Run**.
2. Enter `powershell_ise.exe` and press *Enter*.
3. In the **Windows PowerShell ISE** window, begin entering cmdlets to create your PowerShell script (see *Figure 15.21*):

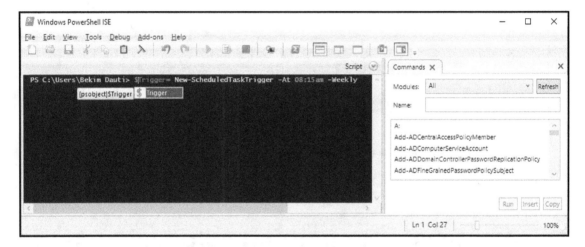

Figure 15.21: Creating Powershell scripts using Windows PowerShell (ISE) in Windows 10

 To learn how to create and run scripts in Windows PowerShell, refer to the following URL: `https://docs.microsoft.com/en-gb/powershell/`.

Converting Group Policy Objects to MDM policies using the MDM Migration Analysis tool

To run the MDM Migration Analysis in Windows Server 2016 via Remote Desktop Connection from your Windows 10 computer, complete the following steps:

1. Press Windows key + *R* to open **Run**.
2. Enter `mstsc` and press *Enter*.
3. In the **Remote Desktop Connection** dialog box, enter the **name or IP address** of your Windows Server 2019 and then click **Connect**.
4. In the **Windows Security** dialog box, enter the **username and password** and click **OK**.
5. Once you get connected to your Windows Server 2016, open Internet Explorer and enter `https://github.com/WindowsDeviceManagement/MMAT` in the address bar to download the **Mobile Device Management** (**MDM**) **Migration Analysis Tool** (**MMAT**).
6. In the `WindowsDeviceManagement/MMAT` page of the **GitHub** web site, click the **Clone or download** green button and then select **Download ZIP**.
7. Once the download completes, extract the ZIP file to your preferred location on the server's disk(s).
8. Open **Windows PowerShell** with elevated privileges.
9. In the **Administrator: Windows PowerShell** window, navigate the path where the `MMAT-master` folder is stored.
10. Enter the `Set-ExecutionPolicy -ExecutionPolicy Unrestricted -Scope Process` command, and then press *Enter*.
11. When asked about the execution policy change, enter `Y` and press *Enter*.
12. Enter the `$VerbosePreference="Continue"` command, and then press *Enter*.

13. Enter the `./Invoke-MdmMigrationAnalysisTool.ps1 -collectGPOReports -runAnalysisTool` command, and then press *Enter* (see *Figure 15.22*):

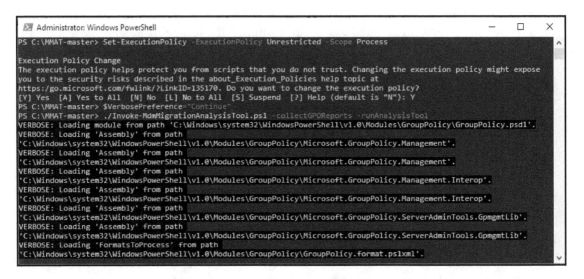

Figure 15.22: Executing the MdmMigrationAnalysisTool script in Windows PowerShell

14. Once the execution of the Windows PowerShell script completes, open the `MDMMigrationAnalysis.html` file from the `MMAT-master` folder to view the *Report Information*, **Group Policy To MDM Analysis Results** tab, as shown in *Figure 15.23*:

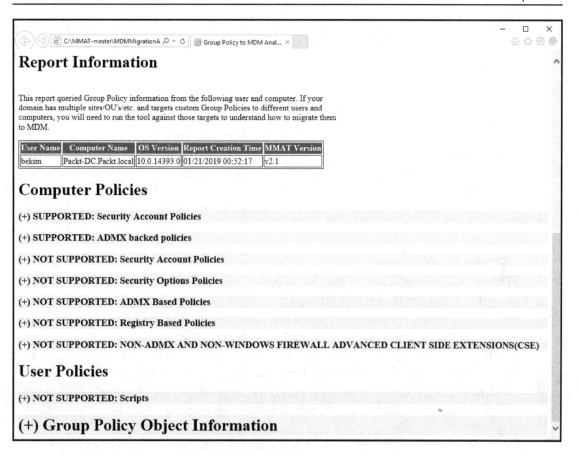

Figure 15.23: Report Information: Group Policy To MDM Analysis Results

Summary

We can summarize the chapter with the following points:

- A system resource is any computer component, both physical and virtual, and internal or external.
- The operating system is responsible for managing the system resources, whereas users use system resources to open programs and utilities.

- Once the device is plugged in to a Windows 10 device, the device is immediately recognized by the operating system.
- The path to driver store in Windows 10 can be found at `\Windows\System32\DriverStore`.
- An **Interrupt Request** (**IRQ**) is a signal sent by a device through communication channels to get the attention of a processor whenever that device requires processing.
- **Direct Memory Access** (**DMA**) is a system resource used by a device to bypass the processor whenever that device needs direct access to device's memory (RAM)
- Driver signing represents the device's driver digital signature that identifies the publisher of the driver package.
- Windows Services are the long-running background process that keeps the Windows programs and utilities alive.
- Windows Services can be stopped, paused, started, delayed, or resumed through Windows Services Control Manager.
- Windows Registry acts as a hierarchical database that stores the hardware and software configurations and system security information.
- Once you access Windows Registry, you will notice that its root keys pane has five registry keys known as hives (that is, HKEYs).
- Often, when you fix an issue or add a new feature in your Windows 10 device, you might end up adding a new registry key or a registry value in Windows Registry.
- The service accounts are the Windows 10 native accounts or accounts created by an administrator to manage the Log on as services.
- As far as service dependencies are concerned, there are applications that use more than one service.
- The MMC serves as a platform for the majority of administrative and management tools.
- Task Scheduler allows system administrators and advanced users to perform automated tasks on a chosen computer.

Questions

1. **Direct Memory Access** (**DMA**) is a system resource used by a device to bypass the processor whenever that device needs direct access to the device's memory (RAM).
    1. True
    2. False

2. The path to driver store in Windows 10 is at:
    _____.

3. Which of the following services accounts are available in Windows 10?
    1. Local System
    2. NT Authority\LocalService
    3. NT Authority\NetworkService
    4. All of the above

4. The **Microsoft Management Console** (**MMC**) serves as a platform for the majority of administrative and management tools.
    1. True
    2. False

5. The service accounts are the Windows 10 native accounts or accounts created by an administrator to manage the _____.

6. Which of the following registry keys are available in Windows 10? (Choose three):
    - **HKEY_CLASSES_ROOT**
    - **HKEY_MACHINE_LOCAL**
    - **HKEY_CURRENT_USER**
    - **HKEY_CONFIG_CURRENT**
    - **HKEY_LOCAL_MACHINE**
    - **HKEY_ROOT_CLASSES**

7. A system resource is any computer component, both physical and virtual, and internal or external.
    1. True
    2. False

8. The _____ is responsible for managing the system resources, whereas _____ use system resources to open programs and utilities.

9. Which of the following are Windows Services start-up mechanisms in Windows 10? (Choose three):
    - Automatic
    - Idle
    - Manual
    - Start
    - Disable
    - Resume

Further reading

- **About Services**: https://docs.microsoft.com/en-us/windows/desktop/services/about-services
- **Structure of the Registry**: https://docs.microsoft.com/en-us/windows/desktop/sysinfo/structure-of-the-registry
- **Microsoft Management Console (MMC)**: https://docs.microsoft.com/en-us/windows/desktop/srvnodes/microsoft-management-console--mmc-
- **Task Scheduler**: https://docs.microsoft.com/en-us/windows/desktop/taskschd/task-scheduler-start-page
- **Understanding Important PowerShell Concepts**: https://docs.microsoft.com/en-us/powershell/scripting/learn/understanding-important-powershell-concepts?view=powershell-6

16
Studying and Passing Exam 70-698

This chapter is designed to provide you with an overview of the 70-698 exam's objective domain areas. In addition, this chapter contains explanations as to what *Exam 70-698: Installing and Configuring Windows 10* is and how to register for it. Also, this chapter contains suggestions on how to prepare for the exam and considerations that need to be taken into account when sitting the exam. In regard to the 70-698 exam's objective domain areas, you will find the chapter references for each and every objective so that you can find more explanations in the book concerning the respective objective. Last, but not least, learn and practice as much as you can with operating systems in general, and Windows 10 in particular, because only by doing so will you be able to get the needed skills to pass the examination without hurdles, and become a **Microsoft Certified Professional (MCP)**.

The following topics will be covered in this chapter:

- Overview of the 70-698 exam
- Advice on taking the 70-698 exam
- Overview of the 70-698 exam's objective domain areas
- 70-698 exam details
- Tips to prepare for the 70-698 exam
- Registering for the 70-698 exam
- On the day of the 70-698 exam
- Post 70-698 exam certification path

What is the 70-698 exam?

The acronym **MCP** stands for **Microsoft Certified Professional,** and represents the Microsoft Certification Program that enables IT professionals and developers to validate their technical expertise. MCP includes all of the exams required in the **Microsoft Certified Solutions Associate (MCSA), Microsoft Certified Solutions Expert (MCSE), Microsoft Certified Solutions Developer (MCSD),** and Microsoft specialist certifications. That is to say, if you pass one of the exams of any of the aforementioned certificates, then automatically you earn the MCP credential. With that being said, the 70-698 exam qualifies for an MCP credential, as it tests a candidate's knowledge and skills related to Windows 10 technologies, such as installation, configuration, services, maintenance, and troubleshooting. In addition, the MCP 70-698 exam counts toward obtaining your MCSA Windows 10 certification too:

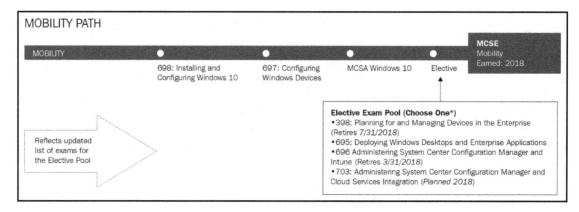

Figure 16.1. Exam 70-698 is a core exam in MCSA Windows 10 certification

Who should take the 70-698 exam?

Candidates for the 70-698 exam are IT professionals who perform installation, configuration, general local management, and maintenance of Windows 10 core services. Candidates may also be exposed to some enterprise scenarios or cloud-integrated services.

What are the 70-698 exam's objective domain areas?

In general, exam objectives, topics, or technical tasks form an unwritten standard that is practiced by the IT industry when it comes to certification exams. Usually, it represents a general guideline for a certain certification exam issued by the exam client (in this case, Microsoft) that is likely to be included in the exam. At the same time, Microsoft will necessarily update exam objective domain areas to better reflect the content of the exam. You will find the following objective domain areas in the 70-698 exam.

You can learn about the objective domain areas of the 70-698 exam at https://youtu.be/XVcmzfxpc-M.

Objective domain area 1 – implementing Windows (30-35%)

To accomplish this objective domain area, the candidate is required to know pre-installation requirements and various ways of installing Windows 10. In addition, the candidate should know how to configure devices and device drivers, how to perform post-installation tasks, and be able to implement Windows in an enterprise environment. When you feel confident that you have mastered this objective domain area, then you can move on to the next objective domain.

Objective 1.1 – preparing for installation requirements (Chapter 1)

This objective may include, but is not limited to, the following:

- Determining hardware requirements and compatibility.
- Choosing between an upgrade and a clean installation.
- Determining appropriate editions according to device type.
- Determining requirements for particular features.
- Determining and creating appropriate installation media.
- What is a client, server, host, and node?

Objective 1.2 – installing Windows (Chapter 2)

This objective may include, but is not limited to:

- Performing clean installations
- Upgrading using installation media
- Configuring native boot scenarios
- Identifying valid upgrade paths
- Migrating from previous versions of Windows
- Installing to a **virtual hard disk** (VHD)
- Booting from a VHD
- Installing on a bootable USB
- Installing additional Windows features
- Configuring Windows for additional regional and language support
- Device drivers

Objective 1.3 – configuring devices and device drivers (Chapter 3)

This objective may include, but is not limited to:

- Installing, updating, disabling, and rolling back drivers
- Resolving driver issues
- Configuring driver settings, including signed and unsigned drivers
- Managing driver packages
- Downloading and importing driver packages
- Using the **Deployment Image Servicing and Management** (**DISM**) tool to add packages

Objective 1.4 – performing post-installation configuration (Chapter 4)

This objective may include, but is not limited to:

- Configuring and customizing the Start menu, desktop, taskbar, and notification settings according to the device type
- Configuring accessibility options

- Configuring Cortana
- Configuring Microsoft Edge
- Configure Internet Explorer
- Configuring the Hyper-V client
- Configuring power settings

Objective 1.5 – implementing Windows in an enterprise environment (Chapter 5)

This objective may include, but is not limited to:

- Provisioning with the Windows Configuration Designer tool
- Implementing Active Directory–based activation
- Implementing volume activation using a **Key Management Service** (KMS)
- Querying and configuring activation states using the command line
- Configuring Active Directory, including Group Policies
- Configuring and optimizing **User Account Control** (UAC)

Objective domain area 2 – configuring and supporting core services (30-35%)

To accomplish this objective domain area, the candidate is required to know how to configure networking and storage in Windows 10. In addition, the candidate should know how to access and use data, how to install and configure apps, and be able to set up remote management in Windows 10. When you feel confident that you have mastered this objective domain area, then you can move on to the next objective domain.

Objective 2.1 – configuring networking (Chapter 6)

This objective may include, but is not limited to:

- Configuring and supporting IPv4 and IPv6 network settings
- Configuring name resolutions
- Connecting to a network
- Configuring network locations

- Configuring Windows Firewall
- Configuring **Windows Defender Firewall with Advanced Security (WFAS)**
- Configuring Network Discovery
- Configuring Wi-Fi settings
- Configuring Wi-Fi Direct
- Troubleshooting network issues
- Configuring VPNs, including app-triggered VPNs, traffic filters, and lockdown VPNs
- Configuring IPSec
- Configuring DirectAccess

Objective 2.2 – configuring storage (Chapter 7)

This objective may include, but is not limited to:

- Configuring disks, volumes, and filesystem options using Disk Management and Windows PowerShell
- Creating and configuring VHDs
- Configuring removable devices
- Creating and configuring storage spaces
- Troubleshooting storage and removable devices issues

Objective 2.3 – configuring data access and usage (Chapter 8)

This objective may include, but is not limited to:

- Configuring file and printer sharing and HomeGroup connections
- Configuring folder shares, public folders, and OneDrive
- Configuring filesystem permissions
- Configuring OneDrive usage, including Files On-Demand
- Troubleshooting data access and usage

Objective 2.4 – implementing apps (Chapter 9)

This objective may include, but is not limited to:

- Configuring desktop apps
- Configuring startup options
- Configuring Windows features
- Configuring Windows Store
- Implementing Windows Store apps
- Implementing Windows Store for Business
- Implementing Windows Store for Education
- Provisioning packages and creating packages
- Using deployment tools
- Using the Windows **Assessment and Deployment Kit** (**ADK**)

Objective 2.5 – configuring remote management (Chapter 10)

This objective may include, but is not limited to:

- Choosing the appropriate remote management tools
- Configuring remote management settings
- Modifying settings remotely by using the **Microsoft Management Console** (**MMC**) or Windows PowerShell
- Configuring remote assistance including Easy Connect
- Configuring Remote Desktop
- Configure remote PowerShell

Objective domain area 3 – managing and maintaining Windows (30-35%)

To accomplish this objective domain area, the candidate is required to know how to update, monitor, and manage Windows 10. In addition, the candidate should know how to configure system and data recovery, how to configure authentication and authorization, and be able to configure advanced management tools in Windows 10. When you feel confident that you have mastered this objective domain area, then you are ready to take the 70-698 certification exam. So, what are you waiting for? Go on, register the exam, sit it, and pass it proudly. Good luck!

Objective 3.1 – configuring updates (Chapter 11)

This objective may include, but is not limited to:

- Configuring Windows Update options
- Implementing Insider Preview, **Current Branch (CB)**, **Current Branch for Business (CBB)**, and **Long-Term Servicing Branch (LTSB)** scenarios
- Managing update history
- Rolling back updates
- Updating Windows Store apps

Objective 3.2 – monitoring Windows (Chapter 12)

This objective may include, but is not limited to:

- Configuring and analyzing Event Viewer logs
- Configuring event subscriptions
- Monitoring performance using Task Manager
- Monitoring performance using Resource Monitor
- Monitor performance using Performance Monitor and Data Collector Sets
- Monitoring system resources
- Monitoring and managing printers
- Configuring indexing options

- Managing client security by using Windows Defender
- Evaluating system stability using Reliability Monitor
- Troubleshooting performance issues
- Managing security using the Windows Defender Security Center
- Configuring Windows Defender Advanced Threat Detection

Objective 3.3 – configure system and data recovery (Chapter 13)

This objective may include, but is not limited to:

- Configuring a recovery drive
- Configuring a system restore
- Performing a refresh or recycle
- Performing a driver rollback
- Configuring restore points
- Resolve hardware and device issues
- Interpreting data from Device Manager
- Restoring previous versions of files and folders
- Configuring File History
- Recovering files from OneDrive
- Using Windows Backup and Restore
- Performing a backup and restore with WBAdmin
- Performing recovery operations using Windows Recovery

Objective 3.4 – configuring authorization and authentication (Chapter 14)

This objective may include, but is not limited to:

- Configuring Microsoft Passport
- Configuring picture passwords and biometrics
- Configuring workgroups
- Configuring domain settings
- Configuring Azure AD Domain join
- Configuring Homegroup settings

- Configuring Credential Manager
- Configuring local accounts
- Configuring Microsoft accounts
- Configuring Device Registration
- Configuring Windows Hello for Business
- Configuring Device Guard
- Configuring Credential Guard
- Configuring Device Health Attestation
- Configuring UAC behavior
- Configuring Dynamic Lock

Objective 3.5 – configuring advanced management tools (Chapter 15)

This objective may include, but is not limited to:

- Configuring services
- Configuring Device Manager
- Configuring and using the MMC
- Configuring Task Scheduler
- Configuring the automation of management tasks using Windows PowerShell
- Converting Group Policy objects to MDM policies using the MDM Migration Analysis tool

What to expect in the 70-698 exam?

As you already know, exams contains questions, so expect to have between **50-60 questions** for your 70-698 exam. The exam duration is **120 minutes**, including an **additional 30 minutes** for an introduction and survey. The passing score for the 70-698 exam is **700**. Questions do have a mark for review or flag for review option, which means that you can check that box to review the question after you have gone through all the questions. Other than that, you can move back and forth by clicking the **Previous** and **Next** buttons.

How to prepare for the 70-698 exam

In general, there is no written standard on how to prepare for the certification exams, and the 70-698 exam in particular. In fact, that has more to do with the use of best practices for the exam preparation. In the case of the 70-698 exam, they are as follows:

- **Active work experience** in the ICT industry from 1 to 2 years
- Attending **Windows 10 training** at Microsoft Partner for Learning Solutions
- Reading **Windows 10 books**
- **Practicing** with Windows 10
- It helps a lot if you are certified with **CompTIA A+** or **Windows Operating System Fundamentals**
- Taking **practice tests** so that you become familiar with the 70-698 exam format
- Reviewing the **objective domain areas** carefully to identify the points where you have weaknesses
- **Meeting with friends** who have passed the 70-698 certification exam and learning from their experiences

> You can help yourself to prepare for the 70-698 exam by exploring the content at `https://www.microsoft.com/en-eg/learning/exam-70-698.aspx`.

How to register for the 70-698 exam

In general, all Microsoft exams are provided by PearsonVUE. There are two types of exams:

- **Proctored exams** delivered at a test center
- **Self-administered** online exams

The 70-698 exam is a proctored exam that is delivered at a test center. The test center is a facility that has been authorized by PearsonVUE to deliver certification exams. Then, when you feel that you are ready to take the 70-698 exam, you can schedule your test in two ways:

- **Online** through `www.PearsonVUE.com` (requires a web account)
- Contacting a nearby **test center** (requires visiting a test center)

You can schedule your 70-698 exam online at `http://www.pearsonvue.com/microsoft/`.

On the day of the 70-698 exam

Make sure that you have slept well the night before the exam. Do not stress yourself in trying to remind yourself of the things that you have learned while preparing for the exam. Make sure to arrive at the testing center 30 minutes before the exam is scheduled and that you are carrying the required IDs. On entering the testing center, be polite with the test center administrator and carefully read the Pearson VUE Candidate Rules Agreement. When you are sitting in front of the workstation exam delivery, say a prayer because it will help build up your self-confidence, read the exam instructions carefully, and begin the exam. Read each question with high concentration and do not rush to answer the questions before reading each answer with the same concentration too. Remember that you can mark questions for review or hit the **Previous** button to go back to questions that you have already provided an answer for, so do not waste time on the questions you have doubts about. At the same time, be rational with the exam time because even though there is enough time at your disposal, if you do not properly manage it, then it may not suffice you. At any point, do not let panic get in your way, instead enjoy the exam to its fullness by having fun with the exam questions. And like that, question after question, you will be able to complete your 70-698 exam. At the end, you will get the score for the exam. Believe me, it is a joyful feeling when you realize that you have passed the exam. However, if the exam result is not the one you expected, then do not let the exam test your personality. Instead, accept the result as such and, as of the next day, begin preparing to retake the exam by identifying the points at which you have performed insufficiently. Remember that you now have the experience of the exam and that will greatly help you in the preparing for the exam and successfully passing it. **Good luck with your exam!**

 You can familiarize yourself with the Pearson VUE Candidate Rules Agreement by visiting `http://www.pearsonvue.com/fl/doh/PVTC_Rules.pdf`.

Post-70-698 exam certification path

Having passed the 70-698 exam successfully, the candidate automatically obtains the **Microsoft Certified Professional (MCP)** certification. On that occasion, congratulations to you on obtaining the MCP certification! The MCP is a professional certification program by Microsoft that proves that certified individuals are capable of implementing Microsoft products in practical business environments. In addition, the MCP 70-698 certification is the first step toward obtaining the **MCSA Windows 10** certification. To do so, the candidate must pass *Exam 70-697: Configuring Windows Devices*. Good luck with your upcoming Microsoft exams!

You can explore Microsoft certifications at `https://www.microsoft.com/en-us/learning/browse-all-certifications.aspx`.

Useful resources

- **Preparing for Exam 70-698: Installing and Configuring Windows 10**: `https://mva.microsoft.com/en-US/training-courses/preparing-for-exam-70698-installing-and-configuring-windows-10-17591?l=0mzrIl2qD_7705167344`
- **Exam Ref 70-698 Installing and Configuring Windows 10, 2nd Edition**: `https://www.microsoftpressstore.com/store/exam-ref-70-698-installing-and-configuring-windows-9781509307845`
- **Windows 10 for Enterprise Administrators**: `https://www.packtpub.com/networking-and-servers/windows-10-enterprise-administrators`

Assessments

In the following sections you will find answers to the questions of the chapters so that you can compare them with your answers and at the same time will server you as a way to reinforce the topics that you have learned in this book.

Chapter 1: Preparing for Installation

1. True
2. 12 editions
3. (3) Windows 10 Enterprise, (4) Windows 10 Education
4. False
5. An upgrade
6. All of the above
7. True
8. A node
9. All of the above
10. With minimum specifications, your computer will only be able to run the most basic tasks. Hence, if you want to avoid slow performance on your computer, the system requirements are recommended.

Chapter 2: Installing Windows 10

1. True
2. migration
3. All of the above
4. False
5. Clean install
6. All of the above
7. True
8. Native boot
9. (3) Bootable USB flash drive
10. True

11. Turn Windows features on or off
12. (3) Turn Windows features on or off

Chapter 3: Configuring Devices and Device Drivers

1. True
2. answer file
3. All of the above
4. True
5. PnPUtil.exe
6. (3) WSIM
7. True
8. Devices, Device Manager
9. All of the above
10. True
11. Out-of-Box Experience (OOBE)
12. (2) Update driver, (3) Disable device, (4) Uninstall device

Chapter 4: Performing Post-Installation Configuration

1. True
2. Microsoft Edge
3. (1) Desktop mode, (2) Tablet mode
4. False
5. Power & sleep
6. Windows key + C
7. False
8. search box
9. (2) Hub, (3) Reading list, (4) Writing on the web
10. True
11. Magnifier, Narrator, Audio, Speech, On-Screen keyboard

12. (3) Choose what closing the lid does, (4) Create a power plan

Chapter 5: Implement Windows in an Enterprise Environment

1. True
2. Group Policies
3. All of the above
4. True
5. User Account Control (UAC)
6. All of the above
7. True
8. KMS threshold
9. (2) Software license, (3) Software activation
10. True
11. software activation
12. Windows Configuration Designer (WCD)

Chapter 6: Configuring Networking

1. True
2. computer name, IP address
3. (1) App-triggered VPN, (2) Lockdown VPN
4. False
5. virtual private network (VPN)
6. All of the above
7. False
8. Internet Protocol Security (IPsec)
9. (1) Computer name, (3) IP address
10. True

11. Domain Name System (DNS)
12. Dynamic Host Configuration Protocol (DHCP)

Chapter 7: Configuring storage

1. True
2. Disk partitioning, formatting
3. (3) Hardware problems, (4) Software problems
4. True
5. turn off
6. (1) Internal device, (2) External devices
7. False
8. Storage Spaces
9. (3) Disk Management, (4) Windows PowerShell

Chapter 8: Configuring Data Access and Usage

1. True
2. NTFS permissions
3. All of the above
4. True
5. file server
6. (1) File Allocation Table (FAT), (2) New Technology File System (NTFS)
7. True
8. %systemdrive%\Users\Public
9. (1) NTFS permissions, (2) share permissions
10. True
11. Share permissions
12. (1) Modify, (2) Read and Execute, (3) Write

Chapter 9: Implementing Apps

1. False
2. Microsoft Store for Business
3. (1) desktop apps, (2) Microsoft Store apps
4. True
5. General-purpose computer
6. (1) Microsoft Store for Business, (2) Microsoft Store for Education
7. True
8. Fast startup
9. (1) Microsoft Deployment Toolkit (MDT), (2) Group Policy Objects (GPOs)
10. True

Chapter 10: Configuring Remote Management

1. True
2. Remote Desktop Connection
3. (1) Remote Desktop Connection, (4) Windows PowerShell Remoting
4. False
5. Windows Firewall
6. (2) Microsoft Remote Desktop app, (4) Microsoft Management Console (MMC)
7. True
8. Windows PowerShell Remoting
9. Windows Remote Management

Chapter 11: Configuring Updates

1. True
2. Long-Term Servicing Channel (LTSC)
3. (2) Change active hours, (3) Advanced options
4. True
5. Change active hours
6. All of the above

7. True
8. Windows Server Update Services (WSUS)
9. (1) Microsoft Windows Updates server, (3) Windows Server Update Services (WSUS) server
10. True
11. Rolling back updates

Chapter 12: Monitoring Windows 10

1. True
2. baseline
3. (1) Application, (3) System
4. True
5. Windows Defender
6. All of the above
7. True
8. Windows Security
9. All of the above
10. True
11. Counters
12. (1) Counters, (2) Instance

Chapter 13: Configuring System and Data Recovery

1. True
2. Recovery
3. (2) External disk, (3) Network share
4. True
5. Restore
6. System Restore
7. True
8. Volume Shadow Copy Service (VSS)
9. WBAdmin.exe

Chapter 14: Configuring Authorization and Authentication

1. True
2. Windows Hello for Business
3. (3) Picture password, (4) Windows Hello
4. True
5. Dynamic Lock
6. Local Security Authority (LSA)
7. True
8. Personal Identification Number (PIN), Windows Hello
9. Bluetooth
10. True
11. Web Credentials, Windows Credentials
12. (2) Windows Defender Device Guard, (4) Windows Defender Credential Guard

Chapter 15: Configuring Advanced Management tools

1. True
2. C:\Windows\System32\DriverStore
3. All of the above
4. True
5. Log on as services
6. (1) HKEY_CLASSES_ROOT, (3) HKEY_CURRENT_USER, (5) HKEY_LOCAL_MACHINE
7. True
8. operating system, users
9. (1) Automatic, (3) Manual, (5) Disable

Other Books You May Enjoy

If you enjoyed this book, you may be interested in these other books by Packt:

Windows Server 2016 Administration Fundamentals
Bekim Dauti

ISBN: 978-1-78862-656-9

- Become familiar with Windows Server OS concepts
- Learn how to install Windows Server 2016
- Learn how to install device drivers and run services in Windows Server 2016
- Learn how to add and install roles in Windows Server 2016
- Learn how to apply GPO to your Windows Server 2016 environment
- Learn how to tune, maintain, update, and troubleshoot Windows Server 2016
- Prepare for the MTA 98-365 exam

Mastering Windows Server 2016
Jordan Krause

ISBN: 978-1-78588-890-8

- Familiarize yourself with Windows Server 2016 ideology, the core of most datacenters running today
- New functions and benefits provided only by the new Windows Server 2016
- Get comfortable working with Nanoserver
- Secure your network with new technologies in Server 2016
- Harden your Windows Servers to help keep those bad guys out!
- Using new built-in integration for Docker with this latest release of Windows Server 2016
- Virtualize your datacenter with Hyper-V

Leave a review - let other readers know what you think

Please share your thoughts on this book with others by leaving a review on the site that you bought it from. If you purchased the book from Amazon, please leave us an honest review on this book's Amazon page. This is vital so that other potential readers can see and use your unbiased opinion to make purchasing decisions, we can understand what our customers think about our products, and our authors can see your feedback on the title that they have worked with Packt to create. It will only take a few minutes of your time, but is valuable to other potential customers, our authors, and Packt. Thank you!

Index